2024

2024

INDIA IN FREE FALL

SANJAY JHA

HarperCollins *Publishers* India

First published in India by HarperCollins *Publishers* 2024
4th Floor, Tower A, Building No. 10, DLF Cyber City,
DLF Phase II, Gurugram, Haryana – 122002
www.harpercollins.co.in

2 4 6 8 10 9 7 5 3 1

P-ISBN: 978-93-5699-889-6
E-ISBN: 978-93-5699-929-9

Typeset in 11.5/15.2 Bembo Std at
Manipal Technologies Limited, Manipal

Printed and bound at
Replika Press Pvt. Ltd.

This book is dedicated to teachers, authors, journalists, editors, thinkers, historians, public intellectuals, activists, publishers and millions of free-spirited souls who valiantly stand up against threats and tyranny, bullying and bulldozing, for freedom and democracy.

The detailed notes pertaining to this book are available on the HarperCollins website. Scan this QR code to access the same.

CONTENTS

'The tyranny of a prince in an oligarchy is not so dangerous to the public welfare as the apathy of a citizen in a democracy.'

—*Montesquieu*

INTRODUCTION

I AM ASSUMING that almost every Indian was rapturously hooked onto their television screens watching the successful culmination of the historic Chandrayaan 3 mission as it landed on the south polar side of the moon on 23 August 2023. It was a proud and tectonic moment for India's scientists and engineers, especially as the country is still bracketed among the Global South and, at best, is at the lower rung of middle-income nations. But everyone was not that fortunate to experience the extraordinary spectacle. At least twenty-three Indians were most certainly not watching that singular event; they had died earlier during the day in a tragic collapse of an under-construction railway bridge in the Northeastern state of Mizoram, near the capital city of Aizawl. The contrast between the two diametrically opposed episodes was incandescent. The marvel of space engineers and rocket scientists had resulted in a nation trending #OverTheMoon, while India's superstar Bollywood actor Shah Rukh Khan tweeted '*Chaand taare todh laoon*', from one of his many blockbuster hits. At the same time, whether it was criminal negligence in engineering design, or outright corruption leading to faulty safety procedures, or sheer incompetence, human life in India was being reduced to a dull, useless number, which would at most grab a fleeting presence on prime media real estate. India could not yet build a bridge without losing human lives in the bargain; it seemed odd for a country which aspired to be the 'next big thing'. The stentorian voices that boasted of a USD 5 trillion economy in the coming years could not save the lives of twenty-three ordinary labourers building India's big infrastructure story. This was not a one-off happenstance. It had become part of the day-to-day narrative—the contrasts, the contradictions. A hard to unriddle conundrum. As Nobel laureate Prof. Amartya Sen said, "'The frustrating thing about India", I was told by one of my teachers, the great Cambridge economist Joan Robinson, "is that whatever you can rightly say about India, the opposite is also true.'"[1] I experienced a similar sentiment a little earlier during the day when I was visiting New Delhi.

G20 summit billboards had hogged all available public space, from the T3 international airport all the way to Connaught Place. India's Prime Minister Narendra Modi's half-smiling face, clearly shot by a professional photographer who probably told him to look like a commanding leader with a hint of a confident smirk, adorned the capital city. The global get-together of world leaders in New Delhi has been the overriding marketing obsession of the ruling party, the Bhartiya Janata Party (BJP), showboating their leader Modi's 'Vishwa Guru' (spiritual teacher of the world) credentials. Although I disagree with that facetious rhetoric, what troubled me was the fustian tagline: Mother of Democracy. Really? Not far away from where I was in the much-maligned Edward Lutyens' Delhi, there is India's notorious Tihar Jail, whose unfortunate inmates include terrorists, murderers, rapists, hardcore criminals, thieves, drug dealers—a smorgasbord of anti-social characters, whose lives are intertwined by their alleged nefarious motivations. One of them in there is Umar Khalid. A Jawaharlal Nehru University (JNU) scholar. He has been in jail for over a thousand days, accused of being the mastermind of the Delhi riots of 2020, when US President Donald Trump was in Ahmedabad, Gujarat doing a stadium show with Modi. Over sixty people were killed, both Hindus and Muslims, over several days of communal slaughter. Several homes were burnt down. Hundreds, if not thousands, of lives would never be the same again.

I had met Khalid briefly in 2019, when he had come to Mumbai along with his friend and former JNU Students' Union president Kanhaiya Kumar. I was hosting the latter's book launch, ironically titled *From Bihar to Tihar*. Khalid came across as a charged up but soft-spoken activist, brimming with both ideas and visible brio. He had a nondescript, slim frame which belied his public profile of being a wily saboteur of national security interests. He looked more like a distracted bookworm, unused to the media attention and the sudden emergence of his image as a dangerous member of an anti-national cabal, the 'Tukde Tukde Gang', a term that was manufactured by the ruling party's propaganda factory to attack critics of the Modi government. I asked him how he coped with the sustained pressure from a hard-handed state, which seemed determined to frame him. He laughed and then said: 'I know they will come after me. I know they will get me too one day by using their brutal power. But if we don't push back now, then when?'[2] He was confident and possessed an arresting chutzpah. On 20 September 2020, they did come after him. He was charged under the dreaded Unlawful Activities Prevention Act (UAPA).[3] He has been languishing in jail since, and at the time of writing, he has not even been charge-sheeted. His bail application has been repeatedly rejected, even by the Supreme Court of India. In a letter that he wrote from solitary confinement to a concerned citizen, after two years in prison, he said, 'I often wonder, how long is this dark tunnel? Is there any light in sight yet? Am I near the end, or am I only midway through? Or has the ordeal just begun?'[4]

A senior BJP leader and a minister made highly vituperative and vile comments around the same time that the communal violence broke out; the leader who used the slogan '*Desh ke gaddaron ko, goli maaro saalon ko*' is often seen wearing dapper bandh-gala suits and holding press conferences as the government's leading spokesperson. He is not just a free man; he is a celebrity politician. India, honestly, never stops to amaze. Mother of Democracy? That does not just seem to be a creative copywriter's imagination on roller-skates but an attempt at unalloyed subterfuge. Yet, at the G20 Summit being hosted by PM Modi, India's civilizational values of tolerance and compassion, oneness and syncretism would be lauded. Umar Khalid, on the other hand, would be spending his time looking out at the stars in the night from his dark, dingy and desolate cell, while Joe Biden, the US President, will in all probability hail Modi's inspired leadership, his commitment to upholding the highest democratic principles and so on. The usual drivel, the predictable blah blah which happens in these high-sounding meets. India never ceases to amaze me, as does the hypocrisy of global political leadership.

To say that 2024 is a watershed year for global democracy will not be an exaggeration. Three countries go to polls in myriad circumstances. They are all considered to be, theoretically speaking at least, the lodestars of free speech, possessing independent institutions of public governance, a vigilant media and an argumentative civil society. They have also produced incredibly inspiring political leaders, who in their own way, have affected humankind enormously and most certainly their own countries. Abraham Lincoln, Mahatma Gandhi, Winston Churchill, F.D. Roosevelt, Jawaharlal Nehru, John F. Kennedy, Margaret Thatcher and Barack Obama are a few such individuals. The United States, Britain and India will be, at different times of 2024, voting in their general elections either to re-elect their incumbent government or choose a new alternative. The choice will have serious ramifications for global democracy, which has already been haemorrhaging for a while now.

America will be watched with interest, as it appears that the world's current sole superpower is struggling with some alarming internal schisms within its broken society. The country is so sharply fragmented that it is almost a foregone conclusion as to which are the red and blue states, bringing the election of the most powerful CEOs of the world down to just a handful of swing states. Only a few thousand votes would do. When Joe Biden defeated Donald Trump in 2020, he raked in 81 million votes, the highest accumulated number of any president in history. But there was a catch. Trump, with 72 million votes, actually got more popular votes than Barack Obama, the Democrat poster boy of White House statesmanship.[5] Polarization creates an uncanny arithmetic. Despite innumerable violations of law and several convictions for attempting to delegitimize the presidential elections of 2020, inciting riots at Capitol Hill, pressuring officials, violating voting rights, etc., which would have normally forced any political aspirant into certain oblivion, if not forced hibernation, Trump appears to be the front runner to become the Republican nominee to take on the incumbent Biden. The controversial billionaire has literally redefined the traditional Republican as a white supremacist, anti-immigrant, climate-change denier, anti-vaxxer, and worse, a violent insurrectionist if denied. Trump might just return, for good or worse, as the next president in 2024.

Despite giving the Conservatives their biggest majority (after Margaret Thatcher) in the House of Commons in December 2019, Boris Johnson, the floppy-haired unpredictable maverick with a razor-sharp ability to connect to Tory emotions, could not remain prime minister for his full term. While he successfully navigated the Brexit quagmire to stump his critics from both within and outside his party, his mercurial ways and shameless fakery eventually caught up with him. In fact, his own party loyalists turned Judas-like, fearing total electoral annihilation after the Partygate exposé, a downbeat economy and post-Brexit British isolationism in relation to its European neighbours. Johnson, however, still contemplates a comeback. As does India's Narendra Modi.

Modi has already been prime minister since 2014. Someone who wants to usher in what he terms as 'New India'. So far, I have struggled to comprehend what the definition encapsulates. But one thing is apparent, that the Idea of India, as is still traditionally understood, is considered Old India by Modi and his party. It is often derided as an esoteric western-educated elite's fantasy, the Khan Market gang which likes biscotti with their cappuccino, which must be cursorily jettisoned. It already has been. Modi's New India is already an operational reality: fearful, fractured and coloured in a monochromatic flourish across the canvas, obliterating any hues that might impinge on the dominant theme, leaving no one in doubt that the artist seeks to leave the viewer dazzled with a saffron spray.

In his epic book, *The Idea of India*, author Sunil Khilnani writes, 'To me, in 1997 and now, the idea of a plural India, open to diverse and competing beliefs, is not an achieved ideal. It is a work in progress: a field of tension, or arena of debate, where differing conceptions of India can encounter one another, seeking to persuade—and willing to listen. Yet that conception, of a nation advancing through self-criticism to a more complex understanding of itself, is regularly threatened by more exclusivist views of nation and of community.'[6] This Idea of India is under a regular treadmill test in India these days.

Pandit Jawaharlal Nehru, India's first prime minister, constructed a modern democracy from the embers of a bloody Partition, a plundered economy and an imperious monarchy that had stripped it off its self-confidence. The post-Partition, post-Gandhi phase would end up being called Nehruvian India. Nehru was able to successfully create an inclusive social infrastructure because besides his own indomitable pursuit of a pluralistic India, he also received a public mandate to do so in three successive general elections. He was prime minister for seventeen years until his death on 27 May 1964. If Nehru did not have parliamentary longevity, it is possible that India could have taken on an altogether different course long earlier, as evidenced by the Congress under a vacillating and ultimately autocratic Indira Gandhi. Essentially, to reconstruct or recalibrate a nation, continuity in office is a prerequisite. It helps for sure. One needs time to make seminal changes. Were Modi to win a record-equalling third term, he would have the opportunity to completely reimagine the country as he deems fit. A metamorphosis of sorts is possible, albeit the metabolism may be ugly. The manifestations of the first ten years presents a tenebrous prospect. Nothing else could match how much India has changed since Modi became the country's self-proclaimed Pradhan Sevak than two gory episodes that were both morally revulsive and embroiled visceral repugnance with their object of hate.

On 3 May 2023, unknown to the rest of India, two women were paraded naked by a revanchist mob numbering about a thousand in Manipur. One of them was later gangraped.[7] Publicly. By the mob. No one knows how many. Two of the relatives who tried to come to the women's aid were butchered in cold blood. This horrific episode was apparently, shockingly enough, not known to either the state government or New Delhi. If it was not for a video that went viral on social media, perhaps India would have never heard of the barbarism of biblical proportions happening within its territorial boundaries. Was this justice for all in the New India envisaged by Modi?

As the Jaipur-Mumbai Central Superfast Express train neared Palghar on the outskirts of suburban Mumbai on 31 July 2023, a thirty-three-year-old railway police officer by the name of Chetan Singh went rogue, transforming into a terrifying monster. He literally hunted down Muslims identifiable by the beard, skull cap and lungi or pyjama that they wore and shot them dead. He also pummelled bullets into his senior, a Hindu, who perhaps tried to stop him.[8] He then used the vestibules to saunter across several coaches while tracking his hapless prey. Co-passengers appeared remarkably unaffected as they shot pictures on their mobile videos, while the murderer stood like a bounty hunter lording over the massacre that he had perpetrated. Singh then announced to the world, 'If you want to live and vote in Hindustan, I am telling you, it's only Modi and Yogi.'[9] In short, he was telling the world, through his sickening, cruel ways, that the Muslims had to support India's prime minister and the Uttar Pradesh Chief Minister Yogi Adityanath if they wanted to live in India. Among those whom he killed was forty-three-year-old Saifuddin Mainuddin. He was the only breadwinner of his family, and left behind his wife and three young daughters, lamentably and so unnecessarily orphaned. Their ages are six years, two years and six months. The six-month-old child is the lucky one; she had a providential escape from perpetual nightmares; she is too young to decipher the rage that led to her father's mutilation. When hate goes retail and lone wolves walk around fearlessly in search of imagined demons, a nation steps closer to the precipice. That is the story of New India.

I meet people who talk of India's rapid digitization, expanded expressways, the fifth-largest economy in the world status, continuing Foreign Direct Investments (FDIs), the rise of new dollar multi-millionaires, rising sales of Electric Vehicles (EVs) and a booming stock market as proof of India's global standing, its invincibility. With more than a modicum of regret, they wish that maybe social welfare expenditure for those living below the poverty line was significantly curtailed. The demagogic incendiary and sectarian schisms of the politicians do not feature high in their table menus. They miss the woods for the trees. It appears in the opinions of some that if we live in a self-created giant bubble where one can buy luxury goods online and order avocadoes and cheese platters on the fly, then India is an unstoppable nation headed for destination Davos. It is a myopic, flawed and inward-looking mindset. If India were to abandon its diverse character, allow mobs to go on a wild rampage and permit sulphuric rage to escalate across the country, then it could be staring at a potential apocalypse. Those who foolishly believe that this is India's big bang moment, irrespective of the civil war in Manipur and the social divides within the rest, besides flagrant income inequalities and overall institutional emasculation, could be doing their dear country a great disservice. Religious majoritarianism and populist nationalism are not some meaningless nugatory of an intellectual's imagination; they are India's reality. And the truth is always like a bitter pill—hard to swallow. There is a famous saying that you can wake a man who is asleep, but what do you do with someone who is only pretending to be?

This book is not like the innumerable books on India which recapture its baronial history from time immemorial. In fact, it is a focused look at a critical period, from 2020 to 2024, as India heads to its eighteenth general election. During this period, India experienced among others, the sapping Covid pandemic, year-long farmer protests, a resurrection of the for-long sluggish Congress, the construction and inauguration of the Ram temple (BJP's political rehabilitation began with the Ayodhya agitation in 1989), the dramatic rise of plutocracy and the virtual knuckling under of India's Big Media to the government. Mother of Democracy seems like black humour, given the goings-on in the country. If you wish to get a thorough timeline of India since Modi became prime minister, then I suggest you read this book in conjunction with my previous, *2014: The Great Unravelling*.

The year 2024 thus becomes India's moment of truth. The 800-pound gorilla in the room is whether India can survive this ongoing unrelenting assailment of a minority section of its own, while it browbeats the few remaining voices of reason and sanity under its iron-fisted ruthlessness. On the face of it, it remains an unsustainable model, but stranger things have happened, and people have acquiesced with repressive regimes by popular choice, Turkey being a recent example. The tryst with destiny of 1947 built the foundations of a liberal democracy and a secular society, although there were occasional aberrations like the Emergency of 1975. But India always found its way back, largely because the people, civil society, Opposition parties, media and the judiciary were its guardrails. As India is overwhelmed with the hallucination of a perfidious Amrit Kaal and the perennial reminder that the past must be rewritten to create New India, it enters a slippery slope. After that, it is usually followed by a free fall.

PROLOGUE

*'A patriot must always be ready to defend his country
against his government.'*
—*Edward Abbey*

IT WAS ONE of the hottest days of the year in the UK. Red alerts were frequently broadcast, and a country unaccustomed to 40° centigrade summer temperatures moved about with nervous trepidation, sweating profusely under the collar. The iridescent blue cloudless sky matched the colours of the jersey worn by the city's celebrated champion football team, Manchester City. There was a cautionary warning: stay indoors, unless you must. I had no choice. I was scheduled to fly back to Mumbai that night after a quirky mix of football watching, book writing, cricket binging and endless long walks with my younger daughter who studied there. Taxis were understandably in short supply, and so I waited anxiously for my Uber driver to show up. On the App, the driver looked a confounded mess, judging by the way the small rectangular beetle-shaped miniature car moved around the hotel block on my mobile screen, like a headless chicken attempting a merry-go-round. I was getting increasingly irritable; the Avanti Westcoast Express from Manchester Piccadilly station to Euston, London was to depart in less than thirty minutes. The weather fulminated, and I fumed. Then suddenly, the digital toy-car popped out of my screen and arrived in the shape of a midsized white Volkswagen sedan, its taillights flashing incessantly. I thought that was being rather audacious; after all, I had been waiting inordinately long, and now the driver was being discourteous enough to tell me to hurry up. It was like the proverbial pot calling the kettle black. But I was relieved, nevertheless.

A man about his mid-forties emerged from the driver's seat, wearing a creasy white shirt and crumpled beige-coloured chinos, the latter matching the furrowed lines on his dry cheeks. It was apparent, looking at him, that he perhaps looked older than he really was. He avoided eye contact but said: 'Sorry! I just dropped a passenger at Oxford Street and rushed. There are so few of us on the road today. Everyone is staying at home, I think. Too hot to handle.' I didn't say anything, mentally calculating that I had approximately twenty-four minutes to board the usually punctual southbound train. Hollow pleasantries were beyond me, as I belong in the category of those who are pathologically obsessed about reaching transport destinations way ahead of time. Missing a train or a flight is blasphemous in my books. I have a spotless record, and I was not about to besmirch that accomplishment. But I had quickly glanced to see his badge, an oblong white plastic card, double the size of a credit card, hanging round his neck girded by a blue ribbon: Shahnawaaz Khan (name changed) it read.

There was an awkward silence in the car as we drove past the several buildings that form the University of Manchester campus: an impatient passenger in the backseat, checking his mobile phone watch frequently and a cautious but seemingly talkative driver in the front. 'Where are you going, Sir?' the driver blurted, perhaps surprising himself too but eager to douse the impenetrable tension in the car that added to the rising afternoon glaze. 'London,' I said, my monosyllabic response meant to articulate my intention, which was to be left alone. But Khan had other ideas. 'I guessed that,' he said, 'but what I meant was where are you from?' I am usually loquacious when travelling as I find cab drivers are the best city-guide brochure; everything of import is locked in their experience membrane. They also have a sixth sense of the public mood. But today I was restless, exasperated. Small talk was not my thing. 'Sir?' he implored. The Google map showed me that the short journey was to end in nine minutes. I could survive this torturous barrage for that long for sure, I told myself. 'India,' I said. 'Me too, Sir, I am from India, too.' And I could sense the abrupt animation in his voice. In a second, almost preternaturally, the insurmountable walls that separated us had eviscerated. We were linked. Khan and I were brothers from the same land. Had I avoided conversation with him earlier because I presumed he was a Pakistani as Manchester has a huge population of them? An unconscious bias maybe?

'How long have you been living here?' I asked, peppering my pithy linguistic expressions with a first full sentence. He was thrilled that I had at last evinced an interest to engage. 'I have been here for twenty years, Sir. It has been a very long time.' 'Do you go back to India from time to time?' 'No, sir,' he said wistfully, his initial blithely disposition, dramatically punctured. 'I have been home just once since I came here. And that was about ten years ago.' I sensed an antsy tone, an allusion to anguish. I probed further, almost genuinely keen to know what had stopped a man from returning to the homeland he seemed to be so hopped-up about just a few minutes earlier. Strangely, now it was me who wanted a conversation. 'And why is that?'

We were now about three minutes away from reaching the train terminus. 'Sir, I left along with my brother in 2002. He has decided to never go back. And my wife and children don't want me to go back either. That's why.' He sounded choked, overwhelmed maybe that he was sharing a deep personal excruciation with a complete stranger who not long ago would have preferred to have no dialogue with him whatsoever. 'Are you from Gujarat?' He nodded; 'Yes,' he said. 'What happened?' The taxi had slowed considerably as it neared the entry gate to Piccadilly station. We were almost there. 'Nothing,' he said, as he shook his head vigorously from left to right and back. And then he began to cry. A soft sob, followed by a guttural sigh. 'I am sorry,' I said. There was nothing else I could have uttered but that word that often sounds nothing more than moronic helplessness, a false sympathy. The driver did not have to say anything. I knew.

He helped me with my luggage and waited for me to pull out my credit card for contactless payment on his mobile machine. 'Listen, there are many people in India who are fighting hard to create a society of oneness. It is not easy, but we will get there. Hopefully soon.' I tried to assuage him and convince myself too, I guess. 'I wish you luck, sir. I wish everyone luck, sir. Thank you for talking to me so sweetly.' He held out his quivering hands, seeking solace from a man he would probably never see again. 'Goodbye,' I said, 'and I hope you will visit your ancestral home soon.' He held my right hand with both of his own, not willing to let go. We were two Indians in Manchester, thousands of miles away from our own country, bonding over a ten-minute taxi ride.

He waited for me to leave, waving gently until I had disappeared from his sight. I trudged my luggage up the escalator and wondered what it felt like to live with the fear of never seeing the neighbourhood one grew up in, the playground where a cricket carnival with tennis balls once crowded out the rest, the kites soaring into the skies for a frenetic duel with colourful adversaries and the familiar smell of home-made pickles in the kitchen. A kaleidoscope of memories, closed forever.

I checked my watch. My earlier disquiet was unwarranted. The fastidious man was very much in time. While the taxi driver returned to his duties on the wretched surly afternoon, I ordered a cold lemonade while waiting for my train to take me to London, from where I would later head to my homeland: India.

1

THE BLOODSTAINED EARTH

*'There are moments in your life when you must act, even
though you cannot carry your best friends with you.
The "still small voice" within you must always be the final
arbiter when there is a conflict of duty.'*

—*Mahatma Gandhi*

THEY SAY THAT the most excruciating human experience is that
of a parent losing their child. Honestly, it must be an unbearable
trauma; hard to even contemplate. But for Fatima Hussain,* it was
made even more sepulchral, doused with savagery as it was. Her
three-year-old daughter, perhaps not more than two feet tall, was
slaughtered in front of her eyes by a bloodthirsty mob comprising
of several rapacious men,[1] for whom death was their only salvation.
Eleven monsters gangraped Fatima Hussain, her mother and her
sister; they were not just viscerally revengeful, they were determined
to exterminate her dignity, leave her scarred for perpetuity were
she to survive. At the time when she was experiencing a nauseating

---

* Owing to a legal prohibition on mentioning the names of survivors of
crimes of this nature, a pseudonymous name has been used.

avalanche of sexual violence, Hussain was five months pregnant. Many of those beastly men were her neighbours, people whom she knew, people who had purchased milk from her. They were now transmogrified demons. It was 3 March 2002.

The Gujarat riots of 2002 was an apotheosis of hate, as all communal holocausts are. Innocents from both Hindu and Muslim communities were massacred. Fatima's tiny toddler was among them. The cold-blooded brutalization of Fatima did not end there. Seven of her family members met the same fate, reduced to lifeless limbs, as the violent lynching continued unabated and human fury assumed ghoulish proportions. Official records indicate that 1,400 people were killed, belonging to both religious communities of Hindus and Muslims.[2] Unreported, unofficial estimates suggest a much larger depressing statistic.

If Hussain survived, it had a lot to do with divine intervention perhaps, or a fluke occurrence. But her miserableness did not end there. Local police stations in Gujarat refused to lodge a complaint against the perpetrators of the butcherly homicide. To use the hackneyed expression, she had to run from pillar to post in several police stations. Even in despair and having suffered depravity and unimaginable injury, Hussain was all alone. Helpless. Indian democracy was just a bystander, a nomenclature only for intellectual confabulations and political grandstanding, a constitutional guarantee that meant nothing. Hussain had been raped twenty-two times. Her arm was broken. So was the great Indian republic.

That the criminal justice system was being flagrantly flouted by the state administration was apparent when the Supreme Court transferred Hussain's rape case out of Gujarat to Mumbai, Maharashtra in August 2004. A special court later convicted eleven rapists to life imprisonment in 2008, providing Hussain and her family a sliver of hope that there was indeed comeuppance in this parallel universe. But it took till 2019, when the Supreme Court ultimately gave her a financial compensation of Rs 50 lakhs to rebuild her life, to rehabilitate her smashed home. It appeared, momentarily at least, that there was an end to this sordid nightmare, for Fatima Hussain—one that had begun in Randhikpur village near Ahmedabad seventeen years earlier. But it was not to be.

On 15 August 2022, the BJP was popularizing the shibboleth of Amrit Kaal (a period of purity). Allegedly, India under Modi and the BJP, was now in that divine period of supreme blissfulness, untainted by animus, untarnished by sectarianism, a superlative society of unrivalled goodness and prosperity, a flowing river of milk and honey. Mahatma Gandhi, Netaji Bose, Sardar Patel, Maulana Azad, Pandit Nehru and the other freedom fighters, and of course, the principal architect of the Constitution, Dr Babasaheb Ambedkar, would have huddled together in heaven to watch the grand exultations below. After all, it was a historic day. What they saw, must have left them devastated. The eleven rapists of Fatima Hussain were released from prison, ahead of time. A stunned nation watched the astonishing betrayal of Hussain on prime-time news. India was celebrating its haloed seventy-fifth year of Independence.

The BJP ruled government of Gujarat had, of course, done its legal homework and found that as per the remission policy of 1992, the convicted rapists were legally entitled to being prematurely released. Their case was buttressed by a Supreme Court order that overturned a Gujarat High Court verdict earlier that gave the administrative jurisdiction to decide on the case to Maharashtra, where the trial had been held in the first place.[3] The revised remission policy of 2014 (which is currently applicable) prohibits felons of heinous crimes such as rape and murder from being treated with any exception; for them, life imprisonment is permanent, a cul-de-sac. Since Hussain's rapists were sentenced and convicted in 2008, the new rules did not apply was the reasoning of the Chief Minister Bhupendra Patel government.[4] It was done with contemptuous disregard for not just political propriety but of human decency itself. Of course, the Gujarat assembly elections were due a few months later in December 2022. But the farcical pantomime did not end there.

When the eleven rapists walked out of prison, what awaited them was a red-carpet welcome, a warm, effusive homecoming,[5] which would have left an Olympic gold medallist returning home from foreign shores chafed with the outrageousness of it all. It was not a moment for sober introspection, or for atonement as it should have been; the hurried release symbolized the moral decadence of a society which had degenerated into a cesspool. Sweets distributed, garlands buffering their necks, the prisoners appeared to be part of a noisy society tamasha.[6] Fatima Hussain's dastardly ugly memories of the past were naturally reignited. Justice was eluding her all over again. The government in New Delhi was silent even as millions of Indians were stunned by the perversity of the travesty. Of course, there were equally many if not more who were clapping and dancing in joy all over the state.

Justifications for the rapists' release poured in like an unstoppable deluge. People change, they have a right to be reformed, was the popular refrain. Among others, there was this peculiar reasoning: 'We must show compassion towards them. After all, they are Brahmins. They have intrinsic Sanskar.'[7] The superior caste hubris was uttered by a BJP MLA who was part of the committee that recommended the early remission. Incidentally, he is an elected lawmaker from the Godhra constituency, the same controversial place where the Sabarmati Express bogey number two was burnt down on 26 February 2002, which triggered India's first state-sponsored genocide.[8]

Fatima Hussain released the following statement after hearing of the rapists' and murderers' release. 'The release of these convicts has taken from me my peace and shaken my faith in justice. My sorrow and my wavering faith is not for myself alone but for every woman who is struggling for justice in courts. I was bereft of words. I am still numb. Today, I can say only this—how can justice for any woman end like this? I trusted the highest courts in our land. I trusted the system, and I was learning slowly to live with my trauma.'[9] She added: 'No one enquired about my safety and well-being, before taking such a big and unjust decision. I appeal to the Gujarat Government, please undo this harm. Give me back my right to live without fear and in peace. Please ensure that my family and I are kept safe,' said Hussain.[10] A few weeks later, India quietly, unaffectedly, moved on. PM Modi did not say a word. It was unconscionable, but India had other pressing priorities clearly.

The problem with a terminal, moral crisis of a nation, which is an aggregation of individual righteousness, is that there is no easy nostrum. It is a work in progress; normally epiphanies don't happen, because finding a messiah in today's politics in India is like looking for a needle in a haystack. They are there, but they are usually sidelined or neglected in our hierarchy driven social systems and political structures. I have seen wonderful people with utopian dreams who have meekly surrendered to realpolitik, to the debased cesspool that Indian politics has become. Lifting a country whose inner conscience is on tired legs will require a herculean effort from someone who is an alchemist seeking nothing for himself but everything for the soil of the country of his birth. Like Gandhi, in whose state of birth, Fatima Hussain stood shamed.

2

THE POLICEMAN COMES KNOCKING

'I learned that courage was not the absence of fear, but the triumph over it. The brave man is not he who does not feel afraid, but he who conquers that fear.'

—*Nelson Mandela*

THE HULLABALOO WHICH happened when the Assam police suddenly swooped into the Delhi airport to arrest my former colleague Pawan Khera, chief spokesperson of the Congress party, on 23 February 2023 should have been expected. It was an absurd overreaction. Nothing justified the sanctimonious outrage of the ruling Bhartiya Janata Party at Khera's sardonic dig at the Prime Minister Narendra Modi's alleged buddy-buddy relationship with the controversial businessman, Gautam Adani. Police state? Yes. Illiberal democracy? Totally. Bodacious dictatorship? Almost there.

It is clear that liberalism has been in retreat in recent years. According to Freedom House, political rights and civil liberties around the world rose during the three and a half decades

6

between 1974 and the early 2000s, but have been falling for fifteen straight years prior to 2021 in what has been labeled a democratic recession or even depression.[1]

India fitted the global trend perfectly.

Politics is about both subtle and overt messaging; the several FIRs filed against Khera, a television busybody who commands loquacious answers to all of the BJP barbs, was an unambiguous message to everyone else out there in India's hyperventilating political ecosystem: we can come after you. Straight and simple. The fangs of an authoritarian bully were being showboated. Take it or lump it. Be scared.

Khera had, in a press conference held earlier in Mumbai, wickedly used some wordplay with Modi's father's name, pretending to inadvertently call him Gautam Das instead of his real name Damodar Das. The innuendo was on the Modani relationship, but to call it slander, was an overstatement (the matter is sub judice in the SC). Given the bizarre histrionics we see in the Parliament from elected members of the House, wherein even Modi speaks in disparaging terms about the Nehru surname, as if it is an albatross round the neck of the Gandhi family, what Khera said was relatively innocuous. Khera was only playing by the standard rules of contemporary political speak. Should Khera have, however, given himself a green card to join the substandard conversations that define our public discourse today? Probably not. It was, in retrospect, completely unwarranted. But then it is not easy being the national spokesperson of a party. One is daily, gingerly, navigating a minefield. You are expected to deliver an annihilated opponent, bludgeoned to bits to your party bosses. In the nightly blood-fest ritual that happens on prime-time TV, there can be only one man standing when the curtains fall. The pressure is enormous. It was there earlier too, but it has got nauseatingly toxic now.

Long before I became an official voice of the grand old party in 2013, I had been articulating the Congress position—ever since Anna Hazare and Arvind Kejriwal were daily hammering an unusually tepid UPA government in 2011 on the Lok Pal bill. The regulars representing the Congress were Abhishek Manu Singhvi, Manish Tewari, Jayanthi Natarajan and the humble author himself. Occasionally, Renuka Chowdhury and Rajiv Shukla joined in. The BJP fielded the veteran Ravi Shankar Prasad, Nirmala Sitharaman, Prakash Javadekar and Piyush Goyal. When it came to serious heavy lifting, Arun Jaitley made his commanding presence felt. Trust me, there was no love lost, and it was often acrid, but we unwittingly, subconsciously knew where to draw the line. Javadekar was always humble, and although Prasad found me an exasperating gate-crasher into the elite club, he never got nasty. The others were equally sufferable. Things changed dramatically after the monstrous emergence of social media, particularly Twitter, in the post-2014 phase.

> A party emboldened by a favourable election result or motivated by ideology, or both, might change the system from within. When fascists or Nazis or communists did well in the elections in the 1930s or '40s, what followed was some combination of spectacle, repression, and salami tactics—slicing off layers of opposition one by one. Most people were distracted, some were imprisoned, and others were outmatched.[2]

Khera was not the sole collateral damage of a targeted witch-hunt. Several Opposition leaders, such as Manish Sisodia and Satyendra Jain of AAP, Nawab Malik of NCP, Sanjay Raut of Shiv Sena, Congress leaders D.K. Shivakumar and Karti Chidambaram, TMC's Abhishek Banerjee, were being regularly questioned.[3] The BJP's intention of demolishing the Opposition and making India a one-party state was a work in progress, it seemed.

For spokespersons from the Opposition, 2014 was a turning point. With most TV channels embracing the new dispensation, social media became the agony aunt that everyone needed. A new trend emerged. The moment a programme concluded, spokespersons would rush to their social media accounts to seek validation from their equally demanding if not trenchant echo chambers on their performance. The louder the applause and appreciation got, the higher the aggression and combativeness from the bruised gladiators in the nightly circus. The motivation to indulge in exaggerated theatrics and name-calling had suddenly become de rigueur. Spokespersons had to become actors. News became politainment, like a Netflix spectacle pregnant with sound bites, whataboutery, fake news and dialogue-baazi. Bellicosity becomes a badge of honour. I often encounter this spokesperson from the BJP, who comes prepared with a C-grade Bollywood script and mouths the dialogues with professional agency. I believe he is a superhit with a cult following in his charmed constituency. But honestly, we do a great disservice to non-aligned television viewers.

Spokespersons are also given an instant assessment by their party superiors or colleagues following a political slugfest; the more caustic or ill-tempered, the better. The decline in standards is startling. Pawan Khera, in my opinion, was a victim of the ballooning age of competitive muckraking. It is the new playground. The gloves are off; détente is a distant dream. While some of my former colleagues have sometimes trespassed the red lines that define a civilized dialogue, I need to regretfully state that the BJP is more guilty of being deliberately coarse and crude, thereby creating a corrosive environment of mutual recriminations. Khera and team, honestly, had limited elbowroom to make their case on most shows.

For the Congress, the crucial lesson from the Khera episode was not to fall for the BJP's tit for tat culture. As for the BJP, it might be worth remembering that their biggest heartthrob got the first name of the Father of the Nation wrong. Modi had referred to Gandhi as Mohanlal Karamchand Gandhi. Mohandas must have squirmed in his grave. The Sabarmati Ashram is in Ahmedabad, incidentally. A slip of the tongue is not unusual, perhaps. The SC quickly intervened and cut short the intent of the Assam and UP police (both under BJP state governments) to arrest Khera after forcibly deplaning him. Khera got interim relief, but unknown to many, was someone putting his ear to the keyhole and eavesdropping on freewheeling conversations, ostensibly for reasons of national security?

The hashtag #PegasusSnoopGate trended on Twitter on 27 October 2021, following the Supreme Court of India's observations (it was a long 46-page order) on the several petitions filed before it. The petitioners were allegedly being spied upon by the Modi government.[4] It was a watershed moment which only confirmed the rumours of ongoing surveillance circulating in several drawing rooms. Several TV pundits were divided on whether it was India's 'Watergate' moment. The Opposition was understandably livid. Until the issue met a proper legal consummation, it was expected that both camps would take their traditional positions. At stake was individual liberty and the right to privacy, among a host of other fundamental rights.

US President Richard Nixon was impeached because of the organized conspiracy of wire-tapping phones and robbing documents in the Democratic National Committee headquarters in Washington in June 1972. It was, at that time, an unprecedented political scandal of egregious immorality, which understandably shocked the world. #PegasusSnoopGate however could be worse if it established that the government was indeed playing the

George Orwellian Big Brother, because the targets here were not just Opposition leaders (Rahul Gandhi) but included freelancers like Prashant Kishor, journalists like Siddharth Varadarajan (whose online portal The Wire was part of the global consortium of new organizations that collected data for the secret project), activists, bureaucrats and even a Supreme Court judge. It was an eclectic list with a disturbing commonality; almost everyone had been vociferously questioning the government and its anti-democratic conduct. This was a citizen of India versus the State issue. India was now in the discredited company of Azerbaijan, Kazakhstan, Saudi Arabia, UAE, Rwanda, Morocco, Mexico, Hungary, Bahrain, etc. which are infamous for their police-state infrastructure. Significantly, the three-judge SC bench looking into Pegasus spyware was headed by Chief Justice of India N.V. Ramana, signaling the importance of the contentious subject that was at the core of civil liberties and free speech in India. The court was already grappling with similar cases. Snooping was alleged by several Left-wing activists who languished in jails on the Bhima-Koregaon issue.

That was not the end of the cyberattack on the Bhima Koregaon accused and their supporters. Citizen Lab, a Canada-based institution that examines such breaches, said that, between January and October 2019, nine human rights defenders were targeted with emails containing malicious links. Three of the nine were also targeted By Pegasus spyware through WhatsApp in 2019. The NSO group, which manufactures Pegasus spyware, told the court that they only sell to government intelligence and law enforcement agencies.

Who was responsible for this expensive, long-drawn-out manipulation of evidence and targeting of individuals? The only logical answer is that it has to have been one or more government agencies. Which ones though? There are numerous intelligence agencies and security forces that have intelligence operations. A conservative count puts at least twenty-two intelligence arms at the Union level, besides the police at the state level. All of them have some kind of cyber operations, while some of them, like NTRO, R&AW and even IB, have significant capabilities in that area.[5]

The government's defence was languid at best, disingenuous at worst and left a lot to wild speculation. As the SC correctly stated, it was at best a 'limited affidavit' which was submitted by the Modi government to the SC.[6] It neither confirmed nor denied the use of Pegasus. BJP-led NDA was tergiversating; it was being abstruse on a matter of great import. The government refused to answer the primal question: Did the government acquire the Pegasus Spyware from NSO, the Israeli firm which has a powerful client list worldwide? Crucially, NSO sells its powerful software directly to sovereign governments only and not to private third parties. Thus, if the published material was true then it was impossible that individual mobile phones were hacked into without direct state authorization, or through one of its security agencies. The government was publicly ambivalent on this, while its spokespeople did the usual foggy-dodgy bit. Even the minister of Information Technology in Parliament was equivocating on the subject. But why? As usual, the ruling party took sanctuary under the pretext of 'national security'. Various BJP-ruled state governments have frequently abused existing statutory laws in a draconian fashion, using national security, sedition and threat to public order as an excuse. There has been a cavalier disregard for protecting an individual's fundamental rights as guaranteed under the Indian Constitution.

Interestingly, the SC refused to accede to the government's request to form a special panel of experts on its own to get to the bottom of the proposed Pegasus investigation.[7] There is a humongous trust-deficit with the current dispensation in India, and it is not limited to traditional political adversaries. Large sections of mainstream media, NGOs, Left-leaning intellectuals, artistes, think tanks, activists and authors have been incessantly harangued by the vindictive establishment. The cases of sedition charges being imposed on Muslims who, in different parts of the country, celebrated Pakistan's victory over India in a T20 World Cup match and the unwarranted harassment of actor Shah Rukh Khan's son Aryan Khan in a drug case in Mumbai reflected that there was rampant institutional intimidation at work. The law was being flagrantly abused; to use a cliché, the process is the punishment. When we juxtapose the assortment of cases targeting marginalized or prominent individuals against the Pegasus spying of political stakeholders, one can comprehend the authoritarian atmosphere in India. Fishing expeditions were the rule, not the exception.

The SC selected a distinguished panel comprising former SC judge R.V. Raveendran, former IPS officer Alok Joshi and cybersecurity expert Sundeep Oberoi to probe into the mass surveillance issue which had rocked and rattled India.[8] The roles were temporarily reversed; for a change, the government was being frisked, under the supervision of the SC. The future of a dwindling democracy was being watched with deep interest. It was time India confronted some inconvenient truths. But as has happened several times earlier, it all ended with an embarrassing whimper, a stunning noncommittal verdict which got the Modi government to get away scot-free, albeit the government did get a dressing down. The panel concluded in the August of 2022 that of the meagre twenty-nine mobile phones which went through forensic scrutiny, they could not specifically detect Pegasus spyware on them, although there were five cases where malware was explicitly detected. It added, 'We will say [it] in one sentence—the government did not cooperate with the technical committee on the scrutiny of the devices for Pegasus spyware.' There were thus two apparent conclusions; the government sidestepped the Pegasus investigations; but why would it do that? Malware was found in 16 per cent of the mobile phones under observation, and while the results were inconclusive, it did not outright reject the infiltration of Pegasus either? That left the final outcome as hazy as it was before, when the SC had strongly defended an individual's right to privacy, which the Modi government had churlishly repudiated as irrelevant in the larger context of national security. In fact, the government had cited the latter as a ruse to escape a judicial review. None of this sounded right, but tragically, in India's fast-moving news bulletin age, in what could have been the most scandalous case of state surveillance, the explosive revelations got summarily buried. But a body far more powerful than the winged horse Pegasus, the namesake of the monstrous organization, was making its formidable presence felt in the political battlefield; it was called the Enforcement Directorate (ED).

India seemed to be on an overdrive to establish itself as a hybrid model of an elected autocracy. Thus, the government led by Prime Minister Modi took another stupefying decision that brought democracy's doomsday even closer. Through an Ordinance, it empowered India's political executive 'to increase the tenure of the chiefs of Central Bureau of Investigation (CBI) and the Enforcement Directorate (ED) to up to five years, from the previous two years as prescribed by a Supreme Court order (Vineet Narain case, 1997). This was atrocious, and manifested the barefaced authoritarianism of a repressive regime, which was incorrigibly in a clampdown mode. The government was conveying a crystal-clear message to the people of India; it was no different from tin-pot dictatorships. We will do as we please, damn constitutional proprietary and political ethics (the expected whataboutery that even the Congress had done it in the past was extravagantly employed), was the explicit political messaging.

The Winter Session of Parliament which followed, was predictably shambolic. That an ordinance of such grave import needed parliamentary deliberations, which in any case was a procedural requirement, was never on the table. The tyranny of the majority rule was there for all to see. So why was the BJP/ NDA in such a tearing hurry to proclaim an Ordinance (this was its 83rd Ordinance since 2014). It has an absolute majority in Lok Sabha with 303 seats. The needle of suspicion fell on its obvious intent to provide Sanjay Mishra, ED director, with a longer stint on the top job. Mishra was to retire on 19 November 2021. Institutional emasculation of a democratic frameworks does not need a more classic instance than this. This was BJP's open call to subvert the administration of India's powerful investigative agencies for keeping more pliant favorites in the top jobs. Citizen interest could wait. It was a good time to talk about 'caged parrots'. The Supreme Court described the CBI as one during UPA's last days. The parrot was now a mummified, voiceless creature deserving our sincerest commiserations. The vulgar internal warfare within the corrupted CBI was on full public display in an unbecoming brawl between two police veterans, Aloke Verma and Rakesh Asthana. The midnight-hour putsch happened, resulting in a dramatic transfer of power. It seemed as if we were watching a Martin Scorsese directed thriller on the unholy nexus between political grandmasters and the underworld mafia. Sadly, the Supreme Court's intervention went nowhere; it remained couched in hollow talk (Chief Justice Ranjan Gogoi would go on later to become a member of the Rajya Sabha). The loser was India's governance model, which stood atrophied.

It is often said that the health of a democracy is determined by the integrity and independence of its institutions. India's were more fragile than China vase. The embarrassing spectacle of the

Narcotics Control Bureau (NCB) in the celebrity-harassment case of Aryan Khan, son of actor Shah Rukh Khan, was damning. From extortion, pay-offs, selfie-taking and a media witch-hunt to recklessly violating prescribed protocols of search and arrest, the case was a frightful reminder to Indians of the state's unlimited wherewithal for freewheeling intimidation. The soap opera lasted for several weeks as a prime-time top of the charts, just like the actor Sushant Singh Rajput case. The innocent-looking and visibly dumbstruck Aryan Khan was converted into a political football. The man who allegedly orchestrated the entire jamboree was the zonal director of the Narcotics Control Bureau (NCB), Sameer Wankhede, who arrested Khan Jr on allegations of being involved in the 'consumption, sale and purchase' of illegal drugs. From the very beginning, the entire case looked suspiciously like a celebrity witch-hunt, reminiscent of the Rhea Chakravorty case following actor Sushant Singh Rajput's suicide in June 2021. It ended up with a poached egg on the NCB's flushed face.

In May 2022, Khan Jr was given a clean chit by the NCB, now in a U-turn confirming what the world already knew: 'lack of sufficient evidence' and more significantly, 'shortcomings' in its investigation. Wankhede had been earlier moved out of NCB itself, and before long, faced the humiliating ordeal of being charged by the CBI for a Rs 25 crore extortion for Khan Jr's release. The pendulum of political-bureaucratic vicious nexus and its scurrilous ways had swung the other way. There were several cases of harassment of ordinary Indians just doing their regular day job. Social activist Teesta Setalvad, who courageously fought the cases of Gujarat 2002 riot victims, including that of Zakia Jafri, the widow of the slain Congress MP Ehsan Jafri who was killed in the Gulberg Society massacre, was repeatedly harassed, threatened, and even arrested.

After serving two years of his jail term, after he was arrested by the Uttar Pradesh Police while heading to the Hathras household of a Dalit girl who was allegedly gangraped, murdered, and then cremated clandestinely, journalist Siddique Kappan walked a free man in February 2023. India's criminal justice system needs a herculean makeover. Joining Kappan was Dr Kafeel Khan, the thirty-eight-year-old pediatrician from Gorakhpur, who was booked for making an allegedly 'incendiary speech' on the government's citizenship law in a gathering in Aligarh, Uttar Pradesh. To understand the brutality of the government, one had to read what the verdict that eventually led to Dr Khan's release stated. For one, 'he did not promote hatred or violence', and more significantly, the doctor actually gave a call for 'unity among citizens'. It was hard to disassociate the callous bogarting of Dr Khan from the shocking incident of 2017 at the Gorakhpur public hospital where more than sixty children died on account of lack of oxygen supply. Although he claimed in several interviews that he brought 250 cylinders in twenty-four hours to save lives, he had been clearly done in by political vendetta.

The Leh correspondent of the State Times, Tsewang Rigzin, was arrested for a comment against the BJP member of Parliament from Ladakh. The interesting aspect about his arrest is the fact that it wasn't even Rigzin who made the comment. He was arrested solely because the comment was made on a Facebook group of which he was the administrator.[9]

The number of such random cases of unabashed strongarm tactics was staggering.

Muckraking thus became the new game in town. For the ED, the Income Tax and the CBI, given their enormous powers, they can easily destroy reputations, whatever the end outcome of their probes. According to a report, of the 5,906 cases of money-laundering being investigated by the ED, only twenty-five had a successful conviction.[10] That was a miserable 0.42 per cent, meaning that it was more an instrument for political score settling than recovering black money. In a risible diversion of the data, the ED or the government claimed that the twenty-five cases, out of the twenty-six it had successfully concluded, constituted an outstanding performance of 96 per cent conviction rate.[11] It was a desperate effort to circumvent reality. An *Indian Express* investigation exposed the orchestrated prosecution: between 2019 and 2023, out of the 129 cases registered against political leaders, 95 per cent of them targeted the Opposition. Two Congress leaders, Sanjay Patil and Harshvardhan Patil, who joined the BJP in Maharashtra went on record to say that they could sleep peacefully once they had joined Modi's party as the threat of the ED and CBI had receded.[12] In the Shiv Sena Leader Sanjay Raut's case, the special court stated that the arrest of Raut by the ED was illegal. Raut spent two months in jail. In Parliament, senior BJP minister Meenakshi Lekhi threatened Opposition leaders who interrupted her speech with 'Stop, or the ED will come after you.'

The truth is, India is an ersatz democracy; like a gorgeously dolled-up mannequin with a plastic body. Inanimate. Soulless. The ED and CBI are like the government's Rottweilers; they will come after you with their sharp ferocious teeth the moment the master abandons the leash and says Go! Practically all Opposition leaders or political parties are under their penetrative watch—Samajwadi Party leaders, Farooq Abdullah, Congress leaders such as D.K. Shiva Kumar, B.S. Hooda and P. Chidambaram, the Dravida Munnetra Kazhagham (DMK), Bahujan Samaj Party (BSP), Trinamool Congress (TMC), etc. Miraculously, BJP leaders were, of course, as white as Swiss snow. And those from other parties whom BJP either forced or beguiled into joining them had all their past black sin, overnight obliterated from public view. A magical transformation happened. Not surprisingly, political vocabulary came up with a tantalizing insertion for BJP's barefaced hypocrisy: The Great Washing Machine of India. The corrupt had become the cleanest. There were several examples of unscrupulous defectors from other parties on whom further police action ceased altogether; Himanta Biswa Sarma, Suvendu Adhikari, Mukul Roy, Narayan Rane and perhaps the most glittering priceless acquisition of the BJP, Ajit Pawar, formerly of the 'Naturally Corrupt Party (NCP)' as charitably described by PM Modi himself.[13] Indian politics resembled a crime entertainment show, like *Breaking Bad*, with several twists and turns. Ashok Lavasa, formerly of the Election Commission, featured among those who were being snooped on in the #PegasusSnoopGate scandal. Lavasa had strongly dissented (one among three other EC colleagues) in five cases of alleged contraventions of the Model Code of Conduct by Modi and Amit Shah during the 2019 general elections. While the BJP continued to reactivate the Emergency to corner the Congress (a tactic that lasted for twenty-one months) whenever attacked, the truth was that India had entered into its 110 and counting months of unofficial, undeclared Emergency. The gradual dismemberment of Indian democracy was stealthy, mostly indiscernible.

Article 14, an online news portal, showed that 96 per cent of the sedition cases filed against 405 Indians for criticizing political leaders and governments occurred after 2014.[14] The two leaders who prominently stood out were Modi and Uttar Pradesh Chief Minister Yogi Adityanath; criticizing them lead to instantaneous legal action. The major events triggering the onerous law were primarily the farmers protests, Hathras gangrape, Pulwama terror attack and CAA nationwide dharnas. Not surprisingly, those who were on the hit list were all vocal critics of the government: Opposition leaders, journalists, authors, activists, students, public intellectuals, etc. The role of the BJP-ruled states was stark in its audaciousness; with reference to the Pulwama attack, for instance, twenty-six of the twenty-seven sedition cases were filed in states where the party was in power.[15]

Ask any ordinary Indian and they will tell you forthrightly that they do not trust the police, the Income Tax Department or most government departments when it comes to probity. Most have become terribly cynical of even India's last remaining rampart of hope: the judiciary. While the Supreme Court of India has been periodically keeping the unprincipled, unscrupulous governments, both past and present in check, the lower courts have largely disappointed with their anodyne play-it-safe approach which has compromised individual liberties. UAPA has been wantonly abused. Accusations of sedition have been generously interspersed on ordinary civilians: Dr Kafeel Khan, Siddique Kappan, Disha Ravi, Left-wing intellectuals in the Bhima-Koregaon case like Sudha Bharadwaj, Gautam Navlakha, Anand Teltumbe, Varavara Rao, JNU student activist Umar Khalid and Arun Ferriera, among many others. But in terms of the sheer scale of unmitigated shamelessness, the most heartbreaking, tragic case was that of the late Stan Swamy.

Eighty-four-year-old Jesuit priest and human rights activist Father Stan Swamy had spent five decades fighting mining and steel companies as they destroyed the forests, water, and livelihoods of the Adivasis, the tribal population, in the eastern state of Jharkhand, In early October 2020, the National Investigation Agency (NIA)-India's counterterrorism task force-arrested Swamy under the Unlawful Activities Prevention Act, which denied him both bail and a speedy trial. They accused him of instigating violence after the January 2018 Dalit celebration at Bhima Koregaon near Pune in Maharashtra. The NIA described him and fifteen others similarly accused as 'Maoist' terrorists. Swamy, who had advanced Parkinson's disease, was unable to hold a glass of drinking water. With COVID-19 rampant in his overcrowded jail and his frail health making him an easy victim of the deadly disease, he appealed for bail. The NIA curtly countered that he was taking 'undue benefit' of the pandemic, using it merely as 'a ruse.' The courts repeatedly denied Swamy bail, although in late May 2021, they transferred him to a hospital. There, on July 5, he died of COVID-related complications. In truth, a ruthless state had killed 'a caged bird,' as he described himself.[16]

India is living in a dystopian nightmare. And a nightmare only ends when people wake up. But of that there was little sign. It baffled me, the stunning impassiveness to naked coercion from the powers that be. Most seemed happily reconciled to their fate even if they did fret and fume occasionally, probably hoping that some brave soul(s) would pull the country out of the deep black hole. In the meantime, as long as they were not at the receiving end of the khaki-clad stone-faced policeman's wrath, it was okay.

3

THE FINAL FAREWELL

*'Politics is not the art of the possible. It consists in choosing
between the disastrous and the unpalatable.'*

—*J.K. Galbraith*

THE DAY WAS 20 May 2020. It was a strange headache, the kind I had never had before. I am not prone to them, barring an occasional sinus that causes the area above my right eye to throb. This one was indecipherable, both in its intensity, from mild to strong, and its origins, which were totally unknown. Normally, I get a runny nose as an early sign of a cold. This time I had no real sniffle, none of the irascibility in mood that precedes the exasperating bug. None. I was on a Zoom conference call with my senior colleague and Member of Parliament from Thiruvananthapuram Dr Shashi Tharoor, easily India's most flamboyant, articulate and cerebral politician who was also the chairperson of the All-India Professionals Congress. The latter was the Indian National Congress party's new outreach programme for attracting the vast middle class urban population that had recently deserted it, opting instead for Prime Minister Narendra Modi's rhetoric of 'Achhe Din' and 'Maximum Governance and Minimum Government'. I headed the

Maharashtra chapter of AIPC as its president. Our goal was to attract independent professionals such as lawyers, corporate executives, doctors, businessmen, teachers, activists, etc. into our fold. As the Zoom call progressed, I felt a sudden deterioration in my mood, a weird fatigue setting in and disorienting me considerably. Unknown to me, I was coming down with Covid. It would soon usurp India in its asphyxiating grip. And the world.

Like individuals, countries too need to learn from their experiences, particularly when they are hurting. The year 2020 was an outlandish year for all of humanity, leaving most bewildered, baffled at what lay ahead as everyone downed shutters. We remained closeted, frightened of a cough and a sneeze, and got our body temperatures checked more often in one month than we had done in our entire life aggregated together. It was surreal, like watching a doomsday fantasy, dark and cataclysmic. But this was not on Netflix, it was for real. And it was not going away in a hurry.

It was a discombobulating year for India as well, made worse by its own doing. For one, it remained a fatalistic country, believing that some heavenly benedictions would provide a protective shield against the coronavirus monster. A leader from a BJP alliance partner asked people to repeat the positive affirmation, 'Go Corona Go'. Local cures with cow dung, cow urine and Baba Ramdev's Patanjali company's 'breakthrough remedies' were suggested for developing antibodies.

Prime Minister Narendra Modi announced a three-week lockdown on 25 March 2020. The chaotic, cacophonous streets of Mumbai went dead. The silence was impregnated with a satanic eeriness. The bark of a lonely dog broke through the impenetrable quietness. Everyone looked nervous, but no one thought the virus would actually come visiting them. Many opened their mobile calculators to check the law of averages and measure their chances of being infected. The PM, always an assiduous player of doublespeak, talked of a three-week triumph over the virus, reminiscent of the Mahabharata mythology. But by December of 2020, India had over 10 million cases and 1,47,000 Indians were dead.[1] Indeed, there were lessons to be learnt. And it was not just about better public health infrastructure. It was also about politics in the time of calamity.

India had the sui generis distinction of being a thoroughly fractured country right in the middle of a pandemic which was destroying the world. It was playing its favourite spectator sport: the communal trapeze-act. The Tablighi Jamaat (a Muslim missionary group) were accused of a deadly conspiracy to spread the virus in India. Around 3,000 of them had attended an event at Nizamuddin Mosque, Delhi in the middle of March. And while several did test positive, religious animosity was not called for. It was bizarre, but the way mainstream media shoved that malicious propaganda down people's throats, there were several takers for the balderdash. Hate had just received an instant laboratory-approved vaccination. Covid-19 was secular, India's ruling party was not. At least the deadly virus was infecting people without discriminating on the basis of religion, caste, gender, income, class, ethnicity, language or customs. #CoronaJihad was a disgusting slur used to refer to the Muslims of India.

Covid-19 upended India: The GDP for the quarter of April–June 2020 saw a massive 23 per cent contraction; young people were committing suicide because of being jobless; migrants were walking hundreds of miles under the blistering sun and dying along the highways. Some desperate travellers would come under a goods train while they slept on railways tracks. In the meantime, the virus's feral tentacles were ferociously spreading everywhere. In a normal world, people huddle together in an hour of crisis. For India, social distancing included the religious segregation of 200 million citizens of Muslim faith. Not surprisingly by the end of the year, several

BJP-ruled states were actually passing legislations on inter-faith marriages. Ratan Tata, India's celebrated mega-business tycoon, had his crown jewel Titan hastily remove a television commercial which depicted religious compatibility. The commercial was a charming commentary on inter-faith marriage with one terrible flaw in the eyes of the lunatics: a Hindu woman was shown as being pregnant with the child of her Muslim husband. Sacrilege screamed the trolls! How could Titan promote love jihad? Blasphemous, was the social media roar. Love in India was now a four-letter tabooed word. Few spoke up. Covid and communalism were accelerating in tandem.

Earlier, the year had seen communal riots in Delhi and pre-planned attacks by organized mobs on university campuses. As usual, Jawaharlal Nehru University (JNU) was the soft target. In 2020, hate and violence were harmoniously normalized. The state appeared not just as a disinterested party but an accessory in the goings-on. That the entire grotesqueness at JNU, India's most prestigious educational institution was not to be missed. The cops watched and did nothing.[2] Even before wearing masks became a compulsory diktat that Modi himself advised all to adhere to, the perpetrators of the abhorrent attack, from the student wing of the RSS, wore them to conceal their hideous identity.

Amidst the madness, India had state elections in Bihar where all Covid protocols such as mask wearing, social distancing and hand sanitizing seemed like a frivolous prescription. No one cared. Soon, farmers from Punjab and Haryana took to the streets. A cocky government neglected them, treating their remonstrance with supercilious disinterestedness. It even called them Khalistani terrorists, insidious separatists, anti-nationals and apostates. Abuse and puerile allegations were hurled at them. But the protests ballooned. Once upon a time, UPA's political arrogance over the Lok Pal bill had torpedoed its otherwise noble intentions. The NDA's hubris, discarding parliamentary protocol and constitutional traditions on the farm bills, was coming to bite them. But it was the ham-handed manner with which the government responded to the medical emergency crisis that pulverized India.

After imposing a unilateral lockdown on the evening of 24 March 2020, without practising cooperative federalism and that too at a four-hour notice, Modi faced a tough Hobson's choice as the lockdown versus lives binary reached a flash point on 17 May 2020, when Lockdown 3.0 came to an end. He then announced an extension to Lockdown 4.0 but with a promise of a substantial reduction in restrictions and a whopping Rs 20 lakh crore fiscal package to be announced in a phased manner. The government had belatedly woken up to the naked truth: India was failing the medical emergency test and self-destructing by creating an economic washout. Since 25 March 2020, when the national curfew commenced, the number of infected cases had risen rapidly. Given the unpredictable nature of Covid-19 (a second wave seemed to be occurring in South Korea and Germany already), it was futile to engage in the puerile debate on whether India had triumphed or was losing the fight against the diabolical pathogen. However, two facts were irrefutable: human suffering had reached disconcerting levels, and the Indian economy was in serious trouble. It was a good time for the government to recalibrate its Covid-19 strategy. In imposing back-to-back rigorous lockdowns without any breathing space, the government was placing all its eggs in the lockdown basket. It had clearly backfired. What then could be the strategic way out?

First, one had to recognize that the RAG model (Red, Amber and Green) of the Covid risk measurement grid had inherent limitations because the economy is inter-connected. If Mumbai, Delhi, Pune, Ahmedabad, Bengaluru and Chennai are in the red zone with zero economic activity, even if the rest of the country were in the green zone, it would be preposterous to assume

India's GDP would rebound. Production is a complex process; intermediate goods may have several supply vendors scattered all over the country. As much as 32 per cent of overall tax collections come from Mumbai -headquartered companies alone, for instance.[3] There was thus only one option: radically decontrol by removing all proscriptions and let business recommence. Of course, the usual safeguards on mask, sanitizers, social distancing and Section 144 would need to be strictly adhered to. Micro-targeting of hotspots in a red zone with quarantine was recommended as opposed to a blanket ban which had proved counterproductive. An aggressive public awareness campaign had to be sustained. India also had to be prepared for a sudden spike in cases, but that could be temporary, as people realize the concomitant risk of being in the public space all over again. Over a fourteen-day cycle a discernible trend would establish the cost-benefit of the lives versus livelihood argument. In economics, a fundamental assumption of microeconomic theory is that human beings are rational. The government had to trust the fact that no one wishes to be on the ventilator and that self-preservation would be the primordial obsession of every individual. Policies could always be revised later. But being alarmists was imprudent. If it worked, India could start breathing again.

Second, the government's financial rescue package had to prioritize expenditure expectations on medical infrastructure, direct cash transfers to the poor agriculture labour, cash in hand to the luckless migrants, middle-class relief on unemployment allowance, EMI moratoriums, substantial credit and liabilities relief to the bleeding MSME sector, among others. Extraordinary situations demand extraordinary solutions. It could take a leaf from the UPA during the global financial crisis of 2008 following the Lehman Brothers implosion that led to the Great Recession. As the mortgage crisis plundered the world economy, India's GDP fell from a staggering high of 9.3 per cent in 2007–08 to 6.7 per cent in 2008–09 even as inflation sky-rocketed from 4.7 per cent to 8.1 per cent.[4] It was a double whammy. But the government did not panic. Instead, its fiscal and monetary stimulus which was countercyclical resulted in the GDP bouncing back to 8.6 per cent in 2009–10 and inflation was lower at 3.8 per cent as well.[5] The key to the dramatic turnaround was the fiscal risk the government took; the centre's fiscal deficit which was at an all-time low of 2.5 per cent in 2007–08 doubled and more to 6 per cent in 2008–09.[6] Economics is about trade-offs; you can't have the cake and eat it too. Incidentally, the GDP bounce-back was not a one-off. In 2010–11, India's GDP climbed even higher to 8.9 per cent.[7] Several critics will point out that subsequently the economy slowed. But the UPA faced the terrible headwinds of a global slowdown, parliamentary gridlock, high oil prices and a coalition government. The Modi dispensation had greater headroom for tougher decisions.

Third, at some point, the government had to bite the bullet on tax revenues to fund the fiscal deficit; it always is better than government borrowing and monetizing debt. GST is a regressive tax. The government had to avoid this lazy, inelastic source of revenue as it could pauperize the middle class and the poor further, other than perhaps on luxury goods. Clearly, the Rs 1,45,000 crore tax write-offs to the corporate sector in the previous fiscal year was thoughtless in an aggregate demand-starved economy.[8] But direct taxes were the government's only alternative, including wealth tax, inheritance tax, progressive taxation of the super-elites, and cutting back on wasteful non-plan expenditure. In a bear stock-market, public divestments would not give commensurate returns, and monetizing of government real estate assets would give lower returns as it would probably be under-valued, given the fact that it would be seen like a distress sale. There was little elbowroom.

Lastly, the NDA needed to formulate a National Exit plan. Its strategy of letting lockdown unravel district by district through official commandments called guidelines appeared thoughtless. The granular opening flexibility that the chief ministers were demanding would lead to more confusion than resolution. For example, for the economy to kickstart, inter-state movement of goods and services had to be on a National E-Pass, which had to be honoured by all states. Without interstate movement, the economy would remain sub-optimal with low productivity as incremental steps would only create bottlenecks. India also needed to learn from the Sikkim model of handling Covid-19; both their caseload and deaths were at zero. Ultimately, humility is better than hubris for governments during crisis situations. The cardinal error the Modi government made was that it had convinced itself that it could slay the virus in twenty-one days.[9] Had it understood that the virus, a diameter of 60 nanometres—or 60 billionths of a metre—was different from the usual suspects this government picked on, India would have been in a better place. But it wasn't. And it wouldn't be. As subsequent events would prove, India descended from hope to hell, plunging into an immensurable dark pit. Many would die. A quick fix-it attitude marinated with foolish optimism would cause total havoc. India has its own term for it: Jugaad.

I first heard the word 'jugaad' in the mid-1990s. 'How do you intend to get the IPO application forms to Rajkot by the morning?' I asked, incredulous at my broker's exuberant confidence that this could be accomplished. The very idea seemed out of la-la land.

I worked in Alliance Capital then, a global investment management firm bullish on India's yet fledgling mutual fund industry. It was past sunset and picking up a big chunk of forms from the printer in suburban Mumbai, then delivering it on time at the stock market and to other sub-brokers by 9 a.m. looked far-fetched. It was a long twelve-hour drive. 'Don't worry. *Iska jugaad ho chuka hai*' was the cool as a watermelon-on-ice response. And indeed, my broker delivered.

But I remained far from convinced that working in 24x7 emergency-like situations is a smart business model. Nevertheless, many Ivy-League type CEOs serenaded this operating style, citing India's rustic survival instincts and its unique creativity under duress to pull it off. 'If it ain't broke, don't fix it' was the popular mantra. Modern Standard Operating Procedures (SOPs) had to coexist with the stickiness of local practices that were basically shortcuts. The risks were enormous, as business susceptibility to extraneous factors ought to have been controlled with a Plan B or Plan C earlier. However, even Harvard heavyweights eulogized jugaad as Indian exceptionalism in frugal engineering, as if we should patent it. The reality is, India has romanticized a casual fix-it approach to serious problem solving. The second Covid wave shattered that suspect glorification.

This was not a hard-to-imagine nightmare India lived through; this smog of cataclysmic doom was for real. Several unsuspecting Covid-infected Indians did not die because the dangerous virus usurped their lungs with incurable pneumonia;[10] they died because their political leadership could not provide them with oxygen supply, ICU beds, life-saving ventilators and crucial medicines. The poignant stories of people begging for oxygen were innumerable, and heartbreaking. They are immortalized forever in social media posts and will be a permanent reminder to the people about the country's unpardonable failures. Indians have paid a price for this jugaadu attitude, inherently fatalistic and foolishly rose-coloured.

If India, fearing a deadly virus onslaught in March 2020, pushed for the most heavy-handed lockdown ever, what led to the extraordinary complacency in January 2021 when most countries faced a lethal second wave? Wasn't the government aware of USA's Operation Warp Speed, where former president Donald Trump engaged in a partnership model with private sector pharmaceutical companies like Pfizer, Novartis, Johnson & Johnson, etc. to incentivize production of vaccines and give Americans first rights? Why was the Serum Institute of India (SII), India's biggest vaccine manufacturer, given a measly order of 11 million vaccines as late as January 2021 and Pfizer forced to withdraw its application? Why were private sector hospitals not engaged from the very beginning as part of vaccine distribution? Why didn't India place orders with other foreign vaccine manufacturers when even Canada had ordered 414 million vaccines for its meagre 38 million population?[11] Was India under-reporting deaths in certain states? Whatever happened to the celebrated 'pharmacy of the world' slogan when locally it had a vaccine shortage? The list of unanswerable questions was endless.

It was also the jugaad predisposition that led to the super-spreader Maha Kumbh Mela in Haridwar, Uttarakhand, which was sponsored by the ruling BJP, while politicians defied Election Commission (EC) proscriptions in Bengal and elsewhere and continued campaigning. In a terse order, the Madras High Court (HC) observed that the EC should be booked for murder for going ahead with the five assembly elections (Kerala, Puducherry, Assam, West Bengal and Tamil Nadu) amidst the raging pandemic. The situation was so out of control that one heard of cryogenic oxygen tankers travelling hundreds of miles to meet the last mile requirement of helpless patients. Jugaad hadn't worked: India was gasping for breath. The 'we are like that only' flippant refrain had clearly boomeranged.

If the Supreme Court and high courts have to intervene in public interest to ensure basic essentials like oxygen supply for the suffering Indian, it demonstrated a failed executive and a distressed polity. The citizen-state trust deficit was at a Himalayan peak. India needs bulletproof SOPs with a robust Plan B in all aspects of public interest: health, security, delivery of public services and natural disasters. It cannot handle emergencies with old-fashioned ad hoc decision-making. The post-pandemic governments of the future will need the mentality of an ambitious startup: performance-driven, fully transparent, nimble-footed, quick decision makers and disruptive dreamers thinking a generation ahead. Donald Trump and Brazilian President Jair Bolsonaro epitomized the fall of the bombastic bullies, who mishandled Covid. Boris Johnson, the British prime minister, joined them too, albeit for a personal peccadillo. For Trump, Bolsonaro and Johnson, Covid was like a coup de grace. For Modi, it was a gold medal.

Trump mocked the virus from the very beginning, plunging his country into an unpardonable lethargy and smugness even as the world burned under the rampaging health crisis. It would cost America dear in the final count (a total caseload of over 33 million and over 6,00,000 dead).[12] Albeit in all fairness Trump displayed smart business sense through his Operation Warp Speed to get vaccine manufacturers to guarantee USA first rights and full access to vaccine supply, the damage had been done and it was irreversible. The lesser said about President Bolsonaro, the better. Sao Paulo and Rio de Janeiro rose in unison to put their head of state under a commission of inquiry for crimes against humanity. In effect, it was not very different from the Nuremberg trials where the Nazis stood implicated for their gas chamber genocide during the Holocaust. Bolsonaro demonstrated shocking apathy. His statements were preposterous, he refused to wear a mask and get vaccinated. Brazil suffered a humongous headcount (finally at over 7,00,000 dead and counting).[13] The people assembled in Sao Paulo wanted justice. India with over 44 million cases, officially had a casualty list of over half a million.[14] The state had failed, government claims notwithstanding.

There was palpable anger against an insouciant state, which underestimated the second Covid wave and appeared clueless on elementary medical availabilities of oxygen supply and ventilators. Its approach to ensuring vaccine supply for its vulnerable population was abecedarian, borne out of both intrinsic hubris and incompetence. India's summer of 2021 is an unforgettable nightmare for its trusting population, a devastating consequence of government callousness. While reams have already been documented on the subject, the Delhi High Court's observation was perhaps the most trenchant: 'Someone needs to be booked for manslaughter.'[15] In other words, a venerable court in India's capital city explicitly categorized the tragic deaths (bodies floating down the sacred Ganga river, families struggling to get crematorium space and finally settling for car parks), vaccine shortage, etc. as nothing short of institutionalized murder. The Supreme Court was equally unequivocal about the 'arbitrary and irrational vaccination policy'.[16] The government was compelled to revise its bizarre policies and stop sleepwalking, but can a bereaved family resurrect its dead? Worse, the government added grievous insult to still bleeding wounds even when it came to a token financial compensation.

In response to a petition in the Supreme Court demanding a meagre Rs 4 lakh for every family that lost a member to Covid, the government of Prime Minister Modi expressed its reluctance to do so in a written affidavit to the SC.[17] In the history of India's parliamentary democracy, this must rank as its most abysmal moment of shame. Assuming just one member died per family, India had to pay Rs 20,000 crores as ex-gratia compensation (nearly 5,00,000 dead x Rs 4 lakh). It was peanuts given the fact that we are talking of a once-in-a-lifetime medical calamity. But the NDA government contested it. The glitzy Central Vista Project of course continued with a reported budgetary outlay of Rs 20,000 crores.[18] Could there by anything more humiliating and insulting to the grieving families? In 2019, Finance Minister Nirmala Sitharaman gave tax concessions of Rs 1,45,000 crores per annum to India's corporate sector.[19] Billions of cash change hands in crony deal-making, slush money, dodgy political funding, money laundering, etc. India is awash with a booming parallel economy; demonetization was mere eyewash. If the government had even an iota of sensitivity and empathy, it would have just printed cash and paid families Rs 10 lakhs each, much higher than the Rs 4 lakhs that most were expecting. Instead, they found a flimsy technical pretext to circumvent their responsibilities; apparently, Covid was not included in the initial 'classification of natural disasters' created years ago, and of course, we must look at 'optimum utilization of resources'.[20] In the meantime, there were questions raised about the government's prestidigitation which had led to an under-reporting of virus-related deaths. But could anyone ignore the dead as they floated down India's most sacred river, the Ganga?

Lifeless bodies floated down the blue river. The disturbing images made one gasp in disbelief. It appeared ghoulish. In early 2020, the rural population of India had heard of a Chinese virus, which could make people cough and fall sick. Even die. Although they unfailingly obeyed the prime minister's diktats to light a candle and bang their kitchen vessels, which they perhaps saw as superstitious activities to keep the evil spirits away, they did not quite know much about coronavirus until much later. It was when the first national lockdown was announced on 24 March 2020 that they realized that something was gravely amiss. They were abruptly dumped from India's national mainstream conversations as big cities catapulted to Covid-19. Many of them trudged the lonely national highways, enduring parched throats and an inexorable summer sun. Many died. But many survived. It was in the big cities that people were getting infected; those who drove fancy cars, travelled abroad, lived in luxurious apartments and loved the fast life. Or lived in urban slums, the cosmopolitan ghettos. The nocuous virus appeared to have spared the less prosperous, the more modest villagers. The serene country landscape, miles away from the concrete jungles, was breathing fresh air. No masks were deemed necessary. People huddled together during weekends to have community gatherings and discuss what was being told in the news or what they had heard from their family members in Mumbai and Delhi. Social distancing would seem an anomaly here, a clear oddity. Life rolled along. And then ... Suddenly, everything went wrong as summer dawned in 2021. There were panchayat elections, assembly elections and a huge religious congregation where millions gathered to take a holy dip. Of course, one repeatedly heard on television that India was an exceptional success story which had successfully vanquished the virus, as claimed by the highfalutin speeches of the prime minister. It was good news that had a giddying effect. The danger was past, they were told. It was time for a celebratory get-together. But unknown to them, many would soon be dead. They would never know that they were tragic victims of a government's shallow agitprop. And blazing arrogance.

The world's largest vaccine manufacturer was broke. Queues of anxious people, desperate to get a jab, returned home disappointed as several inoculation centers had no supply of the two life-saving vaccines that were being used in India, Covishield (made by the Serum Institute of India under license from Oxford-AstraZeneca) and Covaxin (local manufacturer Bharat Biotech). With the second wave of coronavirus on a dangerous trajectory, people were terribly frightened. They ought to have been. India's caseload reached a staggering 26 million.[21] India had established dubious records in daily cases (over 4,00,000), daily deaths (4,522) and the fastest vertical progression in infection rate in the month of April 2021. Dead bodies buried hurriedly along river embankments, lack of oxygen supply, inadequate ICU beds, black-marketing of life-saving drugs, the average Indian had experienced a dystopian nightmare, a Kafkaesque disorientation. It can be unequivocally stated that Indians were let down by their central government in its shocking exhibition of political hubris and administrative torpor. The undermentioned example is worth pondering upon.

India's population was estimated to be 138 crores in 2020. The targeted group due for vaccination, those above the age of 18 years, was 940 million. India had approved vaccines that had to be given in two doses (like most vaccines in the world, other than the single-dose Johnson & Johnson). Thus, even a toddler using a calculator could extrapolate that India should thus have ordered (from both domestic manufacturers and foreign suppliers) 940x2=1,880 million doses at the earliest, preferably in December 2020–January 2021 itself. It was again basic knowledge that vaccination was the best preventive measure to stop transmission of the virus, save lives, reduce pressure on a creaky public/private health infrastructure and thus create herd immunity. But the government was caught napping. Like the Titanic crew, they missed the emerging iceberg.

Both the Serum Institute of India and Bharat Biotech, who were given emergency use authorizations, were awaiting government orders to manufacture and ship the vaccines demanded. SII received official orders till January–February 2021, of only a miserly 21 million doses (only 1.1 per cent of India's needs).[22] It was a ludicrous low, a laughable underestimation. Bharat Biotech's production capacity was limited to just 20 million doses per month. Was the government living in a fool's paradise? Were they not aware of the malignant second and third wave that had pillaged USA, UK, Brazil and Europe by then? The answer lay in investing significant funds in both SII (which had taken the business risk) and Bharat Biotech so that they could ramp up production capacity (it takes a time lag of two to three months for them to source raw materials and create the technical foundations) to about 150 million a month and 50 million respectively at the barest minimum.[23] Despite allocating Rs 35,000 crores in the budget for vaccines, the government did nothing right until April 2021, when suddenly India began haemorrhaging as the second wave became a spine-chilling reality. Foreign vaccine makers like those behind Sputnik V were not even talked to, while Pfizer, which came knocking on India's doors, was returned because of the government's contumacious reluctance to acknowledge its shortfalls. The government thought that India's war against the virus was over. Game, set and match, BJP. Bring on the champagne, was their collective chorus of jocundity. It was foolish. The people of India paid with their lives.

The real tragedy is that India could have saved many lives had the government focused on governance instead of grand theatrics. The BJP hailed PM Modi as the ultimate superhero, and the PM himself boasted of India being the 'pharmacy of the world'.[24] It was a self-goal. In its attempt at boosting Modi's global appeal, India even exported 67 million vaccines (more than what it used locally till then).[25] BJP spokespersons talked of India's altruistic manifestations, but in that case why did they suddenly stop helping poorer countries thereafter when India suddenly got swamped by the virus during the second wave? Eventually, India had failed not just its own denizens but even vaccine-starved poor nations in Africa with a vulnerable population. AstraZeneca, UK was forced to send SII a legal notice for non-delivery against contractual obligations, as the government forced it to stop deliveries abroad.[26] It was a snake pit.

Dr S. Jaishankar, External Affairs Minister went travelling abroad with a shopping bag hoping for the charitable dispositions of multinational pharmaceutical companies, whose global commitments now restricted them from obliging India. Of course, by the end of the year 2021 there would indeed be an over-supply of vaccines worldwide, but that's precisely what made the period from June 2021 onwards crucial for India. As 70 per cent of the population needed to be vaccinated for herd immunity to develop, India had to vaccinate approximately 65 crores of its population with at least a single dose.[27] By May 2021 it had touched only a 20 crores threshold; so, the gap was 45 crores. Ideally, if India was doing even 5 million vaccinations a day, it could have opened up like the USA/UK by August 2021.[28] But the daily vaccination levels collapsed to a dismal 1.5 lakhs a day even as virus fatalities rose to alarming levels. At that rate, it would take India ten months, that is till March 2022, to hit the herd immunity benchmark.[29] It could not afford to take such a mammoth risk with human lives. Therefore, the only way forward was to back SII through assured orders and financial support, and through compulsory licensing widen the manufacturing base of Covaxin, even as it urgently facilitated conditions for the import of foreign vaccines. Another Indian company, Wockhardt had volunteered to make 500 million doses by February 2022.[30] But was anybody listening? The question that needed to be asked was why was the government not engaging with the private sector for augmenting supply all these months? It was a fatal error of judgement.

In a normal universe, a Commission of Inquiry would be needed to investigate if human life had perished because of criminal negligence. After all, there must be consequences for those who failed innocent Indians at their critical hour of need. Instead, India had the outrageous situation of the prime minister's face being promoted on Covid vaccination certificates. The head reeled in disbelief.

In May 2022, the World Health Organization (WHO) officially stated that, directly or indirectly, there were 4.7 million deaths (about nine times the official figure) attributable to Covid-19 in India during 2020 and 2021. It would be the highest casualty number in the whole world. Within minutes of the report, the Indian government trashed the report, raising objection to the 'methodology'.

4

THE ROGUE FACE OF CAPITALISM

*'We hang the petty thieves and appoint the great ones
to public office.'*

—*Aesop*

IN THE BLOCKBUSTER Bollywood hit *Drishyam*, the catchphrase is: 'Visuals can be deceptive.' What you see is not what you get. As a country, India has become either astonishingly brazen or completely disinterested in obvious frailties around it, no matter its unmissable gigantic presence. There is a third possibility; it has chosen to get blindsided, partly because it is easier to ignore the inconvenient truth, or maybe posture a deliberate ennui towards issues that cause serious personal discomfort. The bottom line is: It is a nation adrift. What stunned me following Congress leader Rahul Gandhi's fusillade against Prime Minister Narendra Modi on business baron Gautam Adani's fantastical rise to global fortunes (it peaked at USD 154.7 billion) was not the laundry list of allegations that he made (they had been circulating in the public square from time immemorial), but the rectitudinous demonstrated by the treasury benches on them; 'Expunge the remarks,' they roared. 'Show us documentary evidence.'[1] Rahul, evidently rejuvenated by the stupendous success of the Bharat Jodo Yatra, looked like a man transformed. His war cry on the Adani-Modi *jodi* playing footsie while India languorously watched in despair, had seemingly hit the bull's eye. But the Adani rhubarb is beyond the typical BJP-Congress political slugfest; it was about India's national character. A deep dive is necessitated.

Adani and Modi go in tandem. Their sharp vertical progression simultaneously was not a celestial coincidence. The business group was a generous recipient of Gujarat government favours, among others, such as receiving environmental clearances, subsidized land at throwaway price, to a blanket first-among-equals treatment. The Mundhra port is considered to be possessing exceptional facilities, but its meteoric success was skilfully engineered using state power. Serious allegations against Adani were frequently roadblocked, a perfect example being the Directorate of Revenue Intelligence (DRI) investigation into coal imports done illegally. It is a long list.

The Financial Times called him 'Modi's Rockefeller'.[2] They could not have been more direct. But Modi was not at all embarrassed. Buoyant with his raging domestic popularity and convinced that he would rule India till perpetuity, Adani had front-row seats as part of Modi's entourage whenever he travelled abroad. Large cross-border government contracts, whether in Australia, Sri Lanka or Israel, were easy pickings. India had dumped the Congress in 2014 for alleged corruption in 2G telecom case (this was finally thrown out by the courts) and coal-allocations (nothing was proved, but queerly, BJP-ruled states escaped scrutiny), but Modi-Adani's bonhomie, suspiciously bordering on sweetheart arrangements, seemed kosher to them.[3] One alleged corruption was awful, the other, appeared to be acceptable. Morality is elastic in India, it can be made bespoke. But it can have deleterious implications for a country, especially, when carpetbaggers monopolize state contracts and its natural resources.

Nations fail economically because of extractive institutions. These institutions keep poor countries poor and prevent them from embarking on a path to economic growth. The basis of these institutions is an elite who design economic institutions in order to enrich themselves and perpetuate their power at the expense of the vast majority of people in society. The different histories and social structures of the countries lead to the differences in the nature of the elites and in the details of the extractive institutions. But the reason why these extractive institutions persist is always related to the vicious circle, and the implications of these institutions in terms of impoverishing their citizens are similar—even if their intensity differs.[4]

Since I have been both a part of the corporate grid and the political ecosystem, I can confidently tell you that the business-political relationship has an asymmetrical imbalance. Unlike western democracies where even the president courts Big Business and Hollywood stars, seeking political endorsement for promoting themselves in popular company, in India, it is the other way round. Most industrialists have the backbone of a chocolate éclair (Rahul Bajaj and Kiran Mazumdar Shaw are rare exceptions). Capital-intensive projects requiring a public-private participation model have an intrinsic nepotism built into them. The political party in power plays sugar daddy to its wide-eyed favourites by giving them cozy deals while arm-twisting those who appear to have a less friendly disposition. It all links in to quid pro quos, as in outright corruption or surreptitious campaign financing. Opacity rules (electoral bonds, anyone?). That is the source of the problem. White crime, barring the occasional Yes Bank, ILFS, DHFL, Punjab and Maharashtra Cooperative Bank scams, remains blurred in public imagination.

Was Adani group the 'biggest con in corporate history' which engaged wantonly in a 'brazen stock manipulation and accounting fraud scheme', as alleged by the US short-seller, Hindenburg Research?[5] It would have normally got any government panicky, especially if it was transparently mentioned that it had to do with the chummy relationship between the country's prime minister and the embattled industrialist. But not the Modi government. Rahul Gandhi pursued the matter with the same zeal that he had done for Rafale jets in 2019, but with a kowtowing media, a fractured Opposition and a large middle class that has an uncanny tolerance for sophisticated white-collar crimes, it was going to be a Himalayan task.

Modi was adhering to a well-tested model from time immemorial (Gilded Age in America being the perfect starting point) of creating first-among-equals, 'national champions', especially in the areas of Big Infrastructure (ports, airports, bridges, expressways, industrial parks), telecom, green-technology, oil and gas, who would get out of turn government favours. They could also enrich themselves with convenient policy tweaks that suited their industrial enterprise. In South Korea, they call them chaebols.

> The risk is that Modi will follow the path commonly charted by other conservative nationalists before him. In their own ways both Vladimir Putin in Russia and Recep Tayyip Erdoğan in Turkey took power by promising economic reform and hinting that they might move their countries in more liberal directions. But rare is the strongman leader who grows less autocratic the longer he stays in office.

Others held their noses and voted for the BJP, calculating that Modi's promises of development were worth the dangers of the potential social upheaval that he might bring. 'I was aware of the risks,' as Gurcharan Das, a socially liberal author and ex-businessman, said of his own voting decision in 2014.'Modi was polarising, sectarian and authoritarian. But I felt the risk in not voting for him was greater.'[6]

Adani Group published a 413-page voluminous rebuttal of serious fraud allegations by Hindenburg Research. It was mostly bunkum, all fire and brimstone, but at core, vacuous. It was similar to a peeved, petulant political leader caught with his hands in the till but unwilling to acknowledge the malfeasance. Ultimately, Adani adopted his best friends' standard strategy when embarrassed; he raised the bogey of 'national pride', and a concerted devious attack on 'India'. 'This is not merely an unwarranted attack on any specific company but a calculated attack on India, the independence, integrity and quality of Indian institutions, and the growth story and ambition of India,' said the yawn-inducing report,[7] which failed to answer the fundamental questions of round-tripping, shady ownership in tax havens abroad, violation of statutory public holding rules and most importantly, share-price rigging to inflate asset values and purchase cheaper debt. Once the Congress was bludgeoned for the 'India is Indira and Indira is India' slogan. BJP spokespersons on TV shows were defending the shibboleth but altered it to include Modi's blue-eyed businessman friend: 'India was Adani and Adani was India.' Modani became a superhit. However, the ham-handed attempt to assuage worried shareholders by Adani fell flat, and barring the BJP, there were no takers for the infantile, propaganda spiel. The group lost an earth-shattering value in market capitalization within weeks after the 24 January expose. It was like an Alaskan meltdown. The markets were sending out a clear message: crony capitalism had resulted in the creation of big business empires that had feet of clay. The impact was immediate and cyclopean. The Adani group's attempt to successfully raise a USD 2.5 billion share sale, an FPO for Adani Enterprises, had to be cancelled and monies refunded, after a carefully 'managed operation' to salvage it by using government-nudged cartels to subscribe became obvious.[8]

A cursory glance at Adani's mega-empire is enough to indicate plutocracy is in fast-track mode; the infrastructure sector comprising ports, airports, green energy, highways, etc. all require public policy intervention. They are all unsurprisingly mired in controversies. But these are citizens' resources; the Modi government is accountable to the 140 crores people of India on their transparent allocation. Bludgeoning discussions on Adani Group, using whataboutery of Opposition scandals, resorting to sarcastic rhetoric to lambast the Gandhi family's alleged corruption and sandbagging an independent investigation by a Joint Parliamentary Committee (JPC) which the Opposition was correctly asking for, were all bullying tactics by a paranoid government. It is time civil society stepped up to demand integrity from its dodgy political representatives. Just because Modi has won two Lok Sabha general elections, it does not make him an insuperable law unto himself. As a society, India needs to stop being so supine and subservient to the very people who come to them with folded hands, back half-bent, sporting a nauseatingly kowtowing smile begging for votes. Politicians perpetuate their brutal stranglehold on Indians because people let them; there is little pushback. Something needs to change. The Adani affair was an opportunity to do so.

Just how many times has India seen a corporate group get thwacked by a USD 110 billion market capitalization wipe-out in six trading days alone? When Adani became the second richest man in the world, overtaking Jeff Bezos (annual revenue of Amazon was USD 500 billion; the Adani Group is not even a fraction of it), how come the unreasonableness of his skyrocketing net worth did not raise eyebrows (85 per cent of his massive wealth accrued in just three years)? If nearly 80 per cent of market capitalization growth of

Indian stocks in 2022 was largely on account of one business group (Adani), was that not off-kilter? Why did the government override the objections of the Ministry of Finance and NITI Aayog when giving six airport contracts to Adani who had no prior experience of running them? Why did it require a small research firm called Hindenburg to question the glaring financial irregularities while the market regulator, Securities and Exchange Board of India or SEBI (and the Reserve Bank of India or RBI and the government), slept? How come no one looked at the bizarre PE ratios of Adani companies (800) compared to their industry average (24) in one case, for example? Who operates the foreign entities based in tax havens which only invest in Adani stocks? Why did the Life Insurance Corporation (LIC) invest a huge corpus in Adani while the private sector mutual funds stayed away?

It was Rahul's questioning of the Mumbai airport takeover by Adani from the original owners, the GVK group, that needed further probe and could have added to BJP woes. Prima facie, it appeared like a hit job; an anonymous letter accusing GVK of corporate malfeasance was followed by the usual process of the ED/CBI/Income Tax Department juggernaut unleashed on the debt-ridden, troubled group who suddenly capitulated to the hostile takeover. It appeared to be a well-oiled plot, all smokes and mirrors. Adani got immediate access to India's hottest transport property and the proposed Navi Mumbai airport for a throwaway price (they promised to honour the debt liabilities amounting to approximately Rs 12,000 crores).[9] In hushed whispers, India Inc. expressed their fears of the mafioso operation, appearing terrified. Ease of business? Years later, no one has any idea about the status of the criminal investigations against GVK. This was straight out of a criminal syndicate storyboard. Rahul Gandhi had cornered Modi on the Rafale scam, which had never been forensically investigated. The Chowkidaar Chor Hai campaign may have got buried under the Pulwama–Balakot rubble, but the case was far from dead. French investigating authorities had smelt rotten fish and were digging deep into the awkwardly struck defence deal. But with the Adani Group's financial flimflam out in the public space, Rahul knew that the prime minister had a lot to explain for.

The Adani meltdown was not just about vulgar cronyism; it was about political arrogance, Big Business skulduggery, regulatory takeover, mockery of corporate governance and a dysfunctional democracy. Beyond Adani, India stared at a can of creeping crawling worms. The Pandora's box needs to be opened, though. India needs more start-up role models, Infosys and Wipro, Nyka and Unicorns, not gangster capitalists, as multi-billionaire buddies are now being christened. The Modi government's opacity reached a high-water mark when it told the Supreme Court in November 2023 that the citizens of India did not have a right to know about who funds political parties in the electoral bonds case. It was a shocking statement which exposed its hush-hush cover-up attitude and an intent to continue with the policy of corporate chauvinism, which invariably is linked to rent-seeking and quid pro quo structured deals of mutual convenience.

SEBI should be rechristened as the Sleeping Exchange Board of India. It's stupefying silence on Adani's irrational, exponential wealth gain was inexplicable. It had chosen to look the other way at one of the most spectacular rises in market capitalization of an infrastructure group, where such PE valuations are rare, if not non-existent. Adani was no start-up Silicon Valley act of technological creativity; it was a conglomerate built on intriguing buyouts, massive debt leverage, controversial share price premiums and an opaque ownership structure. While future investigations will doubtlessly reveal the truth behind the can of worms, it was easy to surmise that SEBI had succumbed to the perceived proximity of Adani to Modi. There could be absolutely no justification for its wilful disinterestedness in starting a formal inquiry long ago. Adani's wealth grew from USD 4.5 billion (2014), USD 11 billion (2020) and USD 76 billion (2021) to an astronomical USD 150 billion (2022).[10] But for SEBI it was just a proforma development.

The Adani financial numbers were staggeringly greasy; a snapshot is important to highlight SEBI's clear failure to be a stock market watchdog. The group's market capitalization went up from USD 10 billion to USD 120 billion in just three years;[11] for a bricks and mortar commodities/infrastructure firm with huge debts, this was unheard of. In 2022, seven Adani group companies accounted for 80 per cent of BSE listed companies market capitalization;[12] SEBI seemed to think that was par for the course. Further, the PE multiples were bizarrely skewed: While Adani Power's PE was 769, its peer Tata Power traded at a PE of 34; it made little commercial sense. Similarly, while Adani Gas had a PE of 747, Indraprastha Gas's PE was 17. This, when the revenues of the comparable companies were nearly the same.

If the BJP was a discerning political party, which it is often assumed to be, they would understand after Rahul's outstanding performance in the Lok Sabha on 7 February 2023, the Pappufication of Gandhi project was now over. He had survived the shellacking. The man had clearly arrived. The answers on Adani needed to follow. But that was, as subsequent events were to prove, far easier said than done. Adani was not the only beneficiary of the charitable government's large purse. There were others.

There are spasmodic outbursts in the national media from time to time about India's celebrated fugitive absconders being extradited back home to be sent to the dingy coolers at either Tihar Jail or Arthur Road, Mumbai. Among the celebrated names are, principally, former liquor baron Vijay Mallya, the creator of the Indian Premier League (IPL), Lalit Modi, and diamond czars Mehul Choksi and Nirav Modi, an uncle and nephew duo who collectively swindled India's compromised and vulnerable banking system. There are others in the rogue's gallery, like Jatin Mehta and Vikram Kothari, but they have not yet captured the flashing bulbs yet. The list of racketeers is long, but the dominant cast are those mentioned above. At the time of writing none have returned home, although every time there is a headline banner on TV (which appears when the government is in a serious disorder), broadcasting their imminent capture, it seems as if we will see them handcuffed and cordoned off by khaki-clad pot-bellied cops—a far cry from their days of Louis Vuitton suits and Maybach car rides, accompanied by superstar models. But there is a feeling of déjà vu here. These choreographed shows have been seen often before. The Modi government believes periodic assertions reinforce its 'neeyat', its intent to fix financial skulduggery. And in an information and news overloaded world, nothing works better than calibrated repetition. The average viewer probably tells himself or herself, 'Kuch to hoga'. The government's objective meets the bull's eye. It can be said with reasonable certitude that not a single offender will return to the country's shores. In May 2021, the government sent a rented private Gulfstream Bombardier Global 500 jet, allegedly costing the Indian taxpayer Rs 8.45 lakhs an hour, to fetch Choksi from Dominica where he was allegedly nabbed by the local police (for several days it made Narendra Modi look like a Messiah in the press).[13] Finally, it came back empty-handed. For a while, the potential size of the assets seized from Choksi, worth Rs 9,000 crores, made hurricane-like waves.[14] Even if the speculation was true, what nobody tells the poor Indian citizen is that repossessed properties and assets are hugely discounted at auction time, given the enormous hidden litigation risks. Recoveries, if at all, are only fractional. But the atmospherics are alluring for the government.

While most businessmen play a balancing role to keep all political parties pleased, Choksi and Nirav Modi were rather close to the BJP.

They were chaperoned abroad to their cherished destinations with the help of political patronage. It is hardly a public secret that the security apparatus at international airports was lowered to facilitate their movement to their First Class cabins with fine champagne on the menu.[15] And to Antigua (Choksi got a clearance from border patrol, local police, SEBI, etc., to obtain citizenship in the serene Caribbean islands) as well, despite complaints about his larceny, which were given to the Prime Minister's Office in 2015. Modi blithely appeared in Davos, Switzerland for a photo-op with Prime Minister Narendra Modi. Davos symbolizes modern capitalism at its affluent yet hypocritical best; they talk climate change after arriving in their private jets in the Swiss Alps. Money talks. That explained Nirav Modi's hobnobbing with the crème de la crème of global Richie Riches who saw him as part of the Indian entourage. Of course, the BJP would have Indians believe that Modi-Modi presence was just a cosmic coincidence. Or that one Modi was a gate-crasher.

If the government was serious about recovering black money, work would have started at home. Former Reserve Bank of India Governor Raghuram Rajan gave a list of India's biggest loan defaulters to the PMO in 2015. To this date, that secret file has not seen the light of day (mysteriously, the 'independent RBI' refuses to make its contents public). Compared to the illustrious heavyweights speculated to be on that file, Modi and Choksi may be like Mary's little lamb. India's public sector banking loot can be called the Great Indian Bank Robbery. Politicians of all hues are involved. But Modi, who accused the UPA of 'phone-banking', was equally guilty of 'PayTM-withdrawals' as the Opposition called it. Public Sector Undertaking (PSU) banks remained tightly under the control of the apparatchiks of the Finance Ministry. No one dared to ask the tough questions of the BJP-led NDA government. Not even on their highly problematic source of political funding.

I watched two outstanding mini-TV series recently. Both were biopics on those putative wicked villains of the past who end up appearing as star-crossed tragic heroes. *A Very Private English Scandal* is about Jeremy Thorpe, former numero uno of Britain's Liberal Party who was accused of murdering his homosexual lover. The other was *Scam 1992: The Harshad Mehta Story,* an eponymous narrative of India's first celebrity Big Bull who upended Dalal Street. By the time he dies of a heart attack in the Thane Civil Hospital in Mumbai on New Year's eve of 2001, director Hansal Mehta makes you root for the besieged forty-seven year old who saw both dizzying heights and bottomless lows. *The Times of India's* Sucheta Dalal exposed not just Mehta but India's breezy affair with easy institutional money. It was more than a one-night stand.

Madhuli on Worli was once a residential address peopled doffed their hat to when they drove past it. The frisson at seeing Mehta's Toyota Lexus at traffic junctions was noticeable. The world of high finance though is shark infested and requires ruthless ambition and an unquenchable lust for profits. The destruction of an adversary elicits schadenfreude. Harshad Mehta possessed the audacity to defang the bear cartel. He was the Shakespeare of relationship management and deal making. He was an outlier. He would soon make enemies.

I have the dubious distinction of having worked with two foreign banks, ANZ Grindlays and the Bank of America, which were both neck-deep in what came to be known as the 'Harshad Mehta securities scam'. Both banks pretended otherwise. I remember BankAm's dapper CEO Vikram Talwar holding an impromptu office meeting to explain that the San Francisco-headquartered leviathan was as pure as running water. It was laughable. In layman's language, Mehta was simply playing around with idle cash balances (bankers call it 'float') in Dalal Street's undervalued stocks, while awaiting the physical settlement of stock certificates. It was relatively easy to create a bull run as everyone wanted a share of the burgeoning pie. Especially bored avaricious bankers.

Is hamam me sab nange hai is an aphorism that applies to most if not all in India's dodgy business-politics nexus. Equity research is a subterfuge for boardroom leaks. It was when I joined New York-based Alliance Capital that I saw how India's biggest brokers openly insinuated about the 'big names' they hobnobbed with who wanted their share prices massaged. The real battle was between the natural business savvy of the traditional Gujarati stockbrokers and the repressed ambitions of foreign bankers and foreign portfolio investors seeking freedom from India's labyrinthine laws. They smartly decided to hold hands. The politician was not too far away either.

Harshad Mehta took an unprecedented step of holding a press conference on 16 June 1993 where he accused former Congress PM P.V. Narasimha Rao of taking a bribe of Rs 1 crore for political guardianship of his business travails.[16] Thirty-one years later the truth remains buried. Both Rao and Mehta are dead. Election funding in the world's largest democracy remains as opaque as trying to look through a sheet of steel. The Indian Renaissance is not even visible on the horizon. Most Big Bulls have a friendly equation with the ruling political masters. A self-confessed Modi bhakt was the late market maker Rakesh Jhunjhunwala, who once famously said that that democracy hindered India's economic growth. The proximity between business and politics was palpable.

Greed is good, is how conservative economists cleverly interpreted and twisted Adam Smith's free-market philosophy. Mehta was India's Big Bull, but the real wolves who influence Dalal Street operate from faraway Mumbai, cheek by jowl to the murky Lutyens corridors. Ultimately, in a non-transparent world of election bankrolling, there are several stakeholders. The political class is the most powerful of them. Quid pro quo transactions are based on verbal assurances. It is like a parallel underworld operation. I have been in politics long enough to know that the system is a stink bomb. Electoral bonds, the financial instrument considered legitimate for raising campaign contributions, is a daylight heist. The BJP cares two hoots (because it gets 95 per cent of corporate donations). Since the Congress gets a beggarly 5 per cent it should ideally, aggressively seek a public investigation of anonymous donors.[17] But it appears contented with paltry crumbs in the hope that the questionable instrument will serve it well when it returns to power. The BJP and Congress are not sworn enemies; sometimes they are unfortunately joined at the hip. A corporate friend sarcastically joked about the shady bond scheme: 'The Congress should have been a counterfoil to the fraudulent scheme. But it remained silent, happy to play a flunky, even as BJP has elevated fund raising to an efficient legalized mafia operation with bulletproof SOPs.' The Supreme Court is yet to pass a verdict on PILs challenging the electoral bonds scheme. It is over three years. India waits.

State funding of elections, which is touted as an alternative, can be an option, but the truth is India need less government, and more translucency. If a political party can successfully monopolize individual donors and large corporate contributors, it should be kosher, but full disclosure must be made mandatory. Companies are logically likely to fund the front runner more than the laggard; a pure market dynamic. Concealment of even one rupee, however, should be a criminal offense. India needs an independent, empowered Election Commission with the powers to investigate the sources of funds, not a toothless paper lion. Corruption is institutionalized in India, and at the core is campaign financing. Right now, anything in India can be rigged. It is a vibrant civil society that will have to do the heavy lifting. Opacity rules.

The PM-Cares fund, floated opportunistically right at the beginning of the pandemic in March 2020, was sold as a resourcemobilizer to help combat the crippling financial crunch and enable Covid-19-related amelioration efforts. Albeit over 60 per cent of its funds were corporate donations (approximately Rs 3,000 crores) from government owned public sector undertakings, the fund was not obligated to submit itself to Comptroller and Auditor General (CAG) audits or come under the ambit of Right to Information (RTI) Act.[18] It was more than mystifying; it was thoroughly frosty. But why? The corpus of the fund crossed a sizeable Rs 10,000 crore in 2020–21, but the Prime Minister's Office refused to make any disclosures, citing legalese that it was not a 'public authority'.[19] It sounded ridiculous, and disingenuous. Among the investors were private corporate entities who had made generous contributions from their Corporate Social Responsibility (CSR) mandatory budgets. But the Modi government rebuffed all calls for full transparency. The courts said nothing. It appeared like a murky enterprise being floated in broad daylight, but under Modi, the new normal meant that he could do as he wished, and no one ought to question his duplicitous decisions. Among the many cases that required investigation but were probably ensconced in moth balls were Paradise Papers, Panama Papers, Pandora Papers, the zero recovery of black money despite the oppressive demonetization, source of electoral bonds funding, the sale of distressed assets to new buyers under the Insolvency and Bankruptcy Code (IBC), Non-Performing Asset (NPA) write-offs and willful large defaulters in the list given by Raghuram Rajan to the PMO. The romance between government and business corruption had many onlookers, but no sentries. Adani's whirlwind rise needed an explanation; the people of India deserved to know the truth.

Narasimha Rao famously said that he would survive Mehta's bribery allegation like goddess Sita's trial by fire. He did. But until India sorts out its political funding train wreck, its democracy will remain embryonic, feeble. In the meantime, as time passed and public memory became foggy, Adani's stock rose once again, and soon he was back among the Richie Rich billionaires club at rank 20.[20] Adani Group's net worth, however, was down at nearly one-third of the Group's vertiginous peak of over USD 150 billion. In October 2023, the reputed *The Financial Times*, London broke an explosive story on how the Adani Group, India's largest coal importer, was over-invoicing imports, to make massive windfall gains. It was the Indian consumer who paid a higher cost of electricity as a result. Adani rubbished the report. BJP spokespersons batted brilliantly for him. India just moved on.

5

BROKEN PROMISES

'The price good men pay for indifference to public affairs is to be ruled by evil men.'

—*Plato*

B Y SEPTEMBER 2020, even as the Covid pandemic disarranged the country, sending everything into a crazy tailspin, the acronym APMC (for the Agriculture Produce Marketing Committee) had become an exasperating intrusion into people's television time, the prime alphabet soup of the departing monsoon season. One reason it needed a prompt burial, for was the archaic name itself (pregnant with bureaucratic cholesterol) that was in sync with an antiquated practice of supply chain management of agricultural produce. But not surprisingly, India's home-grown jousting between the ruling BJP and the Opposition Congress turned the Modi government's farm reforms into a hot political potato. It was complicated. A rewind is necessary to understand the flaming gridlock over India's famous Jai Kisan.

In 2012, when I was just an unofficial voice of the Congress, one of my principal responsibilities was to argue in favour of the UPA's FDI in multi-brand retail policy. In fact, in an unprecedented development, Prime Minister Dr Manmohan Singh went on national television to address the people of India on an economic agenda, to assuage agitating farmers that their livelihood would be ameliorated and not compromised by the historic liberalization. The proposed changes allowed transnational behemoths such as Walmart, Tesco, Carrefour, Target, etc. to enter India and set up their giant retail stores interspersed across the country and adopt the farm-to-fork model.[1] It was truly refreshingly path breaking. It was predicated on the assumption of a dismantled APMC, giving Indian farmers access to corporate buyers, for whom grocery sales would be a crucial component of their revenue targets. Cold storages, modern warehousing, mechanization of farms, transport logistics, rural infrastructure, branded consumer packaging—that was all part of the new paradigm. Farmers were being incentivized to move away from traditional rice and wheat production to fruits, flowers and vegetables, as part of a crop diversification strategy. Dr Singh, who pioneered the 1991 reforms and fought relentlessly for civil nuclear energy, knew what he was doing contemplated. One political party opposed FDI in retail, tooth and nail? The BJP!

Political pundits harped on BJP's paranoia about losing a big chunk of its 'middlemen' vote bank who would be overnight rendered penniless as a consequence, besides the usual strategy of fearmongering among the small retailers about multinational vampires. And then of course there was the nationalistic RSS think-tank Swadeshi Jagran Manch promoting economic autarky. But come 2020, and both Congress and BJP had reversed their erstwhile positions in a nonplussing U-turn.

There was naturally predictable hullabaloo following the Modi government's multi-pronged farm reforms bills, which replaced ordinances enacted during the draconian lockdown. Some hard data is germane for a dispassionate appraisal of the three laws: The Farmers' Trade and Produce (Promotion and Facilitation),

The Farmers (Empowerment and Protection) Agreement of Price Assurance and Farm Services, and the amendment to Essential Commodities Act. Seventy per cent of India lives in the rural backcountry, which is a mega-mighty 1,000 million people.[2] Eighty-six per cent of India's vast farming community are small and marginal farmers (owning less than 1 hectare of land).[3] Fifty-five per cent of consumption expenditure emerges from the farm belt.[4] During the full-term of NDA-1, agricultural growth was an insipid 2.9 per cent, and the shimmering mirage of doubling farmer income by 2022 was always far-fetched, an illusion. Farmer suicides were at a discomfiting 11,390 in 2016, the last available official data from the National Crime Research Bureau (NCRB).[5] It could be estimated to be much higher, of course. The Modi government had promised during their 2014 election campaign, a Minimum Support Price (MSP) of cost plus 50 per cent as a profit margin; they reneged on that assurance with extraordinary heartlessness. But the truth also is that only a small fraction (barely 7 per cent) benefit from the MSP; as for the teeming majority,[6] their production mostly matches consumption, thus leaving hardly any surplus produce for a commercial sale. The whopping crash in GDP by 23.9 per cent in Q1 of 2020–21 following the pandemic was a lethal body blow.[7] The economic ramifications on landless farm labour and small farmers were devastating, pushing many of them into abject penury and below the dreaded poverty line. In a nutshell, Indian farmers needed an urgent inoculation from depleting incomes and the monopsonist, antediluvian structure called the APMC. Did the farm bills truly achieve the seminal breakthrough that the agricultural sector so desperately needed given the heavy headwinds? The short answer is a surprising yes! Of course, as with everything in India, it boils down to implementation (the nightmarish instances of NDA government's demonetization, GST and the pandemic control disaster are legendary evidence of mismanagement). The path to hell is paved with good intentions. The permanent bugbear is India's characteristic political roadblock to economic reforms.

The farm bills were the one singular reform of Modi (all others, including the Insolvency and Bankruptcy Code, were mired in an executional mess) which ought to have received unanimous political approbation. The fears of ruthless mega corporations (like Adani, Ambani, Tatas, etc.) usurping cheap land and exploiting innocent small farmers while being genuine and worrisome, were enormously exaggerated. For example, it was possible to incorporate stringent safeguards with serious criminal charges for those caught violating small farmer interests. If the farmers were indeed being bamboozled by the deadly combination of the powerful politician-crony capitalist mix, the BJP would pay a massive cost at the hustings. Would they risk it?

At closer scrutiny, all the three new farm laws were in effect a smartly adapted version of the UPA's own brainchild, FDI in multi-brand retail. Of course, for the BJP, large domestic corporates (many with foreign shareholding) were kosher; only foreign firms could do predatory pricing, it seemed (their principal grouse against the UPA's farm reforms). Double standards had been redefined with a capital D.

As expected, the BJP began facing organized nationwide protests[8] in what could be called 'political just desserts'. For six years, mostly on account of obdurate obtuseness, it disallowed UPA's pragmatic FDI in retail reform from being implemented, even as FDI in e-commerce changed consumer market behaviour and Walmart continued its wholesale B2B business. It was political hypocrisy. Now it was passionately propagating the same through a hybrid of progressive reform laws. It was reminiscent of the recalcitrance the BJP showed with the GST bill (tabled first in 2011 by UPA) for purely tactical short-term gains. For Congress though, the bull-headed pushback on the farm bills was equally ill-conceived and smacked of petty tactical play. For sure, it was playing a tit-for-tat game, a perfectly legitimate democratic contestation strategy, but sadly, it was also saying goodbye to Manmohanomics in the process.

The Congress manifesto of 2019 was a comprehensive document which the party proudly declared was conceptualized following a 'bottom up' approach; affected parties' opinions were incorporated during its construction. Repealing the APMC Acts and Essential Commodities Act (both listed in the manifesto) was considered key to giving farmers a liberated economic landscape to boost incomes. Thus, it was astonishing to find senior leaders utter homilies on 'the missing assured MRP architecture' in the farm bills,[9] which was conspicuously absent in the party's own manifesto. I am not sure if those who do the heavy lifting for the party on economic policy issues were comfortable with this unwarranted public mud wrestling. The party was jettisoning what it had proudly documented in its sacred manifesto; this smacked of an incoherent, incongruous approach to serious national issues. But then one way of looking at it was that the Congress was paying the duplicitous BJP back in its own coin; in war, it is only the last man standing who counts.

BJP of course was a victim of its own two-faced approach, brazen opacity and supercilious disinterestedness in parliamentary processes—which only ended up making a rudderless Opposition more bellicose. A much-needed agricultural reform was being torpedoed through a powerful misinformation and disinformation campaign by one, and the prodigious hubris of the other.

In an ideal world, Congress would have ideally taken maximum credit (like it did for GST, Aadhaar, Jan Dhan, etc., which are the UPA's creations) for its manifesto commitment and forced the BJP to institutionalize safeguards for protecting farmers from organized lobbies and unscrupulous corporate mercenaries. The fear of a few rotten apples was no reason to scrap the reforms altogether.

Abandoning APMC would make more sense than abandoning the man who changed India's growth trajectory forever in 1991. But post-2014, the Opposition was like a drowning man clutching at a straw. Disillusioned farmers are an electoral windfall. Everyone wanted a share of that coveted vote bank.

Thus, when BJP's reliable partner suddenly ditched the party, it was a crystal-clear signal to the entire Opposition to join the bandwagon. They did. But why Harsimrat Kaur Badal (Food Processing minister in the Union cabinet) of the Shiromani Akali Dal (SAD) party remained silent since the ordinance was first announced in June 2020 was befuddling. Almost everyone had picked on one issue: Why isn't the MSP embedded in law with an assurance that private corporate buyers would purchase at least at that assured price? Fair enough, but it was a specious argument. For one, the current MSP architecture would continue to co-exist as a parallel practice to open-market pricing; it is a benchmark price that could enable price discovery for traders, state procurement agencies and corporate buyers. Why should farmers voluntarily sell below a publicly announced translucent price when they can always go the closest APMC mandi? Also, over time, as collective bargaining strengthens after farmer producer organizations gather momentum, some could enter into bulk demand contracts, either higher or below MSP, to capitalize on high volume commitments that is mutually acceptable to both parties? Incidentally, the law had built-in provisions to prevent corporate exploitation, but it was also true that an organized business conglomerate can be a slippery customer to an ill-informed, disorganized aggregation of farmers. This is where the role of even state governments in enforcing legislation would have been crucial. What can be prognosticated with some certitude is that the food pie itself would become bigger over time, with price competitiveness depending upon quality of product and minimum quantum of production that farm procurement centres called Farmer Producer Organizations (FPOs) could deliver on a sustainable basis. The APMC regime would remain, thus giving farmers the assured MSP fall-back option anyway. It was a win-win. Anyone who believed the APMC mandis would be promptly substituted or would necessarily languish before becoming obsolescent were being naïve; in fact, there was a compelling argument that higher competition would result in better business practices and a more robust open mechanism (including less extortion and price collusion) that would help farmers. Farmers from Punjab, Haryana, Uttar Pradesh, etc. could benefit considerably at the cost of government revenues. It was a good bill, but very badly handled by the ruling party.

I was surprised by the BJP's aggressive push on the farm bills for two reasons; it indeed would have impacted the lucrative commission market in the APMCs that duplicitous middlemen made plenteous profits from. But were not small traders the saffron party's core vote banks? Thus, it was the vote-hungry BJP which was taking a bigger political risk (obviously on the assumption of creating a farm revolution and thus guaranteeing itself a rural vote avalanche). They were also fully aware that if the farm protests became a genuine movement sans political propping, then it would have damaging electoral consequences for the BJP. Secondly, with more open market purchases across various regional territories it could be rationally presumed that there would be a rise in food inflation as farmers get more attractive remunerations. This again could have eroded the low urban inflation rates that had kept the middle class's romance with Modi fairly intimate. Politically, it was Modi who had chosen to skate on thin ice (as he did with demonetization, GST execution and the lockdown). Once again, Modi was chasing what appears to be his instinctive penchant: going for a big-risk gamble, convinced that if the proposition boomeranged, he would ride it using his titanic might of mainstream propagandists and oratorical spin mastering. But the party's uncouth arrogance had backfired.

The BJP's inherent condescension, its authoritarian ham-handed my-way-or-the-highway attitude in the Rajya Sabha muddied the waters. The political hubris of the party had resulted in a nationwide farmer protest against the bills. Once again, India was missing the woods for the trees. The BJP had self-perished on its farm laws just like the rotten tomatoes on the highway dumped by furious farmers. What compounded matters were two horrific incidents of mindless violence.

It was a gruesome sight. It would take some courage to watch the video that showed unspeakable horror of a man being lynched to death by an angry mob. It was ghastly. It appeared that the man had allegedly desecrated the holy Guru Granth Sahib, leading to mob fury. What was particularly disconcerting was the brutality; the human conscience for all practical purposes was non-existent. The unfortunate victim called Lakhbir Singh, a Dalit who lived in Punjab's Tarn Taran district, was literally chopped to death over several hours, with sadistic voyeuristic men even taking mobile videos of his murder.[10] The incident happened in Sonepat, Haryana close to the Delhi-Haryana Singhu border, where for several months, farmers had successfully protested against the government's farm laws. A Nihang Sikh surrendered, claiming full responsibility for the horrendous act. The sordid event instantaneously assumed a political character. Mayhem ensued.

A while later, some people were arrested for the heinous crime. The core leadership team of the farmers' agitation, the Samyukt Kisan Morcha (SKM) washed their hands off the episode, attributing it to a religious affront.[11] An investigation was ordered, but given India's non-stop, breathless 24x7 news cycle, the killing of Lakhbir Singh quietly disappeared from national attention. India's flawed criminal justice system would ensure that its labyrinthine ways would keep the perpetrators of the crime footloose and fancy free. Singh left behind a wife and three children. The politics then began in deadly earnest. The ruling BJP party's IT cell, notorious for fanning flames, attacked the Congress for not condemning 'substantially' Lakhbir's death.[12] The insinuation was loaded with an electoral slant; after all, the Congress had indeed done a ballyhoo on the Dalit origins of its then new chief minister of Punjab, Charanjit Singh Channi (Dalits are 32 per cent of the state's population).[13] But Lakhbir's death was probably overshadowed by another hideous carnage of farmers which had happened just a few days earlier.

In Lakhimpur-Kheri in the state of Uttar Pradesh, a dangerous convoy simply ruthlessly ran over protesting farmers, mowing them to death. It all happened in a split second. In retaliation, the farmers lynched the driver and a few others they suspected of being part of the controversial minister's (Ajay Kumar Mishra, minister of State for Home Affairs) entourage.[14] The sun was shining bright on 3 October 2021 when the dastardly madness played out. This was like a Wild West cowboy film where wantonness ruled.

The high-handedness of BJP Union Minister Mishra was apparent in his provocative speech, which allegedly triggered the anarchy that followed. In his speech to his followers, Mishra said that he would fix the farmers protesting in his parliamentary constituency in just 'two minutes' if he wished to.[15] If that was not a flagrant instance of political hectoring, what is? It was downright insulting to the suffering farmers, who were being marinated with brazen browbeating. To make matters Mishra exacerbated matters by an act of shocking imprudence; he actually showed a thumbs-down sign to the aggrieved farmers.[16] Thereafter, it was a downhill journey.

The videos were mind-numbing, reminiscent of brutal tribal warfare in war-ravaged African republics in the 1970s. Wildly driven jeeps savagely crushed protesting farmers. In a raging backlash, the farmers lynched four people, including a journalist. The fields were soaked in red. But this was not Rwanda or Zaire, it was a G20 member country with a nearly USD 3.75 trillion economy and foreign exchange reserves of USD 600 billion, and an emerging market democratic lodestar.

BJP leader Varun Gandhi cautioned his party against turning the disgraceful bloodbath into an 'immoral and false narrative' of a Hindu versus Sikh communal conflict. He was promptly dumped from the powerful decision-making body of his party. But Lakhimpur-Kheri had overnight become an embodiment of India's grave fault-lines, usually lost amidst the ruling party's hyperbole underpinned by supine cheerleaders of the Fourth Estate.

In effect, India has an ersatz democracy, corrupted at the core. A new low was the arrest of a twenty-two-year young girl from Bengaluru named Disha Ravi. It was alleged by the powerful politicians in New Delhi that Disha was part of a global conspiracy, nicknamed by a furious media as the #ToolKit gang, to apparently defame India, in the notorious company of green activist Greta Thunberg and international popstar Rihanna.

> The campaign against her took an ugly turn when tweets appeared claiming that her real name was Disha Ravi Joseph and that she was a Syrian Christian from Kerala. The intention must have been to suggest that being a 'Syrian Christian', she was less loyal to the ethos of India. The trick did not work because fact checkers came out quickly, saying that she was not a 'Joseph' of any kind. She was Disha Annappa Ravi, daughter of Ravi Annappa, an athletics coach, and Manjula Nanjiah, a homemaker. Both are traditional Kannadiga names.[17]

The Modi government made 'many requests' to social media company Twitter during the farmers' protests for the removal of inconvenient content by journalists and analysts critical of government policy.[18] They also threatened to shut down Twitter offices in India and raid its employees' homes if needed, according to Jack Dorsey, Twitter's Co-founder. This was not a trade secret. Everyone knew about it. Dorsey's Twitter had been intrepid enough to suspend the account of former President of the United States Donald Trump for exploiting the popular platform for violent instigations. That takes courage, besides indicating that albeit American democracy was being hammered relentlessly, there were institutional safeguards for those who dissented against political powers that be. The Modi government's authoritarian predispositions were now stripped naked. Everyone could see it. The BJP did not seem bothered, they were so blasé about its crushing execution.

Prime Minister Modi, however, maintained radio silence on the horrendous violence at Lakhimpur-Kheri, wherein one of those charged was the son of Ajay Mishra himself, Ashish Mishra. When the Supreme Court had to step in suo moto to take up the case,[19] it signified that state governance had collapsed. The highest judiciary had zero faith in the political ecosystem to deliver justice for the ordinary Indian. The minister's son was finally arrested after media outcry and public furore. But the minister himself, who incidentally made the provocative speech against the farmers, continued to occupy his haloed position. Can anyone seriously expect an impartial investigation? According to the SIT team probing the matter, the incident was a 'planned conspiracy', making the grisly killings an even murkier commentary. The Supreme Court later rebuked the state police for the lethargic progress of investigations.[20] Did the PM really think that facts cease to exist because we ignore them? That India's political CEO was dismissing the death of eight people (including four farmers) with such casual nonchalance should have worried the citizens of India.

The fact is that both Lakhimpur-Kheri and the Singhu murders reflected a society which had calamitously degenerated. When violence and vitriol become normalized, human sensibilities become inured against hate, divisiveness and bigotry. Law and order collapses. Society is flooded with innumerable instances of state apathy as atavistic marauders take over. Circa eight years ago, on 28 September 2015, when Mohammad Akhlaq was lynched in Dadri. Now lynching has become the preferred option of fearless, hot-headed crackpots on a bloody trail. India was in danger. It was a bleeding republic. And it was all there for anyone who cared to see. The only way out was to be brave and vocal; the farmers proved that aphorism to be true. They had the last laugh against an imperious establishment.

The cost of electoral autocracy was clear. The protest against Modi's farm laws, which began on November 26, 2020, stretched over the course of nearly a year. On November 10, 2021, forty-five-year-old Gurpreet Singh, a landless farmer, hanged himself from a tree just outside New Delhi, near where thousands of farmers were still camping in protest. Gurpreet Singh, forced by circumstances to sell his four acres of land in 2000, made ends meet by renting an acre of land. The long absence from his farming duties drove him to economic despair, leaving him with no options, he concluded. COVID-19, exposure to extreme cold and heat, and suicides killed more than six hundred protesting farmers. In a gruesome incident, a BJP convoy-allegedly commanded by the son of a Modi government minister-mowed down some protestors. Then, in a televised address to the nation in the morning of November 19, Modi abruptly announced that he was repealing the farm laws.[21]

The protesting farmers had done their part, waging a successful battle against a government that had treated them with condescension. Democracy triumphed against all odds. Modi is probably the first prime minister to have so frequently addressed the nation on a nationally televised address. Of course, it helped that the coronavirus pandemic obviously gave him ample opportunity to talk directly with an anxious nation more often. Modi, who has mastered the art of skillful persuasion, courtesy the use of choreographed text and an obliging teleprompter, cultivating a trait that separates a winner from a loser, is effortless before the camera as a result. Forget the frequent prestidigitation of his speeches or the intermittent absurdity of his rhetoric. He coasts through it with insouciant ease. He enjoys the attention and his own striking ability to manipulate public emotions and bring them exactly where he wants them to be. Honestly, you cannot be a consummate politician without verbal dexterity and an extravagant dose of narcissism. He is also blessed with a preternatural seventh sense of gauging the public mood. When he spoke on 19 November 2021, dramatically announcing the withdrawal of the three farm laws, capitulating to a nearly one-year long protests by farmers, Modi was cryptically giving his 2024 general election speech.[22] A consummate politician, he withdrew the farm bills on Guru Nanak's birthday, the founder of Sikhism.

Modi has a fetish for victimhood. It is never his fault; in fact, usually someone is trying to torpedo him. He chose to ruefully castigate a 'small section' of farmers who he could not convince of the revolutionary breakthrough. That was an illuminating confession. Since his government believed that the three bills were so salutary for the farmers, why had they recklessly flouted all norms of parliamentary protocol? There were no discussions or debates; the farmers were never consulted (barring perhaps some pre-selected stakeholders, who are supine pro-government lobbyists). The suggestions of many political parties to let a standing committee of Parliament scrutinize the nitty-gritties of the bills was deemed a superfluous exercise. Reportedly, 750 farmers died during this tumultuous phase and like at the time of demonetization (140 died then),[23] the government even refused to shed the perfunctory crocodile tears. Farmers were vehemently denounced, bracketed as separatists with a diabolical plot to dismember India. Or else they were made out to be part of an international conspiracy to malign India's reputation abroad. It was gibberish. Just like the great boondoggle, doubling of farm income by 2022. But the farmers were not the only ones who had been duped with false promises; so were the youth of India.

On 2 May 2023, India officially became the most populated country in the world at 1,42,57,75,850.[24] It is a young country; over 65 per cent of its population is below 35 years of age. They were mostly jobless, but they had been given a grandiloquent assurance of 20 million jobs per year from 2014 by the BJP.[25]

Those who have religiously followed India's economic growth trajectory, particularly in sexy destinations like the World Economic Forum at Davos, will have heard of the term 'demographic dividend' ad nauseam. India's young skilled workforce was meant to unleash the formidable might of its economic prowess. The middle-income South Asian behemoth (now the fifth largest economy in the world) was meant to be the conjunct to the dazzling China-India century. But it has flattered to deceive. India seriously misunderstood what the unleashing of animal spirits really meant.

Of late, unemployed youth, ranging from 50–55 million as of December 2022, are mostly wasting their best years watching YouTube content, WhatsApp forwards, making Instagram videos (the TikTok ban has barricaded a huge revenue source), and doing odd assignments for measly pocket money.[26] Even gig economy jobs, temporary in nature, are a godsend. Unemployment can become a social menace though; the adage, an idle mind is the devil's workshop comes into play. Several unemployed youths have discovered a darker, more diabolical alternative, which is financially remunerative: cow vigilantism. It is like a quasi-government job. They work as undercover agents[27] of local police forces in states that have legally banned cow slaughter; a subject that is a hot button in BJP's New India. 'However, in the absence of adequate employment opportunities, it is not surprising that a large number of youth find the anarchic capitalism of Hindutva appealing,' Dhirendra K. Jha writes.[28] Joblessness was creating a mental health pandemic as well, but no one even bothered to talk about it. Is it any surprise that the land that exports yoga and meditation to the world languishes at an embarrassing 126 in the latest World Happiness Index?[29]

Despite the big hype, the truth was that India's economy had underperformed. The Gujarat Model, which had promised an economic miracle boilerplate for India, had turned out to be an Alice in Wonderland experience. Modi, whose knowledge of economics, had been once sarcastically dismissed by P. Chidambaram as one 'that could be written at the back of a postage stamp' had voluble cheerleaders who had propagated 'Modinomics' as a counterattack.[30] Only nobody knew what that meant. After the economic Armageddon called demonetization, branding Modi's economic policy appeared to be an act of delicious overkill. Modi had surprisingly followed the Left-leaning economic construct of the Congress, by focusing on welfare subsidies, which had been spun using the local dialect to appeal to Hindi heartland voters as 'labhartis' (beneficiaries). Most TV anchors sold what is staple government subsidy programmes for the underprivileged and those who live below the poverty line, as Modi's far-sighted pro-poor programmes.

After boasting about providing two free gas cylinders, subsidized or free food, cheap housing, and a nominal minimum payout to farmers, Modi suddenly felt discomfited when the Opposition trumpeted him on his own home turf by offering similar programmes in their election manifestoes. The truth is all central and state governments led by whichever political party have the onerous responsibility of bridging income inequalities, alleviating poverty, providing basic minimum living standards, etc. Thus, every political party liberally commits large expenditures on the teeming masses. Modi, taking legerdemain to a new high, called the Opposition initiatives 'revdi' (a famous sweet from the land of Mathura in Uttar Pradesh). In short, he termed them as freebies, devoid of commercial budgeting sense. These would create a black hole in state finances and could end up bankrupting the financial system, just because Opposition parties wanted to attract votes from gullible voters, he alleged. The pot was calling the kettle black. The BJP was the prime proprietor of the freebie culture, especially financially profligate when it came to Big Business. Modi gave it an atrocious electoral pitch: 'freebies are dangerous for the youth'.[31] Coming from a party which had promised the youth of India 200 million jobs by 2023, and provided at best 2 million, it had to be the most Amazonian bluster.

There was a political ploy behind Modi's 'revdi' sales call; it would please the angry middle class, who had suffered enormously on account of poor to dysfunctional governance (with their woes including unemployment, high oil prices, EMI defaults, stressful urban life, corruption, mental health, etc.) and felt cheated, by diverting their attention towards others who could be blamed—the poor and the underprivileged needing social welfare subsidies. The middle class had mostly fallen hook, line and sinker for the Right-liberal leitmotif of 'povertarian economics'; they had been made to believe that their hard work and the taxes they paid were being channelled towards less deserving sections of India who were poor or lazy or both. It is a time-tested formula employed by divisive leaders.

Means-tested programs create the perception among many middle-class citizens that only poor people benefit from social policy. And because race and poverty have historically overlapped in the United States, these policies can be racially stigmatizing. Opponents of social policy have commonly used racially charged rhetoric against means-tested programs-Ronald Reagan's references to 'welfare queens' or 'young bucks' buying steaks with food stamps is a prime example. Welfare became a pejorative term in America because of a perception of recipients as undeserving.[32]

India's marginalized sections were in a woebegone state. The growth in real wages (net of inflation, and therefore the real purchasing power) between 2014 and 2022 was below 1 per cent for agriculture labour, construction workers and non-agricultural urban labour.[33] India was worse off, for over 70 per cent of Indians were living in the periphery and income inequality was worsening. One per cent of Indians own 40 per cent of its wealth,[34] and 1 per cent of Indians use 45 per cent of its aggregate flight-time, but the photo-ops, perception and publicity generated was what mattered to Modi more.[35] Thus, new airports excited him. For sure, India needs to look ahead, but the missing essentials like road safety, urban traffic decongestion, better track maintenance in the railways, proper training for bureaucracy in the services sector—these were not tactile and held little importance in his scheme of things. When railway accidents happened, like the Balasore tragedy in Odisha in June 2023, where 295 people were killed in the multi-train crash, it was conveniently attributed to other factors, like an alleged conspiracy.[36] There were over 3 lakh vacancies in the Indian Railways, including for technical staff from the safety departments, which had not been filled in, probably to smother the huge deficit that would have occurred. This was bad economics; human lives were lost.

Amitabh Kant, the NITI Aayog CEO, famously said that India could not hasten reforms because 'we are too much of a democracy'.[37] These were not Freudian slips; not at all. They were emblematic of the ideological mindset of the Modi government. Parliamentary filibustering reached alarming proportions; 155 MPs were suspended after 2014, the government averaged eleven ordinances per year, the annual financial budgets and farm bills were passed by railroading them, and central ministers were deployed to prevent a meaningful discussion in Parliament. Instead of the Opposition, it was the treasury benches who were disrupting proceedings. The reversal of roles showed how Indian democracy had been reduced to a cringe-inducing caricature of itself. Too much democracy?

That India's economy had hit a dreary stagnation point was evident from the fact that new job creation had completely vanished. India's youth unemployment had reached an agonizing high of 23.2 per cent, only exceeded by Iran, Yemen, Lebanon and Armenia. In what appeared to be a comical interlude to a depressing reality, the rattled prime minister actually started to distribute government appointment letters in a highly televised performance. This was unprecedented even from the dictatorial lows of the Latin American countries. The Modi signature had to be embossed on anything which had a state letterhead.

As 2024 beckoned, farmers were driven to the brink and many unemployed youth to suicide, even as stock markets boomed, Adani grew into the super-richest club of global billionaires and Unicorns received vast sums of private equity. The manner and the number of those who died due to Covid only made India's dismal story, darker.

6

MIRROR MIRROR ON THE WALL

'It seemed the world was divided into good and bad people.
The good ones slept better ... while the bad ones seemed to enjoy
the waking hours much more.'
—*Woody Allen*

IT SEEMED KAFKAESQUE; there were actually armed insurrectionists in a rebellious takeover mood marching menacingly up the steps of the storied US Capitol Hill in Washington. 6 January 2021 was an unforgettable crackpot day not just for America but for a flabbergasted world watching the grotesqueness play out on their television screens. The security infrastructure guarding the historical place where the Congress and US Senate were to certify Democrat candidate Joe Biden as the forty-sixth president of the United States of America was ridiculously feeble, unprepared. The world's putatively most enlightened democracy appeared blissfully nonchalant about the trouble brewing at its gates. The bizarre bedlam that followed was thus inevitable. Five people died, including a police officer who was brutally bashed to death by a frenzied white supremacist mob. Democrat Alexandria Ocasio-Cortez feared for her life. The US commander-in-chief, who was also the chief instigator of the ongoing violence, was probably watching the chaos from his bedroom in the White House.

US President Donald Trump, who had taken an oath four years earlier to protect every American life, had betrayed that faith. Gloating sadistically, the incorrigible narcissist had exhorted his Proud Boys and associated toadies into believing that the elite establishment had surreptitiously cheated him of a re-election. The 'stop the steal' call was the provocative fuelling of raging anger. The Democrats had colluded in an international conspiracy to cheat the true patriots of Uncle Sam, bombarded Trump to his fanatical mob. He made outlandish accusations, in a rabble-rousing speech, of election fraud (more than 50 per cent Republican voters believe the gibberish). QAnon, the conspiracy theory website, was Trump's Man Friday. It was a rigged election as he had with calibrated clairvoyance predicted long before 3 November 2020, Trump said. Thus, it was time for revenge. For war. For claiming victory, thundered the business tycoon who is an inveterate liar, according to his new hero-worshipper Ted Cruz. It was like watching 9/11 in real time—only this time there were domestic terrorists, and none would be going to Guantanamo Bay. It will take America time to be great again, rest assured.

Understandably, a scarred Washington echoed all over the world, prompting its numerous adversaries to lecture them about how to resolve their democratic fault-lines. Iran, Russia and China had a field day. China reminded Americans about US Speaker Nancy Pelosi's 'beautiful sight to behold' remark on Hong Kong's pro-democracy protestors. In India, under sustained global scrutiny for becoming an illiberal democracy under PM Narendra Modi since 2014, the reaction was one of self-righteous indignation. How dare anyone now criticize the largest democracy in the world, cribbed BJP acolytes. The transfer of power in India from one government to another has always been a tranquil exercise, argued the pro-

BJP TV cheerleaders. India was a great democracy under Modi, thundered BJP spokespersons. Look at the USA, they said. But did America's meltdown give people in India a reason for smirking? What were many in the BJP exuberated about?

> The general temper in Delhi started changing in 2014 with Narendra Modi's rise as prime minister. One of the climactic points was reached in 2018 with the arrests of Kabir Kala Manch (KKM) activists. This was a cultural organisation formed in Pune in the wake of the 1992 Gujarat riots. Students and young professionals were the organisers and their principal activity was the presentation of protest poetry and plays in slums and streets. They were jailed on the charge that they were 'Maoists' and 'Naxalites'. In December 2020, when two KKM members challenged their arrest in the Bombay High Court, the National Investigation Agency said that the reason for arresting them was that they sang songs criticising Prime Minister Modi and mocking his radio lecture Mann ki Baat.[1]

This is not a description of an alternate reality; it was for real.

India at various times stood ruptured at its soul. A stand-up comedian from the minority community Munnawar Faruqui was arrested for hurting religious sentiments, even before he had started his comedy show.[2] It was the fear of his controversial past performances which angered the new inspector generals of the moral police force. BJP state governments were busy passing anti-love jihad laws which was an assured recipe for further aggravating social disharmony. When love becomes a tabooed four-letter word in a suspicious society practising bigotry with the confidence of a cheetah sighting a hapless prey, then there is trouble. Like Trump, India was obsessed with its manufactured 'enemy within' narrative; the *Desh ke gaddaron ko, goli maaron salon ko* hyperbole echoed loud.

The unending baloney from those in high places was ominous; did one even care to remember that a year earlier the JNU campus, in the heart of India's capital city, was attacked by armed hoodlums in an episode of pre-planned anarchy pregnant with bloodlust while the bodyguards of society in khaki uniform acted as mere disinterested spectators? Had people forgotten the violent mobs who lynched people across India?

> I refuse to believe that the hate being spewed on social media is an organic construct. It is artificially designed for a purpose. Modi's success lies in his capacity to create an atmosphere of hostility in which he is the slandered and vilified martyr. I don't know if he has read Mein Kampf but he seems to have assimilated what Hitler used to say to his followers: 'They must not be afraid of the hostility which their adversaries manifest towards them but they must take it as a necessary condition on which their own right to existence is based. Modi has been true to every word.[3]

In a sense, the insidious spread of hate had a distinctive pattern. Interestingly, the BJP chose its friends just like they selected their enemies—carefully. It even permeated the governments' foreign policy utterances.

The Modi government actually made an embarrassing diplomatic snafu by serenading Trump and the Republican Party on bent knees in meretricious extravaganzas: Howdy Modi in Houston and Namaste Trump in Ahmedabad. It had the possibility of turning out to be a political disaster or a diplomatic waterloo for the BJP. I am sure President Joe Biden was fully aware of the unprecedented *Ab ki baar Trump sarkar* sloganeering campaign, which was organized to boost Trump among the influential, affluent Indian American community. But Modi simply relished playing the theatrical performer in packed shows abroad, with

NRIs lapping up his hyper-nationalistic rhetoric. All was far from well at home though. India dipped in relation to both the World Press Freedom and the Country Democracy Index, a perturbing reality-check for it. For many, it had become a Republic of Fear. For the diehard Right-wingers of course, India was the fountainhead of ecclesiastical democracy, with a 'Vishwa Guru' at the helm. The supreme leader's primal obsession was his 'image'; everything else could wait. Instagram preceded other items of national interest. And brand building, with all its filter choices, started at home: Varanasi.

'Khaike paan Banaras wala' sang Amitabh Bachchan in Don, giving the green betel leaf an international celebrity status. Shah Rukh Khan did an equally impressive redux. A tourist guide in Modi's parliamentary constituency, perennially chewing away like an insatiable cow on a hungry tummy, casually told me that he consumed sixty paans flavoured with chuna and some tobacco paste in a day. Varanasi is a fascinating city; its historical religious significance apart, it has a distinctive character and a visibly irrepressible human spirit (its cycle-rickshaw ride can be akin to a rollercoaster at the six-mile Long Island in New York), and it is at once remarkably ecumenical. The legendary shehnai player, Ustad Bismillah Khan is part of the city's cultural heritage, as are greats such as Munshi Premchand and Pandit Ravi Shankar. The Ganga river has a magnificent expanse, its famous purity, now available in branded bottles on Amazon and Flipkart. When I was there a few years ago, its byzantine small streets offered scrumptious fare, and I had an astonishingly delicious fruit-flavoured lassi, served by a rotund man with a Zen stoned expression. The gods were magnanimous towards him. In 2021, India's Prime Minister Narendra Modi sought similar invocations from the invisible powers above in his home constituency.

Kashi, Benares, Varanasi, take your pick, became an extraordinary spectacle, as the prime minister momentarily disappeared under the river water, taking a holy dip. Modi was there to inaugurate the Kashi Vishwanath Dham, a project to modernize the sacred place that has millions of Hindu devotees and religious tourists flocking in. Varanasi will require a gigantic makeover to become like Kyoto, considered the cultural capital of Japan, but this was still an impressive beginning. Modi wears his religious passport on his sleeve; there is no nervous fidgeting there, no discernible fogginess.

I remember huge billboards at Chowpatty, Mumbai (during the 2014 general elections) that featured a supremely confident Modi, arms folded, looking directly into your eyeballs, being promoted as the Hindu Hriday Samrat (Emperor of the Hindu Heart). Whatever his abject governance failures and the laundry-list of gaffes notwithstanding, Modi has never shied away from broadcasting his religious credentials. To his credit, he has been an open book (he refused to wear a skull cap). The Kashi extravaganza on display, underpinned by non-stop TV coverage, social media bombardment and massive advertising spends in mainstream dailies, was part of his explicit political messaging; India was already unofficially blurring the line between the Church and the State. Modi is a masterful impresario who leverages publicity with adroit finesse, damn the superficial slapstick imagery. For instance, he hugged Pope France when abroad, while back home there were anguished Christians still recovering from targeted violence against them. The horrific attacks at Roorkee was a perfect example of Modi's legerdemain. Naturally, all the glittering razzmatazz is motivated by a singular purpose: elections. In a few months he was to face a litmus test in the Uttar Pradesh assembly elections. Kashi fitted into the BJP's storybook.

When Modi had done the bhumi pujan for the construction of the Ayodhya temple, he had sent a clear message that his personal faith overrode his constitutional obligations as prime minister. It is expected that India's political chief executive should not create a religious hierarchy that obviously has the majority community sitting atop ivory towers. A secular democracy has certain minimum thresholds; there is a difference between private religious practices and a public articulation of them. Since 2014, Modi has dismantled these sacrosanct lines. His transgressions are innumerable; his comments on Kabristan-Shamshan, electricity consumption during Diwali and Eid, the selection of a Muslim-dominated Wayanad parliamentary constituency by Rahul Gandhi, etc. were cases of dog whistling. In Karnataka, he went ballistic, but more on that later. He has used the bully pulpit to maximum effect, forcing India into a discourse that reinforces the never-ending Hindu-Muslim dichotomy. Come elections, the political lexicon becomes more coarse. It is scripted to play to the gallery.

Ayodhya to sirf jhaanki hai, Kashi Mathura baaki hai has risen into an ear-splitting crescendo, but it has been there for a long while. The BJP has a translucent roadmap; keep the religious tensions simmering. Communal polarization needs perpetual nursing. Divisiveness works brilliantly with intermittent rhetoric, a stray violent episode and sustained frictions. It is a constant reminder that the Other is an exasperating trespasser into your hallowed space. Over a period of time, the divisions get ossified. The words of the Supreme Court of India on the P.V. Narasimha Rao government's The Places of Worship Act, 1991 are significant: 'It [The Act] is a legislative intervention which preserves non-retrogression as an essential feature of our secular values.'[4] But India lives in times when the word secularism has been hectored and many from the Sangh Parivar have called for its deletion from the Indian Constitution. For them, it is excruciating torture to be denied a Hindu Rashtra despite an overwhelming BJP majority in Parliament. The Emperor is their supreme hope for that apparitional universe.

In the months of April and May of 2021, India was vaporized by the deadly second wave of the Covid pandemic. It was a frightening bone-chilling nightmare, an unforgettable horror tale. The prime minister miraculously disappeared from the front pages. His lieutenants railroaded their way through with twisted statistics, besides a shocking scapegoating of the Opposition itself. But there was no escaping India's wretched collapse. As dead bodies floated down the Ganga and people mourned the departed souls, there was no prime minister to console them, to heal their wounds, to mollify them in their hour of grief. Modi missed what could have been a memorable Kodak moment as a true caring Indian leader. What one saw in Kashi, of course, was merely meant for Instagram. But how enduring can the foofaraw of a marketing spectacle be? The mirror often cracks as well.

The famous seven-year itch does not apply just to marital relationships, which after the initial flush of romantic idealism, faces some home truths, like diaper inventory, house-help shortages, a distracting flirty office colleague, diminishing libido and the proverbial mother-in-law's oppressive intrusions. Etc., etc. Similar bugs exist in our political ecosystem as well—the hubris of power, alliance strife, faulty laws, a collapsed economy, motor-mouths on a roll, corruption allegations, etc. Nothing is a constant; dysfunctionality sets in. The experience of both the Congress and the BJP confirmed the prevalence of this exasperating bug in politics as well. It usually forces a course correction. The example of Congress's experience in its seventh year during the UPA-2 phase, more specifically 2011, makes for an interesting analysis with that of the BJP in 2021.

In the 2009 general elections, the Congress made a thumping return with its highest Lok Sabha tally since 1991 when it got 206 seats. Prime Minister Dr Manmohan Singh's obdurate position on the civil nuclear deal wooed middle-class voters who saw in the soft-spoken erudite Sardar, a steely determination, an indissoluble resolve for integrity. Further UPA-1, which had surprised psephologists with a stunning performance to upset BJP's India Shining narrative in 2004, had brought in some landmark reforms (RTI, MNREGA, RTE, Forest Act, Food Security Act, National Health Mission, etc.). The economy had survived the global wreckage caused by the US mortgage crisis. In fact, India was growing at an average rate close to 9 per cent of the GDP;[5] it was by all means a baroque outlier, like its northern neighbour, China. Economists toasted to India at Davos, and Dalal Street acknowledged it with a boom. Several books were authored about the great Asian revivalism and whether the Tiger versus Dragon story would be the defining story of the new millennium. The private sector made ambitious plans, infrastructure investments skyrocketed, start-ups blossomed, the 3Ms—malls, mobile and multiplexes—became a middle-class obsession. Some were extremely bullish; India's golden period had arrived. Then just as suddenly Anna Hazare and Arvind Kejriwal happened to the Congress party, and 2011 became its annus horribilis. Seven years after that unexpected victory, the grand old party caught a bug that gave it a severe itch. It went rapidly downhill.

The RSS-backed Hazare-Kejriwal India Against Corruption protests snowballed into a migraine for the UPA, which succumbed meekly. True there were procedural violations in the allocation of scarce resources in land, spectrum and coal, but the UPA was like a greenhorn in the handling of its crisis. Jantar Mantar and Ram Lila dominated airwaves with frenetic television channels giving the melodramatic, theatrical razzmatazz unlimited airtime to thrash the government. Public outrage rose exponentially. The same middle class that was Manmohan Singh's trump card in 2009 now stood disillusioned. Soon policy paralysis gripped the government, which sacrificed bold governance for 24x7 firefighting for survival. Its reputation in smithereens, the Congress fumbled and stumbled.

The BJP went after it like a hungry lion against an injured deer. In the 2014 elections, the Congress delivered a turkey, slumping from an impressive 206 to its worst ever electoral humiliation at 44 seats.[6] The seed of the rout was sown during 2011, seven years after climbing Himalayan peaks. For the BJP, a similar experience was playing out. Or so it appeared.

Despite an underwhelming performance, which included the mammoth disaster called demonetization, sloppy execution of the GST, rising farmer distress, record unemployment, charges of crony capitalism and the rise of an aggressive majoritarian politics that led to ugly lynchings, Modi returned in 2019 with an even bigger tally. The highly questionable 'Pulwama bump' of course, needs a full-fledged investigation after the sensational disclosures of the former governor of Jammu and Kashmir, Satyapal Malik. For the second time the BJP had a commanding absolute majority with 303 Lok Sabha seats on its own.[7] Pundits forecasted that Modi 2.0 would revolutionize India. His famous slogans, 'Minimum Government, Maximum Government' and 'Sabka Saath Sabka Vikaas' which had remained a mirage if not a travesty in his first five years, would now see fruition. But seven years after his dazzling debut, as India entered the last few weeks of 2021, it was more than apparent that the Modi government looked highly vulnerable. It had caught the flu.

The violent clashes with farmers at Lakhimpuri-Kheri in Uttar Pradesh, where nine innocent people were senselessly killed, exposed the BJP's real problem: its intoxication with power. They sincerely believed they would rule forever (Amit Shah has prognosticated fifty continuous years for the party). The Indian economy, however, continued to stagnate, despite some green shoots. Jobless individuals and bankrupt small businesspeople were committing committed suicide, inflation was rising, oil prices were cruising northwards, fresh private investments were hard to come by, democracy had crumbled, institutions were infiltrated with saffron sympathizers and the BJP continued to blatantly polarize India. In any other democratic country, the BJP government would have been on its last legs. Not in India, largely on account of a sleepy-headed, disorganized Congress. But it was still possible that things could change rather quickly as the other Opposition parties recognized a clear opportunity in the emerging vacuum.

The summer of 2022 was unbearably bothersome. Prices of petrol, diesel and LPG cylinders continued to rise alarmingly, devouring the finances of the poor, even as the stock markets turned as choppy as the Pacific Ocean during a storm, eroding the wealth of those higher up in the food chain. The RBI stated that interest rates would go up further, which was hardly the kind of news that would gladden the heart of free-market liberals. The US Fed obviously is the key driver of global monetary policy. With inflation at a record high in both the US (which was at a 40-year peak) and the UK, the age of negative interest rates, which for long had fueled excess liquidity, was finally over. Cheap money, quantitative easing and unbridled capital flows that sought short-term arbitrage and quick returns may be a thing of the past. Vladimir Putin became the unofficial governor of our long-term fortunes. Ukraine was not just about a European ego war being fought by a recalcitrant autocrat with a fragile ego and a hot head against the duplicitous trans-Atlantic alliance led by a dodgy America seeking fresh pastures for military influence. It had grave implications for countries far and beyond (Sri Lanka being a suitable example), as the disruption in supply chains of essential food items and energy prices proved deleterious. Many countries faced bankruptcy and went belly-up; sovereign defaults could not be ruled out. Public protests became quotidian as several societies were severely shattered, even as they struggled to recover from the pandemic's rupture. The world faced an acid test, an examination of its character, an appraisal of its resilience. If at any time post–World War II there was a need for inspirational, far-sighted global political leadership which commanded ecumenical respect, it was now. Sadly, it was conspicuously missing. No country illustrated this gnawing scarcity of moral leadership better than India.

Modi's government reminded one of the French empress Marie Antoinette's memorable line: Let them eat cake. Whether it was jobs (pakora frying was considered a suitable alternative), farmers, women fighting for sexual justice, Dalits being bullied or police officers harassing ordinary people, the government had a stock answer: Modi was the only one Indians had, and if Modi was a Herculean flop, they had to live with it. There is no alternative to Modi, was repeated by TV anchors with the certainty of a Swiss trains' punctual arrival.

The Gyanvapi mosque controversy (the Archaeological Survey of India has been mandated by the courts to look into its history) has raised the communal temperature. It challenges the Places of Worship Act, 1991, which attempted to freeze the status quo on the religious character of places of worship as of India's Independence Day of 15 August 1947, when India chose to become a pluralistic, multicultural society. The destruction of the Babri Masjid by a violent Hindu mob on 6 December 1992, egged on by the Sangh Parivaar, showed that religious fundamentalists could challenge constitutional proprietary with insouciant ease. The riots that happened thereafter all over the country left 2,000 dead.

Former Prime Minister P.V. Narasimha Rao deserved much more credit for this epochal law (the Places of Worship Act), given the blazing circumstances prevalent at that time. Instead, his adversaries lampooned him for being a saffron sympathizer. The fact that the current gridlock over religious origins is happening in the parliamentary constituency of the prime minister is telling.

Narendra Modi had just completed eight long years in office as prime minister. Not surprisingly, the BJP was proudly propagating Modi's brand of 'New India', which essentially wishes to convey that pre-2014 India was an aberration whose history needs a fresh coat of paint or maybe expunction itself.

If one were to look at the government's economic track record, barring using the UPA's Direct Benefits Transfer efficiently (Aadhaar for instance being a crucial component in welfare distribution), Insolvency and Bankruptcy Code, and increasing digitization (which was in any case inevitable in a post-pandemic world), and a few infrastructure projects (where else would one use government CapEx, by the way), there is little to cheer for one that had ten long uninterrupted years and a full majority in Parliament. Socially, India was burned out, exhausted. Broken.

> There is much more to a positive vision of liberal national identity than successful management of diversity and the absence of violence. Liberals have tended to shy away from appeals to patriotism and cultural tradition, but they should not. National identity as a liberal and open society is something of which liberals can be justly proud, and their tendency to downplay national identity has allowed the extreme right to claim this ground.[8]

The Opposition, particularly the Congress, had not been able to understand how to counterattack the BJP's two-pronged lethal weapon of ultranationalism and aggressive Hindutva. All the secular parties were categorized as 'pro-Pakistan and antinational'. The saffron brigade had monopolized the topic of the territorial integrity of India and national security, portraying them as their unique skillset. But none of the fustian boastfulness could stop Satya Pal Malik.

Satya Pal Malik, who was governor of Jammu and Kashmir during the Pulwama terrorist attack of February 2019 and the scrapping of Article 370 in August later that year, added further fuel to fire by stating that prime minister Modi was 'ill-informed' and 'ignorant' about the Kashmir crisis.[9]

In an interview to Karan Thapar of The Wire, Satya Pal Malik, the last governor of J&K before it was divided and reduced to Union territory status, set the cat amongst the pigeons when he said, 'I can safely say the PM has no real problem with corruption.'[10]

Malik held back no punches as he made an earth-shattering accusation against Modi directly on the deadly Pulwama attack in which forty Central Reserve Police Force (CRPF) personnel were slaughtered. Malik claimed that the CRPF had requested for a special transport plane to ferry the contingent but were refused by the Union Defence minister, Rajnath Singh. The CRPF soldiers were sitting ducks thereafter as they were extremely vulnerable when exposed to navigating roads where a trap to waylay them was easy to execute. This is exactly what happened. On being questioned, Malik then made a stunning revelation, saying that both Modi and National Security Adviser Ajit Doval told him to stay silent on the sensitive subject, instead of talking about it. The BJP, unused to internal rebellion, and unconditioned to damaging news emanating from within its boundaries, was too immobilized to respond. Modi, of course, remained frozen, speechless, but even his garrulous lieutenants appeared dazed. Their only hope was the famous 'Godi Media' (a term founded by ex-NDTV anchor, Ravish Kumar) who were professional artists in the act of smothering anti-BJP news and more specifically, anti-Modi barrages.[11] But good news always awaited Modi when he travelled abroad as he represented the world's most exciting emerging market. Applause, hugs and publicity were guaranteed.

Joe Biden, president of the United States (June 2023), and Emmanuel Macron, president of France (July 2023), gave Modi a rousing reception, state dinners and official salutes, while extolling the 'shared democratic values' of the two countries. The western world, never short on homilies and hypocritical grandstanding, driven by their own paranoia about the emerging Russia-China axis, had nonchalantly dumped the subject of human rights violations within India. Arms sales, consumer markets, cheap labour and looking at India as a strategic military asset, a bulwark against Chinese expansionism, had made them turn a blind eye to the serious democratic recession which prevailed in the world's most populous country. For Modi, foreign policy was always more about domestic brand building; the hugs, teleprompter speeches, banquet dinners and the diaspora razzmatazz, covered by a breathless electronic media on steroids, helped him improve his ratings.

G20 billboards dominated practically every bus stop, bus, newspapers and any available advertising space that was government-controlled. One day while driving to work past Marine Drive in Mumbai, I actually started counting them. In a space of less than a few kilometres alone, I could reach twenty-four; yes, twenty-four ad displays. It was an astounding festival of personality promotion. A friend from London who was visiting Mumbai told me in deadly earnest, 'This would piss off Putin. Or even Xi Jinping' The 'mother of democracy', as the G20 summit to be held in September 2023 was titled, had become a ruse to electrify the positioning of one supreme leader. Even a Latin American dictator would have blushed a beetroot red at the self-aggrandizement.

Freedom House called India, 'partly free', while the University of Gothenburg, Sweden said that it was a top autocratic country and ranked it at 97/179.[12] *The Economist* was more prosaic in calling it a 'flawed democracy'. Reporters without Borders ranked India at a dispiriting 150/180. The democratic recession in India was worse than its economic stagnation.

The abuse of lower-caste Dalits and tribals continued unabated, particularly in BJP-ruled states. After a disgusting video emerged where a man purported to be a local BJP leader urinated on a tribal, Chief Minister of Madhya Pradesh Shivraj Singh Chouhan went on a damage control spree as only politicians can, with camera crews in full attendance. He then went on to wash the victim's feet as a form of apology and atonement.[13] The state was due for elections in a few months, in November 2023.

One of the electoral slogans sold aggressively by the BJP was 'Vote for a double-engine sarkar'.[14] The sales argument was that voters should press the lotus symbol on the EVM in the state elections, as doing so would give them the added benefit of the same party ruling as the centre. It is in these acts that BJP revealed its true autocratic propensities. What if the people voted for the Opposition parties instead? Would the Modi government topple it, deny the state its due resources on time, delay developmental projects requiring central intervention, or generally push the state to the brink by targeting leaders through fictitious charges or by accelerating legal cases through the investigating agencies to weaken their political status? The 'double-engine' catchword revealed Modi's doublespeak; while he pontificated on cooperative federalism, in spirit, there was an implied threat which stood against the salient principles of democratic contestation. In the Karnataka elections, BJP leaders carried the rhetoric to absurd levels, telling voters that if they did not vote BJP, they could forget about receiving central government assistance. They lost.

Modi suggested that the proposed ban on the Bajrang Dal in the Congress manifesto for Karnataka was an affront to Lord Hanuman. Religious chasms have always impregnated Modi's politics; he was using his media clout to conceal Bajrang Dal's communal poisoning of society and instead positioning the restrictions on the militant outfit as Congress's assault on Hindu gods. Minority appeasement, BJP's dial-a-quote on Congress, returned with flourish. But the enlightened voter was not buying the balderdash.

For Modi, development had to be a 'visual experience'; therefore, his paranoia about inaugurating Vande Bharat trains, ports, highways, metro stations, airports, etc. Modi is obsessed with what the people think about him, and this deep pathological insecurity in him, sprouted often, with sometimes disastrous consequences. One of his worst diplomatic faux pas was when he said, after the Chinese Galwan valley intrusion in June 2020, in which twenty Indian soldiers were killed, that no Chinese soldier had entered Indian Territory. It was a blatant lie, and a reprehensible attempt at subterfuge. How could the fountainhead of muscular leadership concede that India's hegemonistic neighbour had sneaked in right under the infallible superhero's nose? In doing so, Modi gave China a carte blanche to claim that Indians indulged in concocting anti-China propaganda to paint them as expansionist. No other prime minister would have survived the colossal compromise on India's territorial sanctity which had been done to rescue the leader's image. It helped that Modi had a loyal army. BJP leaders operate as Modi's factotum. I suspect that is the number one item on their job description. They operate like a cackle of hyenas, ingratiating to everything he expects of them. They are noisy both in Parliament and outside. It helps that the media is at their beck and call. On several TV shows, when the BJP spokesperson speaks, the anchor is frightened of interrupting their monologue.

On an Indigo flight from Mumbai to Bengaluru, the only time I squirmed was when suddenly there was an announcement of a government programme which was followed by a profound acknowledgement of the visionary prime minister's contribution, or some such hyperbole. Every trick in the bag, every conceivable opportunity was being exploited to flood consumers with political publicity. Government platforms like public sector gas stations, railway platforms, airports, bus terminuses and railway stations were bombarded with Modi's visage. But a private sector airline company too? I sent a tweet to Indigo Airlines questioning their decision to feature Modi's image, but they did not even bother to respond. Modi was omnipresent in every conceivable space; one could not miss him.

Politics on television had become like an entertainment sideshow; limited fact checking, unlimited puffery, Bollywood-style dialogue-baazi, shouting matches and sometimes, outright abuse. India was like a reality TV show, a WWF contest, where following the mud wrestling only the most muscled, strongest survived. Everything appeared rigged. Everything was programmable, like an Instagram filter. Modi knew that as long as he controlled the political conversations with his influence over the Big Media he had little to worry about, intermittent unpleasantness notwithstanding. If he asked, 'Mirror mirror on the wall who's the fairest of them all?' he was certain the response would be: 'Narendra Modi'. But as 2023 headed for its last calendar quarter, starting with the world champion wrestlers protests in Delhi and down to the civil war in Manipur, the brittleness of the exaggerated hype began to come into play. Modi had dropped the ball, and even his friendly TV anchors struggled with their panegyrics.

The German governments since World War II have maintained the concentration camps where 6 million Jews were incinerated in gas chambers, shot to death or tortured till they could not take it anymore. Dachau, near Munich, is a good example. They have not tried to obfuscate or obliterate their history of the despicable genocide perpetrated by Adolf Hitler's Nazis. They have let the darkest period of human history exist; it has served as a reminder to them and the world of the consequences of racism, discrimination, prejudice and bigotry when these things assume devilish, diabolical proportions. Perhaps India should do the same; instead of spending billions on creating new government structures, it should build memorials, as a form of atonement to those innocent people who were killed for no fault of theirs in communal riots. It might also help a country, of late perceptibly hot-headed, revengeful and provincial, to recognize the futility of violence and hate. We might also then recognize the evil forces which usually command these pogroms for their ulterior gains. More importantly, one would, hopefully, not make the same mistakes again.

7

LAAL SINGH CHADDHA

*'Nearly all men can stand adversity, but if you want to test a
man's character, give him power.'*

—*Abraham Lincoln*

I MET BOLLYWOOD legend Aamir Khan at his Bandra studio at the
peak of the internet 2000 boom. Aamir, off screen, appears to be
a thinking genius, someone who could be a scholarly Sufi poet, a
movie critic or a resolute activist. Or all three. But in front of me
was one of the superstar Khan trio, who commanded respect and
followership because of not just his acting nous but also a non-
flashy, non-Bollywood, down-to-earth demeanour. Khan took us
around his back office where director Ashutosh Gowariker was
working on some post-production work for a film that would
turn out to be a memorable classic, *Lagaan*. We chatted about the
business proposition that we had in mind (I wanted him to be a
co-founder of our proposed entertainment portal) and sundry stuff.
But among other things, I remember telling him with a modicum
of awkwardness: 'I am a huge fan of yours, Aamir. But you must be
bored of hearing it from everyone.' I still have not forgotten what
Khan answered in return. 'No, not at all. I never get bored. That's

what we exist for. Your appreciation, your faith in us. I never tire of it. None of us do. So I would actually say, bring it on. I love my fans, each one of them.' A decade and more later, that conversation about fans with one of the '3 Idiots', became germane to political developments that began to affect celluloid in ways that none had imagined.

'Life is like a box of chocolates. You never know what you are going to get.' This epochal line from American actor Tom Hanks in the all-time Hollywood classic, *Forrest Gump*, became a quotable quote. The film ended up winning six Oscars, deservedly so. Aamir Khan, considered by most to be the ultimate prototype of method acting and blessed with a cerebral impulse, was bringing out an official remake of *Forrest Gump* (not a dissimulated, unofficial version as most local producers do) as *Laal Singh Chaddha*. Khan is a brilliant performer who has consistently pushes the envelope and yet delivers amazing blockbusters at the box office. The film should have got many excited to head to the nearest multiplexes, especially after them being cocooned in their claustrophobic precincts over a hellish two years. But no! There was a deeply muffed mob of internet trolls who had been meticulously organizing the #BoycottLaalSinghChaddha trend. No one had seen the film obviously (it released on 11 August 2022), so the obnoxious cannonade had nothing to do with artistic merit or creative liberalism gone rogue. So, that begs the question: Why were some piqued souls demonstrating such animus against an innocuous cinematic offering? The truth is, India has weaponized hate and demonized minorities. What we were seeing was partisan trench warfare with Bollywood being the soft target. Aamir was going to be paying a huge price for it.

On being questioned at a media event (by the *Indian Express*) about the state of the nation, the erudite actor known for doing offbeat films along with commercial potboilers talked about the despondent social climate, which had prompted his then better half, Kiran Rao, to contemplate moving abroad. Khan had in fact termed that thought a 'disastrous proposition', explaining that he was terribly troubled that they had even entertained the idea of another country's passport. Khan was hinting at the exclusionary nationalism being practised by the political panjandrums of the ruling party, the BJP. The year was 2015. That was a period that saw rising communal heat in India, the ugly religious bigotry resulting in the dastardly lynching of Mohammad Akhlaq in Dadri village of Uttar Pradesh. The rest is history. As things stand today, Khan was being clairvoyant, especially with the growing metamorphosis of a once peaceful even if occasionally volatile India becoming into a recurring maelstrom of hate. India is a dangerously polarized polity. Facts corroborate that assertion.

While Aamir Khan continues to be an Indian citizen, over 16 lakh citizens have migrated abroad since 2011, surrendering their passports as they seek greener pastures.[1] Among them are a staggering 23,000 dollar-denominated millionaires between 2014 and 2018 alone.[2] If anyone believes they have all made such an important life decision only for better goat cheese, fresher avocadoes, designer clothing and the luxury of tax havens, they are most certainly wrong.

Lynching deaths, popularly associated with the murders of African Americans by the Ku Klux Klan during the days of Mississippi Burning, have been normalized in India, with several such incidents now not even generating a conversation, forget a headline. A systematic attempt to make 200 million Indians feel like second-rate citizens has been underway through a regular dose of divisive propaganda—love jihad, ghar wapsi, beef-eating bans, anti-Romeo squads and attacks on the hijab, halal, aazaan, etc. The freedom to sell merchandise close to places of worship is also being taken away.

The government had to hurriedly apologize to Middle Eastern and other Muslim-dominated countries after a slanderous outburst against Prophet Mohammed by the now-suspended national spokesperson of the ruling party, Nupur Sharma, prompting a strong rebuke from the Supreme Court. The SC was unforgiving on Nupur Sharma, holding her, 'single-handedly responsible for what is happening in the country. She must apologize to the whole country.'[3] The Supreme Court's chief justice also lamented the criminal justice system in India, where institutional harassment and unalloyed intimidation under the current regime has been regularized. Could one blame anyone for believing that the democratic deconsolidation in India may have become irreversible, at least in the near term? At the receiving end are many Muslims, withering away as undertrials in jails. Make no mistake, but there are fundamentalists on both sides; there was a horrific decapitation of a Hindu tailor in Udaipur, exposing the dark underbelly of sleeper cells which could overwhelm society. There were bloodthirsty revanchists who were fearlessly beginning to surface from both communities.

The organized attempt to embargo Aamir Khan's film was another form of ghettoization, marginalization and segregation. Hate rises at an exponential rate, because identity politics has a bottomless depth to it. It feeds on human vulnerabilities. It thrives on identity politics. At the end of *Forrest Gump*, the marathon runner standing at the grave of his departed wife tells her, 'If there is anything you need, I am always there.' Perhaps it would help if people start saying this to each other even as they live. But, for now, Khan had a lot on his plate, which explains his self-imposed hibernation.

In March 2021, Aamir Khan trended for different reasons. He was infected with coronavirus as India was overwhelmed by the second Covid billow. But just a while earlier the popular heartthrob had made headlines for an altogether different reason: Aamir quit social media altogether. Interestingly, few bothered to dive deep, or perhaps they did not have the courage to probe into why would Bollywood's numero uno superstar quit Twitter, Instagram, Facebook, YouTube, etc. at a time when the digital revolution is predicted to reach dizzying levels. Post-pandemic, most social media entrepreneurs are expecting a huge user-tsunami in digital consumption. OTT platforms are the latest sensation, and overnight India has become hooked on to web series, like those afflicted with the couch-potato syndrome. India is headed the US way and will in all probability even redefine expectations, moving away from the multiplex commercial formats that were once cinema's traditional foothold. PVR Inox is experiencing falling footfalls, empty halls, quiet popcorn counters and few green ticks on BookMyShow, although Shah Rukh Khan's *Pathaan* and *Jawan* and Sunny Deol's *Gadar-2* did end up lifting sagging Bollywood spirits.

The user base of smartphones has suddenly mounted to 750 million. Even a normally stodgy government has used the App model to vaccinate millions and manage its public outreach. These highly personalized social media platforms are the smartest, most cost-effective way to promote Friday releases; they possess an exponential ability to establish the kind of mass contact that frankly very few, especially politicians, film actors and others in public life, can really ignore. Khan has always dared to swim against the tide; he should have been the chief marketing officer of the Bollywood digital revolution. Instead, he had closed shop and vanished altogether. But there was more to it than meets the eye in Aamir's abrupt walk away. It was the toxic trolling of hate-spreaders belonging to Right-wing extremist groups that had driven the *Lagaan* superstar away from his own following. It was sad, because Aamir and several of his contemporaries have given us such rollicking fun times to look forward to over popcorn and cappuccino on many a weekend.

I need to make an upfront disclosure; I am a sucker for Bollywood. They provide such dizzying non-stop entertainment that you have to be a thoroughbred bore to dislike them. Just one scene from the masterful creator of fantasy films, Manmohan Desai will be enough to augment your adrenaline. A pumped-up Amitabh Bachchan after bashing several henchmen of the creepy villain chases the escaping lout. There is only one problem, the villain is already on a dirt-track runway aboard a small airplane while Bachchan (in the film, *Mard*) is galloping on a white horse. But for Bachchan any trapeze-artistry required to hop onto the plane zooming ahead was like a walk in the park. He throws a long lasso at the airborne plane which hooks on to its tail promptly in a perfectly rounded knot, throwing it off balance. Bachchan then confidently leaps off the horse and onto the plane, and I leave the rest to your wildest imagination. Thankfully, the poor horse was spared from the pyrotechnics, perhaps on account of certain animal rights violations or the absence of CGI then. While most of us have a raucous laugh at this ridiculous excess now, I remember, being thrilled and clapping with the audience when Bachchan did this mind-boggling stunt (the 'double' I am sure was the real hero). Seriously, how could India now mow down these illogical phantasm-creating dream-merchants under the Modi government? How could any establishment divide the creators of fantasy and dreams? Bollywood has no pretensions of being the epitome of unblemished perfection. It is far from ideal; the films abound with human fallibilities, like the rest of us. The filmmakers even dish-out terrible dishwater stuff sporadically. But Bollywood is yet the country's ultimate stressbuster. Not everyone can afford to go to a Kerala Ayurveda camp, or the verdant five star resorts in Himalayan hill stations to do meditation exercises at the crack of dawn. Bollywood makes us laugh (I remember the entire

Inox theatre literally in the aisles when watching *No Entry*) and cry (the last scene of *Devdas* at New Excelsior had many bringing out their handkerchiefs). Even in its most trashy productions, there is a method in the chaos.

I grew up in the Rajesh Khanna-Amitabh Bachchan age; between them, we got utmost entertainment; the romantic Phenomenon vs the Angry Young Man. It was not so much just the movie experience but the build up to it right from the mahurat shot, and the little tit-bits that followed in the gossip columns of Filmfare, Stardust, Cine Blitz and Star and Style. And then of course there were the huge full-page advertisements that followed in *The Times of India* at release time. I used to be most excited while going to book the tickets, standing in the queue for hours. As we would near the ticket counter, our hearts would palpitate with unrestrained excitement. The tickets were usually of different colours for Stall (front and rear), Dress Circle and Balcony. Once the herculean task was accomplished, we returned with triumphalism written all over our countenance. On the day of the movie, we wore smart clothes and shiny shoes and reached the theatre at least half an hour in advance to have Sosyo or Mangola along with those Irani samosas shaped like an equilateral triangle. It was like a family picnic. And no matter which film you saw, no matter how empty-headed and silly, it made you smile. One such film was *Amar Akbar Anthony* (AAA).

As the eponymous title suggests, it was about the confluence of India's diverse religiosity (it is hard to not imagine social media trolls going berserk in today's sulphuric climate against the film's syncretic title, asking for a ban with a #BoycottAAA hashtag). It was released in 1977 and had three famous heartthrobs in it: Amitabh, Vinod Khanna and Rishi Kapoor. It had three heroines too (Neetu Singh, Shabana Azmi and Parveen Babi, portraying three women who coincidentally belong to the same religious community as their respective heroes in the film); that was symmetrical secularism, synchronized to a T. And each one got the same screen time. For us, multi-starrers were 'total paisa vasool'. AAA has to be seen to be believed; children separated at birth, adopted in three different faiths bumping repeatedly against each other, and lost parents crossing paths yet miraculously missing each other. It was a consummate fairy tale with the most exhilarating twists and turns. The more bizarre it got, the more uproarious was the impact; all three heroes donate blood to their mother in a transfusion scene, and they do so at the same time, lying next to each other, unaware that they are brothers. It was ridiculous, but people cried copiously. Watching AAA, it seemed that the entire city of Mumbai lived in the same crowded chawl. At one point, the perennial mother, Nirupa Roy, magically recovers her eyesight in a temple after some laser-like lights emanate from a Sai Baba statue. Comparatively, multiplexes nowadays are such sanitized bores (despite their curated designer menus), because when AAA played in the theatres (every one of them was single screen then) people would actually dance, stand and clap, and one heard the sound of smattering coins thrown on the floor. It was collective joyousness, and everyone participated in the wild mirth with unbridled abandon. The madness has continued unabated despite competition from news channels, soap operas on the small screen and web-based OTT platforms. Bollywood still reigns supreme, but it's choking. It needs to breathe. *Amar Akbar Anthony* would have met a bitter end in India's current climate of intolerance. The new AAA are probably Akshay Kumar, Ajay Devgn and Anupam Kher, three popular actors who have ardently assumed the role of being the Modi government's HMV record player, bellowing forth whatever the lord and master commanded.

It is this same film industry that has been recently painted as a scatological, hedonistic, drug-consuming doghouse with X-rated characters, sleazy sugar daddies and manipulative oligarchic merchants controlling its treasured infrastructure. Even the death of the unfortunate Sushant Singh Rajput led to national political fisticuffs. For the first time, there appeared to be clear ideological animosity between warring camps. Like India, Bollywood is a divided house, polarized. Once Bollywood reflected India's reality, now that same reality has caught up with it. Deepika Padukone's bikini in the film *Pathaan* caused more heartburn to Hindutva zealots than the scorching aftermath of food inflation. The new voice of absolutely nutcase lessons in Indian history were Bollywood fruitcakes who were given extensive media space on BJP-friendly TV channels. It was a joke. The once spirited free bird which soared into the azure skies, propelled by its magnificent creative wings, had been thoroughly subsumed by India's inexorable 'othering' blueprint.

The word bipartisan is a misnomer in India's political dictionary. Unsurprisingly, the pernicious coronavirus second wave further aggravated the chasm. Bollywood was no exception. Several film personalities like Ajay Devgn, Akshay Kumar, Vivek Agnihotri, etc., made even Covid appear like a political machination by a feckless Opposition to muddy Modi's image. Among the most vocal of these actors was Anupam Kher. I read with some disappointment the feverish defence of the ruling dispensation by the senior actor in the *Indian Express*, 1 May 2021. Kher made some valid observations about dispassionate public conduct, impartial politics, etc. during an unprecedented health emergency, and the responsibility of state governments too. It made sense. But he seemed prodigiously piqued with Opposition parties for their continuous interrogation of the central government led by his hero, Narendra Modi. He shouldn't have been. That's what democracy is all about, isn't it? Perennial scrutiny on a public platform? The family members of the twenty-five Covid patients who died on account of inadequate oxygen supply in Delhi's Ganga Ram hospital may not have quite acquiesced with Kher's commiserations for the BJP-led NDA.

Kher strongly believed that the severe condemnation of PM
Modi's pathetic handling of the pandemic was totally unjustified.
Unfortunately, hard statistics are devoid of rhetorical protection: over
4,00,000 cases in one day, 3,600 deaths and 69 lakh new infections
in April 2021 alone,[4] and a teetering health infrastructure unable
to cope with the endless influx of infected patients. It was hardly a
state secret that more alarming numbers were artificially suppressed.
India itself became a micro-containment zone, sequestered from
the global community. The trust deficit with the government was
so high, Twitter and social media became the new SOS platform.
It was India's biggest humanitarian crisis post-1947, and India was
failing the test. It was not the economy, but the virus which was on
an upward rising vertical V-curve. India had dropped the ball. But
who was accountable? Where did the buck stop?

In a tearful scene in the Mahesh Bhatt-directed *Saraansh*, a
heartbroken Anupam Kher, frustrated by bureaucratic apathy, goes
from pillar to post for his deceased son's ashes, which must travel
through India's cumbersome customs procedures. Kher was brilliant
(he was just twenty-nine years old then) as a broken father grieving
helplessly. The audience wept with him. Perhaps Kher needed to tell
himself that there were many fathers and sons going through the
same hellish nightmare now. They were pleading not just for oxygen
canisters, ICU beds, scarce Remdesivir or precious ventilators, they
were also scrambling for crematorium space, to give dignity to their
lost loves. Even a makeshift parking lot would do. It was wretched,
the bottomless depth of human suffering. It was dehumanizing. And
it was for real, no retakes were necessary.

Actor Kajol recently said something which was discussed
animatedly practically every day in every college and office canteen,
on an airplane or a subway train. Everywhere. 'India needed
educated leaders, not uneducated ones.' A seismic eruption followed
on social media. She had not insinuated about any leader with

doubtful educational qualifications, but Right-wingers assumed that she was targeting Modi, whose college degree was a matter of Himalayan conjecture. Kajol was forced to apologize. Pakistani actors who were once a rage in Hindi cinema had disappeared; even guest appearances were taboo. *Tandav*, a web series which was being shown on Amazon Prime Videos, was viciously attacked for upsetting people's religious sentiments, besides showing the prime minister in an unflattering light. There was a call for a ban in BJP-ruled states, besides the ordeal of legal persecution. *Adhipurush*, a modern remake of the mythological classic, the Ramayana, was a box-office turnip, because it allegedly depicted Hindu gods in an unbecoming fashion. Then of course, there was *Gadar-2*, a jingoistic sequel to the popular original from 2001, which became a monster hit as it played on the familiar storyline of the 'evil' neighbouring state of Pakistan and its allegedly nefarious obsessions. The crowds lapped it up like there was no tomorrow.

I would meet Aamir Khan again at a book launch twenty-three years later. *Laal Singh Chaddha*, as it turned out, was Khan's biggest box office failure in recent memory. As someone who thought the film was a touching version of the original, I asked Aamir, 'Were you disappointed with the results? And didn't the massive boycott Bollywood mob who had targeted you specifically damage the prospects of the film even before release?' Khan thought for a moment and said: 'I think the film itself was not good enough.'

8

RIP VAN WINKLE WAKES UP

'Always be a first-rate version of yourself, instead of a second-rate version of somebody else.'

—*Judy Garland*

FOR A FATHER, buying a gift for a daughter who has just entered her teens is a dicey proposition. Balancing the conflicting roles of a protective dad versus the uber cool one is like skating on thin ice. The BlackBerry mobile phone sorted out that predicament for me. While the USP of the gadget was its push-email (the corporate world was completely addicted to it), it had become a global sensation with adolescents because of a feature called BlackBerry Messenger (BBM). BBM was the first messaging service; it appeared like a private bubble, offering both confidentiality and unlimited texting for free. So prized was the BlackBerry that former US President Barack Obama in his autobiography, *A Promised Land*, talks about a heart-breaking separation from his favourite device for security reasons. The Indian National Congress, the party which inspired the great Indian freedom struggle against the British Raj, was for long, like BlackBerry, India's preferred operating system.

Of course, that was eons ago. BlackBerry does not exist anymore (it has an enterprise software model now). Like BlackBerry in the smartphone industry, Congress once overwhelmingly dominated the political narrative in India. If BlackBerry in 2009 had 50 per cent of the US smartphone market, Congress regularly won absolute majorities on its own in the Lok Sabha; its peak was 404 seats in 1984.[1] By 2014, BlackBerry's market share had nose-dived to less than 1 per cent (with losses at USD 1 billion). In the same year, Congress was reduced to 44 Lok Sabha seats, and WhatsApp, which initially appeared to be a poor third cousin of BBM, got a whopping valuation of USD 19 billion from Facebook. BBM had sunk into a rabbit hole. Do you see the similarities here? Both Congress and BlackBerry remained adamant that all was well in the hope that the slipping customer/voter mindshare, at worse, was a transient aberration. It would naturally fix itself. It did not.

The Congress, plagued by internal hubris, underestimated the regional satrap from Gujarat who was revolutionizing the BJP. It seemed content with delusions of grandeur, of being 'India's natural party of governance'. Once again in 2019, the Congress was vanquished, getting 52 seats, while the BJP won a massive 303.[2] It was time to get seriously concerned.

One of managements' most over-used clichés is 'reinvention'. Periodically, every CEO pays homage to this homily, though few really walk the talk. Politicians more so; in fact, the Congress chose to be fossilized, becoming a reluctant reformist at best. But as the Congress trouble-shooters attempted to put an end to months of infighting between a confident but smug Captain Amarinder Singh and a recalcitrant and trigger-happy Navjot Singh Sidhu, many political pundits applauded the magic formula of brokering peace by the Congress in Punjab as a 'pragmatic bold risk'.[3] It was 2021. Elections were due in the February of 2022.

Was the Congress belatedly waking up to the reality that the good old days of incremental fiddling were over? That perhaps the time had come to take some imaginative strides which might even boomerang in the short term? Or was this just a desperate reaction to being pushed to a corner, an unsustainable frail détente at best? In his seminal work *Think Again*, Adam Grant, an organizational psychologist at Wharton, talks of the 'overconfidence cycle' trap that BlackBerry had fallen into.[4] The Congress had been afflicted by the same bugbear, and many of my former colleagues were convinced in early 2014 that at most the BJP would be a seasonal flavour. They have been proven wrong. Repeatedly.

The Congress must aspire to be an Apple, pushing boundaries, forcing inventions, periodically rejigging its mammoth organization and recalibrating its storytelling. It has limited options, because political depreciation can become a death wish. Unlike BlackBerry that had to contend with several competitors, Congress is the only pan-India alternative to the BJP. The latter's subpar performance (including its pandemic mishandling, Pegasus snooping, ravaged economy, high fuel prices, sectarian tensions, undermined institutions, record unemployment, etc.) could affect its political fortunes in 2024. But the Congress was being unusually magnanimous towards it. There were five things the Congress could do to seize the governance debate: elect a Congress president (it did finally), bring the Congress under RTI and disclose source of funds (a game-changing move to checkmate BJP's electoral bonds chicanery), decentralize administration and election management by appointing vice presidents for different regions, revitalize grassroots by having transparent elections from block levels to the CWC, and instead of focusing on personality politics like the BJP, bring back the original 'Congress collective', a culture of dynamic teams (Gandhi, Nehru, Patel, Bose, Maulana Azad, etc.) who challenged each other, prioritizing nation-building over petty politics. Inner democracy could galvanize the Congress.

The Congress must create an alternative national blueprint and knock on every door to inspire a shared vision. The BJP for all its current hegemony must know that BlackBerry's cataclysmic fall was also because it had just one product category: mobile phones. You have to break eggs to make an omelette; the ball was in the Congress's court, to seize the initiative, create a positive narrative and build a coalition, but that could only happen if it revitalized itself. In politics, breaking bread with people is a significant milestone. Food, incidentally, can be quite an ice-breaker and a good way to kickstart a change. It was good to see Congress leaders doing dinner diplomacy with friendly foes.

One of the most underrated perquisites of being in Indian politics is the big chunks of chicken tikka masala floating gingerly in a placid ocean of high cholesterol, which is served on the luxuriant lawns of what is nowadays perceived to be a notorious elite neighbourhood, Lutyens Delhi. At the home of former Congress MP Kapil Sibal's home there was both gastronomic temptations as well as political confabulation in abundant supply. Exhibit A of Opposition leaders attended the dinner, each of them a formidable regional satrap. There was Sharad Pawar, Lalu Prasad Yadav, Omar Abdullah, Akhilesh Yadav, Pinaki Mishra, Sanjay Singh and Sanjay Raut, among others. In politics, atmospherics frequently overwhelms the message itself. At 8, Teen Murti Lane however they played as a doubles team.

If I were to choose an alliteration to describe the evening's summary, it would be anxiety, anger and apprehension at the state of the nation. There was unanimous agreement that Opposition unity was imperative to dethrone a belligerent BJP. While most chose sombre if not altogether vapid utterances, so as to not upset Congressmen who were for a change in absolute majority there, there were others who preferred to address the elephant in the room: Was the grand old party geared up for the big fight ahead? Omar, most unlikely to eschew home truths, was forthright: If the Congress continued its southward slide, it was game, set and match for the BJP in the 2024 general elections, a consequence of an uneven playing field. Everyone applauded that, clearly relishing the political reality check as much as the papdi chaat with dollops of yoghurt topping which was being served, resembling Alaska facing the brunt of climate change.

For all the Congressmen present (which included P. Chidambaram, Manish Tewari, Prithviraj Chavan, Shashi Tharoor, Mukul Wasnik, etc.) they were reminded of that constant bogeyman, 'time for introspection'. After suffering innumerable knockout blows, Congressmen conceal their sorrow effortlessly by being poker-faced. 'Why is Congress blowing up an excellent opportunity to checkmate the BJP?' was the usual refrain. In a way, the answer to that would define the future of India. It was a conundrum that the G-23, who had their skin in the game and were present in full force, tried hard to crack. Without success.

I skipped the dessert section because the focus of the evening shifted to healthier 'low-hanging fruits'. The Congress actually had no pretext for underperformance, because the electoral calculus gives it a lower bar for government formation. For instance, in the 2004 Lok Sabha elections, the Congress (145 seats) had just seven seats more than the BJP (138), but even at that modest level, the UPA was born (it would continue till 2014). The BJP, comparatively, has a Himalayan climb, probably closer to 185 seats (it has always been a dodgy partner, besides being seen as overtly, unambiguously bigoted). In the head-to-head contests between the two arch rivals, it has been a lopsided battle in both 2014 and 2019, with BJP winning nearly 175 seats out of 195 (roughly 90 per cent) seats. The Congress has experienced electoral ruination in many states in the Lok Sabha (Gujarat, Madhya Pradesh, Rajasthan, Chhattisgarh, Uttarakhand, Himachal Pradesh, Karnataka, Maharashtra, Telangana, Andhra Pradesh etc.), pre-emptively snuffing out any probability of an Opposition resurgence. This has worked as a force multiplier for the BJP even against tougher regional rivals as it is already perceived to be in pole position by the voter, which makes the undecided floating swing voter go with the potential winner. The hard truth is that a Congress whitewash also hurts its allies. The Congress is the leaking cauldron of Opposition unity. It needed to fix its cracks.

'BJP's obituary starts from Uttar Pradesh next year,' proclaimed a seasoned campaigner. Akhilesh Yadav looked pleased with that prognostication. But as someone whispered to me, 'Overconfidence is a passport to Waterloo.' (It would turn out to be prophetic.) That was not TMC's problem however, as a triumphant Derek O'Brien was emphatic, 'BJP is beatable. But are we ready yet nationally?'[5] The Opposition (even Shiromani Akali Dal, TRS and YSRC had joined the dinner party) appeared in combat mode. They appeared confused by Congress's apparent lack of urgency, though. It was evident before the evening wrapped up that it was the Congress that had to do the heavy lifting for an Opposition pushback. Organizational reforms, ideological clarity, alliances strategy, powerhouse leadership, there were many boxes still left to be ticked. 'Two Lok Sabha blowouts, and you still don't have a permanent president?' lamented another. Waiting for Godot found application in the Congress quandary.

In *Why We're Polarized*, author Ezra Klein (cofounder of Vox) talks of 'negative partisanship'; people vote not out of positive feelings for the party they support but from negative feelings for the party they oppose.[6] There is a message for the Congress here: stop obsessing about PM Modi/BJP and rebuild the political brand of the grand old party. It needs resuscitation. Quickly. Kapil Sibal had not had a single conversation with the Congress leadership since 2019; such communication breakdowns had to be reversed.

'We don't have fire in the belly,' said a peeved Congressman, blaming it on India's political culture of entitlement. But after that sumptuous dinner, I sure did. The Congress workers, officials and leaders had all become like lotus eaters, slow and sloppy. Something had to give. That's how the infamous G-23 came into being.

G-23 was not a congregation of international leaders huddled in a swanky getaway in the Swiss Alps confabulating on climate change in a post-Trump world order. Neither was it a ragtag gang of disgruntled old men plotting a midnight putsch. In fact, it was an assemblage of twenty-three passionate politicians with gargantuan self-respect for the political party they represented: the Grand Old Party of India. At various times, they have been uncharitably branded by sycophants as 'BJP agents', or as deceptive Trojan horses. Or self-serving superannuated over-the-hill sort who are looking for cosy sinecures in the December of their flagging political careers, who on being denied the same, were behaving like petulant grumps. Or those who were looking for the last hurrah before walking into the proverbial sunset. But all these imaginative speculations were off the mark. When eight of these political heavyweights, which included Ghulam Nabi Azad, Kapil Sibal, Anand Sharma, B.S. Hooda etc., spoke from a public pulpit in Jammu in February 2021, talking about the Congress's grim future, it created a huge commotion. Effigies were burnt, 'off with their heads' was the vociferous call from lily-livered loyalists. They were missing the woods for the trees. The G-23 spoke for many within the Congress. And outside.

The G-23, I can share from my personal experience, were a thoughtful lot, a committed bunch of Congressmen, ideologically Nehruvian, who were appalled that the Congress had become so lazy and listless that it was quite literally giving the country on a platter to the BJP, which was smashing it to smithereens. Everyone would genuinely express their personal affection for Rahul privately; it was his inaccessibility that gave most a migraine. Although petty grovelers would taunt G-23 as BJP agents or desktop leaders, the truth was otherwise. I often hosted Zoom call meetings with many of them and we would talk for hours on how to fix what seemed like a terminal disintegration.

Rahul Gandhi made a sardonic dig at erstwhile colleague Jyotiraditya Scindia; Rahul called him a backbencher in the BJP. In the Congress, he would have become chief minister (of Madhya Pradesh) had he shown patience and commitment to ideology, according to Rahul. Maybe. Maybe not. But did someone from the Congress assure Scindia of that? Rahul's tardy observation was an exhibition of his leadership misses. Instead of exhibiting schadenfreude at the perceptible discomfiture of the Nawab of Gwalior in the BJP, the more fundamental question remained unaddressed: why did Scindia prefer the alleged mortification of being maltreated by the BJP over remaining and stagnating in the Congress, his first port of call? Why did Rahul allow Scindia, who was his Lok Sabha compatriot, to leave at all? If apparently Scindia could walk into the sprawling 12, Tughlaq Lane bungalow anytime because they were close chums, how come Rahul never sensed that his buddy was upset at being sidelined? It is this communication paralysis in Rahul's handling of Congress generals, in particular, that had led to the cul-de-sac for many in the Congress. Sachin Pilot, another popular Young Turk, almost left the Congress as well in what would have been a serious crisis for the party in Rajasthan. After a serious drubbing in two Lok Sabha elections, losing Scindia and the state of Madhya Pradesh (reclaimed after fifteen long years from Shivraj Singh Chouhan of the BJP), Congress nearly blew away the desert state, which would have been nothing short of kamikaze. The party allowed itself to slip down quicksand but seemed unable to understand the threat of extinction. Maybe there was something Rahul and his cabal knew that ordinary mortals don't.

Nothing illustrated Congress's fatal death wish better than the Gujarat assembly election results of December 2022. In 2017, a pugnacious Rahul brought about a spectacular turnaround in

Congress fortunes in a state where it has been out of power since 1995. Albeit BJP still won, Congress claimed to have bearded the deadly lion-like duo of Amit Shah and Narendra Modi in their own den. Rahul showed that he was willing to take the bull by the horns. Fast forward to 2021 and the Congress was in complete disarrangement. It had not just been obliterated from urban municipalities but deracinated from even its once traditional foothold in the rural councils (which bore the brunt of Modi's flawed Gujarat model). Instead of a mega consolidation post-2017, the Congress had become a dismal mess. By the following year, a smart and nifty Aam Aadmi Party (AAP) had quietly usurped the Congress crevices and in its first serious electoral pitch gathered 40 lakh votes, reducing Congress to a dismal 17 seats, its lowest in three decades, thus giving the BJP the state on a shining silver platter with 156 seats. The inevitable must be asked: Who was responsible for such electoral meltdowns? Very few in the Congress were ballsy enough to ask such questions, being conditioned to years of inglorious obsequiousness at the altars of the Delhi Darbar. It is this lack of organizational robustness, internal democracy and an accountable leadership that sunk the Congress. But was anybody listening? India needed the Congress, but did the Congress know what to do with itself?

The Congress's weakness lay in its being tepid in response to the banal charges made against it, which had little substance. While Modi kept bringing up parivarvad in all his election speeches, the party did not counterattack, despite having hefty weaponry. In fact, dynasts within the BJP were some of their famous leaders: Piyush Goyal, Jayant Sinha, Kiren Rijiju, Devendra Fadnavis, Anurag Thakur, Jyotiraditya Scindia, Poonam Mahajan, Pankaja Munde, and the children of Rajnath Singh, Rao Birendra Singh, Raman Singh, Amit Shah and Kalyan Singh, to name a few. But the icing on the cake was that two of the most famous family names in Modi's BJP were the Gandhis themselves, Maneka Gandhi and Varun Gandhi. There had not been a Gandhi family prime minister since 1989, and Kharge was the ruling president of the party.

India is changing at a remarkably rapid pace, but the Congress's metabolism was not able to keep up with it. There are many political analysts and Left-leaning historians who are convinced that the feudal, monarchical avatar of the Congress was in synchronicity with its historical context, wherein powerful political personalities lorded over simmering inner chasms using their unfettered veto power in the post-Indira Gandhi years. The concentration of power in a divine leader was the new normal. They were the unquestioned decision makers; their verdict was sacrosanct. The Gandhis, according to them, are not a conundrum, but a continuum of the same political culture. They think internal democracy or transparent elections within the party would damage its core unifying threads, create fissures. Funnily, that's precisely what they expect from Modi for India; translucency, openness. What's sauce for the goose is sauce for the gander, right? The first tailwinds for the Congress, however, came from a hilly state, often dismissed condescendingly by heavyweight pundits as a 'small state': Himachal Pradesh. Against all odds (election strategist Prashant Kishor had told me that the BJP would make mincemeat of the Congress once again) the Congress formed the government, winning a considerable 40 seats in the 68-member assembly and an equally impressive 43.9 per cent of the popular vote. It got far less airtime than the BJP victory in Gujarat, yet it told a lot about which way the straws in the wind could blow if the Congress got its act together and the direction it could take if it found a new climate. But if the Congress is to stage a strong comeback nationally it must recognize the importance of wooing the shifty middle class, on bent knees. It is hard work, but they are often a bellwether of the national sentiment.

During one of the recurring internal fracases within the Congress in Rajasthan, one particular diatribe of Chief Minister Ashok Gehlot stood out. Sounding peeved, Gehlot pounced on his erstwhile young deputy, Sachin Pilot, 'Being merely good-looking, speaking English and giving sound bites in not everything in politics.'[7] It was a lowbrow attack, puerile in nature, but it revealed a deeper disdain for the so-called urban, educated politician, often dissed and dismissed as nothing more than an overrated pontificating intellectual elite. It also reveals why the Congress has over the years defenestrated itself from India's crucial middle-class vote. This has proved electorally disastrous for the party since 2009. The irony is the Great Indian Middle Class is a Congress construct.

The P.V. Narasimha Rao-Dr Manmohan Singh liberalization, privatization and foreign direct investment push in 1991 unleashed India's animal spirits. India never looked back. The result was burgeoning economic growth that averaged at 8.4 per cent during the first term of UPA.[8] India's middle class was spellbound by #SinghIsKing; his throwing the gauntlet on the civil nuclear deal made Dr Singh a commanding figure. Congress swept cosmopolitan Mumbai (5/6) and Delhi (6/7) in Lok Sabha seats in 2004. In 2009, it won 12/13 seats between the two cities. In 2014 and 2019, it drew a blank in both.[9]

Citizen empowerment through Rights-based legislation (RTI, RTE, MNREGA, Land Acquisition, National Health Mission, Aadhaar, Direct Benefits Transfer, Lok Pal, Food Security Act, etc.) was a smart strategy, but suddenly the Congress's perception became that of being anti-business. For a country on a fast-track economic growth mode, that appeared incongruous. Instead of having frequent interface with industry forums, such as the Confederation of Indian Industry (CII), the Federation of Indian Chambers of Commerce & Industry (FICCI), etc., the party's image of being hostile towards industry began to stick. True, India has its own Gilded Age with some Big Business houses acquiring natural resources through rent-seeking (Rahul Gandhi's Ambani-Adani jibe was not mere pock-marked rhetoric, he was absolutely right), but the majority of Indian entrepreneurs succeeded because of their technological innovations, business intelligence, product uniqueness and creative talent , not corporate corruption. Politically, the Congress distanced itself from India's big thinking technocrats and also ignored the aspirational middle class experiencing the 3M effect: the mobile-mall-multiplex phenomenon. In a hyper-connected world, the Congress had dialled the wrong number. The neo middle class emerged from Congress accomplishments; over 270 million were lifted out of poverty during UPA. India became a middle-income country for the first time in 2010. But the party seemed unaware of its own successes. Rural voters, already fragmented amongst several regional and local claimants besides the BJP and the Congress, had already deserted it for regional parties. It was a strategic lapse, as the middle class is often considered the 'swing voter'.

The Congress is at core a centrist party, socially and economically, and as Dr Singh proved during 2004–14, most large economies with income inequalities need both a booming market economy and regulated state subsidies. It is a flawed assumption that one needs to be either a socialist welfare state or a free-market capitalistic economy. India needs both John Maynard Keynes and Milton Friedman. But the Congress gave the lopsided impression of being merely pro-poor (300 million do live below the poverty line and need urgent state intervention).[10] The 2019 Lok Sabha campaign of the Congress was consumed by NYAY, a minimum income guarantee scheme meant for the poorest 25 crore Indians, providing them with Rs 72,000 per annum. It was brilliantly conceived, but the middle class felt chagrined that they were being ignored. Barring abstruse promises on jobs and saccharine lip service to

Indian industry, there was nothing tangible for them. The young, middle-class, upwardly mobile, gig economy and industry executives voted completely for Modi. The poor rural and urban voters split their votes amongst several competing alternatives. Congress had shrunk its target audience.

The middle class is ideologically malleable, economically ambitious and socially mobile. They can shift political preferences frequently. The BJP has benefited because of a Congress vacuum. In fact, the middle class got a raw deal of record joblessness, plateaued salaries, high gasoline prices, poor governance and rising urban crime. Even the double whammy of demonetization and GST, which wrecked millions, was not capitalized upon by both the Congress and other Opposition parties. The middle class influences voters both upstream and downstream as they are the ones directing the consumption basket. MNREGA advertisements in Mumbai's Breach Candy billboards by the Congress in 2014 made little sense; the middle class felt it was a case of robbing Peter to pay Paul. It barely propagated FDI in multi-brand retail, a perfect middle-class pitch. Congress had the impressive achievement of getting killed for two diametrically opposing economic models: pro-rich crony capitalism and pro-poor free subsidies. What the Congress saw as a cave in the middle class, Modi saw as an open sesame.

There are variegated estimates on the size of India's middle class, but most agree it is about 25 per cent of India's population (about 350 million).[11] The middle class believes that governments work either for the very rich (crony capitalists investing in electoral bonds) or the very poor (MNREGA, PM-Kisan beneficiaries). Many don't vote either, but when they do, they have a tsunami impact. Psephologists estimate that a single-digit upturn in middle-class voter turnout ended CPM's thirty-four-year reign in West Bengal and Lalu Prasad Yadav's fifteen-year suzerainty in Bihar.[12]

Since 2014 Modi has had the WhatsApp, Tik-Tok (now banned but replaced by Meta's reels and other wannabe social media inventions) and Ayushmann Khurrana aficionados charmed, but that can change. After the global disaster following the coronavirus pandemic, the middle class may want political parties to debate health infrastructure and pollution standards. Those who are taking the middle class for granted do so at their own peril. The Congress for sure needed to reboot its political strategy. Gehlot had to know that it was okay to speak English and read Harry Potter. And if some people have a crush on Sachin Pilot's handsome features, even better. The electoral math dictated that the Congress needed to establish a new equation with the middle class; Karnataka, bustling with young software engineers and start-ups, gave the Congress an opening; an attractive, compelling case that it could successfully replicate, in the critical winter elections of December 2023. It must work smarter. And above all, harder.

In business schools in the 1980s, the Avis marketing case study was legendary; 'We are number 2. But we try harder.' In the cut-throat car rental business (this was the pre-Uber age), Hertz was the market leader. As its nearest competitor, Avis had found a winning catchphrase to reposition its brand as one that cared more for its passengers. It would go that extra mile, literally. Juxtaposed to the Indian political context, the number two national party Congress seemed to be driving in reverse gear with the accelerator on full throttle. Whether R.P.N. Singh is a heavyweight or a cipher, losing another Young Turk to the BJP in the middle of the UP elections did hurt the grand old party. Jyotiraditya Scindia, Jitin Prasada, Sushmita Dev, Kirti Azad, the list was becoming alarmingly long. The Congress's once vaunted talent-warehouse began to rapidly dissipate to BJP's advantage. A political party is not an abstract ideology or an amorphous movement; it is a bricks and mortar political structure which is meant to mold public opinion towards its ideological narrative, and ultimately, win office. It is defined by the people it has. It needs a smorgasbord of leaders, a mix of the experienced old guard and fresh blood, aggressors and defenders, spokespersons, conscience keepers, torch bearers, goal scorers, etc. The Congress needed to stop the talent drain, but it seemed puzzlingly unaffected.

Albeit the Congress has a low tally of just 52 Lok Sabha seats, there is no shame in being the largest Opposition party (it still commands a crucial 20 per cent vote share).[13] In the two comparable democracies, UK and USA, whether through filibustering or parliamentary interventions, public debates or street protests, the leading Opposition party performs like a shadow government-in-waiting. The UK follows the tradition of a shadow cabinet. The Opposition voice dominates airwaves, sets up the daily prime-time news and drives public opinion. The Congress, for too long accustomed to unfettered uninterrupted power, has failed to do enough justice to this pivotal role. For a challenger brand, the key is unflagging pressure mounting on the government and a dynamic, outbound public contact programme. Prashant Kishor was right; waiting for anti-incumbency to defeat BJP would be nothing short of political suicide in slow motion.

Despite a baffling torpor that gripped the party's functioning post-Rahul Gandhi's resignation as Congress president in 2019, it still was a redoubtable competitor to the BJP. At its full potential, it can be a winning machine. The party has extraordinary roots, which had been under-leveraged. Rahul Gandhi's flip-flop on his own role worsened public antipathy towards Congress. In his speech at Jaipur on becoming vice president in 2013 Rahul had said: 'Power is poison.' It is certainly not a cinch. For the party's critical resurrection, Rahul was better suited to do a nationwide padyatra, connecting with the poor and the destitute, the marginalized and the dispossessed, where he appeared more at home. Rahul was not playing to his strengths; he ideally should have been Congress's ideological ambassador, not an impatient head of a clunky organization. Congress was struggling; it has not won an absolute majority in Lok Sabha since 1984.[14] In about seven states (UP, Bihar, Odisha, Bengal, Tamil Nadu, Andhra Pradesh and Telangana), with 260 Lok Sabha seats among them, it is a spent force.[15] It needed an epiphany. Internal party elections proved to be the booster shot the party needed.

The G-23 demand for elections to the post of the Congress President met with party-wide support. There were two candidates: the veteran, eighty-one-year-old warhorse from Karnataka, Mallikarjun Kharge, and the former international civil servant, Shashi Tharoor, a three-time parliamentarian from Thiruvananthapuram. Kharge expectedly won a huge landslide (84 per cent of votes as compared to 12 per cent for Tharoor),[16] but in putting up a valiant fight in a party that had not seen a contest since 2000, when Jitendra Prasada took on Sonia Gandhi, inner-party democracy got a big shot in the arm for the Congress. For the new president Kharge, the big challenge would be to learn from the agonizing shipwreck that the party had created for itself in the border state of Punjab.

The 'captain' was forcibly retired in a coup that surprised many. But Amarinder Singh, who suddenly became a 'former chief minister of Punjab', was not torpedoed by a wily BJP or his traditional bête noire, the Shiromani Akali Dal. He was outwitted and finally outlawed by his own Indian National Congress party. If ever the doctrine that politics is the art of the possible applies, Punjab would be a shining example of it. In the second half of 2021, no one would have thought that the eighty-year-old army veteran would be so unceremoniously dumped. Elections in Punjab were due within six months in March 2022.

The Congress spun the narrative that the newly appointed chief minister, Charanjit Singh Channi, was the first Dalit chief minister of Punjab. Overnight, everyone woke up to the harsh reality of Dalit disenfranchisement (they are a staggering 32 per cent of Punjab's population).[17] It is astounding how political parties attain enlightenment about social marginalization just before the ballot box (or now the EVM) comes closer. If the Congress were to capitalize on the Dalit card, it would be publicized as an electoral masterstroke, but the fact was that it was still early days. On the flip side, would the Jat Sikhs who traditionally were the big chiefs, not feel shortchanged? Such caste permutations and combinations, charitably described by the punditry class as social engineering, are usually a zero-sum game. A gain somewhere is neutralized by a loss elsewhere. The truth is that Channi was a by-product of political expediency. The man who wanted to be king, Navjot Singh Sidhu, India's perennial motor-mouth without brakes, found himself between the proverbial rock and a hard place. If the Congress in Punjab appeared to be in la-la land daze, it was Sidhu who deserved to be given accolades for the inspired chaos. Till Sidhu burst onto the scene like a bull in a china shop, it was all calm waters and smooth sailing for the Congress. Congress's political management strictly complied with Murphy's Law: if anything can go wrong, it will.

Captain Amarinder Singh was publicly disgraced at Sidhu's behest by the Congress leadership. The party's interlocutor Harish Rawat (the former chief minister, who should have been campaigning in his home state of Uttarakhand) said in no unambiguous terms that the captain would be Congress's principal campaigner in the upcoming elections. What changed? For one, it appeared that Sidhu deliberately provoked Singh with his continuous barrage of nasty comments, fully aware that the former army veteran would find the fusillade insufferably hard to bear. The reaction came as expected. When two of Sidhu's lieutenants Balwinder Singh Mali and Pyarelal Garg posted controversial Facebook comments on

Jammu and Kashmir and Pakistan, the captain's team pounced on them, labelling them seditious and betrayers to the Indian state. This was mutually assured destruction for both the captain and Sidhu. An apology was promptly demanded. The BJP, as anticipated, blew up Congress's compromised stance on national security to the Big Media. All hell broke loose. Even then it was not too late for the Congress leadership to douse the raging fires. But instead, they encouraged further dissensions. They were fermenting a battle royale. At some point the cookie had to crumble. It came on the subject of the renovation of the Jallianwala Bagh memorial museum by the NDA government.

Rahul Gandhi joined several historians who lambasted the government for the ostentatious spectacle they had made of the memorial of the 1919 massacre. Some called it the Disneyfication of the bloodbath in the holy city of Amritsar. But astoundingly enough, Captain Amarinder Singh dismissed the criticism with nonchalance, noting that it was okay by him. The Congress naturally took it as a public affront of Rahul, which they believed deserved immediate reprisal. It appeared that the outmanoeuvred captain would soon be a victim of a well-orchestrated palace intrigue. In calling for the Punjab legislature meeting without even informing the CM, the political messaging from the Congress high command was clear: Singh was being told that forget being king, he would now have to accept being thrown under the bus. Singh's time was up. But the Congress had ended up opening a Pandora's Box. And it would pay dearly.

As the state president, Sidhu had to now demonstrate his political nous or become a ridiculed figure. With the captain determined to brand him as a Pakistan sympathizer (for hugging Pakistani Army Chief, General Bajwa) and an anti-national, Sidhu faced an uphill task ahead. The chickens were coming home to roost. Worse, there was no guarantee that the dark horse, Chinni, would quietly abdicate his throne were the Congress win to win, which effectively would stump Sidhu's ambitions. Entertaining fireworks were expected after the election results. The Congress, instead of having an assured triumph in Punjab in their bag, giving them substantial time to focus on Uttarakhand, Goa, Manipur and UP, had to ensure at least a face-saving result. It did not happen. The Congress surrendered its pole position to AAP. Punjab was a debacle. AAP had an unimaginable 92 seats (42 per cent vote share) in the 117-seat assembly while Congress was reduced to a paltry 18 seats (23 per cent vote share). Embroiled in a peculiar burnout, the party struggled with remodeling itself, while unable to respond quickly to both internal demoralization and a rampaging Modi whose political mission was to exterminate his main rival with a rambunctious call for a Congress-Mukt Bharat.

The party held a Chintan Shivir in Udaipur in May 2022, following the elegiac mood in the Congress after the assembly election results, where it drew a blank, losing in all the states. It was unpardonable lethargy that had prevented it from conducting a brainstorming session within a month of the 2014 Lok Sabha elections. But better late than never. The Congress is India's last bulwark against a smoldering BJP election machine. The party had to, however, overcome three myths that had made it into a defanged dinosaur.

Myth 1: The Congress is too big to become extinct.

Statistics don't lie. Two Lok Sabha routs, losing forty of the previous fifty-one state assembly elections, tells a gloomy tale.[18] The party, founded by A.O. Hume in 1885, needed to look at the French presidential elections of April 2022 for a serious wake-up call. The two titanic parties who repeatedly formed the Parisian government, the Socialists and the Republicans, have nearly vanished amidst the Emmanuel Macron phenomenon (his party, Renaissance, is just six years old). Marine Le Pen, a Right-wing ultranationalist is the dominant voice of the disgruntled Opposition. The Congress faces not just a strong BJP but a resurgent AAP in the national sweepstakes. The regional parties have virtually obliterated the Congress in several states like Andhra Pradesh, Telangana, Odisha, Bihar, Bengal, Uttar Pradesh, Tamil Nadu, etc. But the party still had the wherewithal to make a comeback. It needed a big idea. It needed a booster shot. And yet, ironically enough, anyone who wrote off the grand old party did so at great risk.

Myth 2: The BJP will lose on anti-incumbency.

The idea above has been Congress's boogeyman and has revealed its myopic underestimation of its rivals' doggedness. Firstly, the BJP is a ruthlessly efficient machine whose immoral, yet pugnacious attitude permeated through its organizational core. It had overcome several headwinds with aggressive campaigning, using an adroit mix of falsehoods, social polarization and exaggerated successes sold over WhatsApp. For example, on the WHO estimates of Covid deaths in India being allegedly the world's highest at 47 lakh people,[19] the BJP flattened the Congress instead, accusing it of being part of a western global conspiracy to malign India. It was absolutely ridiculous, but the Congress response was typically tepid. Secondly, anti-incumbency works more in two-party western democracies like the US or UK, where there is always a visible and viable alternative, tried and trusted, on the national mainstream. Margaret Thatcher, Tony Blair, Bill Clinton, Ronald Reagan, George Bush Jr had great runs that were abruptly terminated, because there was one clear option available. But in a multi-party, first past-the-post system, there are multiple beneficiaries of anti-incumbency through a splitting of votes, which neutralizes the losses of the front runner Congress is waiting for Godot if it expects the BJP to just crumble.

Myth 3: The Congress is India's default operating system.

In his Jaipur address in 2013, Rahul Gandhi made a forthright disclosure: 'We don't know how we win elections, but we do.'[20] Everyone guffawed, but they had misunderstood what was a loaded confession. Rahul had correctly identified Congress's messy organizational functioning, a chaotic muddle despite electoral winnings, but unfortunately, he did not fix it. The problem was in the execution bug. Just like how Rajiv Gandhi hit the nail on the head in 1985 at the Congress centenary celebrations when he said that 85 per cent of one rupee was being appropriated by greedy middlemen, with only the balance 15 per cent reaching the ultimate beneficiary.[21] Rajiv too did not or could not rigorously execute a robust counter-plan. It would end up becoming an albatross round the Congress's neck, a perfect example of how the path to hell is paved with good intentions. The Congress is a victim of the false belief that it is the natural party of governance. India has of late begun experimenting with different kinds of software. Winning elections, managing the political brand and retaining public trust requires a solid operating plan in the 5G Age.

The Udaipur Declaration was important; it was an opportunity for renewal. The decision to rebut criticism of dynastic stranglehold by announcing a 'one family one ticket' rule and the inclusion of 'one person one post' augured well for the party's future. The Udaipur meet was a step forward in the right direction. But if the Congress believed that the status of the principal leadership of the Opposition that it occupied would be its sole prerogative, it was being presumptuous. There were others, more ambitious and adrenaline-pumping, who were eyeing the vacant space that the Congress had conceded generously.

In political colloquialism, whenever there is a striking departure of a senior leader (such as Sunil Jakhar in Punjab) or a mass exodus (as in Meghalaya MLAs of Congress joining Trinamool Congress), the cliché uttered is 'the rats are deserting a sinking ship'. It is partially true, the capsizing Titanic part of it. But calling them rodents may be an exaggeration. In India, ideological fidelity is an oxymoron; it has become purely transactional. The Right in India is defined not by its love for free markets and less government, but by its religious doctrine of extreme Hindutva, national security, restorative nostalgia and nativism. The Left, for its voluble sympathy for Maoist rebels, anti-Americanism, antediluvian communist de-growth model and minority protection. That leaves the centre, which had become India's default option under the Congress's inclusive political umbrella since Pandit Nehru became the prime minister, although it was always Left leaning. But with the rise of multiple regional parties, each doing a copycat manifesto pledging commitment to secularism, socialism and social justice, it has become a crowded square. Taking full advantage of this ideological amorphousness was TMC's Mamata Banerjee. Her target: the severely depleted Congress party. The reason why many Congress leaders (L. Faleiro, Sushmita Dev, Kirti Azad, etc.) were merrily dancing to Didi's drumbeat was because joining TMC was not causing a bitter heartburn unlike Congress, which was playing footsie with its 'communal nemesis', the BJP. Joining TMC was akin to leaving Facebook for WhatsApp; one was still part of the Meta verse. Banerjee was hoping that the latter's market valuation would soon tip over that of the mothership itself. Her comment in Mumbai that 'there is no UPA' (after meeting Sharad Pawar and Sanjay Raut) was a sardonic assault on the Congress.[22] TMC was creating an alternative arrangement. It wanted to lead it. When Pawan Verma, former Rajya Sabha MP, called me and said he wanted to have a private chat, I kind of figured what he had in mind. Varma, who is an astute debater and a Stephanian wordsmith, did no pussyfooting; 'Join the TMC,' he said. The Congress has become spiritless, limp, old fogey, was what he told me. TMC, under Mamata had the roar of a hungry tiger. TMC would be the new INC; a combative, strategic, streetfighter party that could defeat the BJP. The Goa assembly results would establish that paradigm. Verma, when he speaks in his deep baritone voice, making a persuasive argument which he considers ironclad, can even convince a lion to befriend a goat. I heard him out and promised to call him back.

While it was understandable that Congress targeted the BJP relentlessly given their historical rivalry, it made the cardinal mistake of underestimating its knavish allies or ex-Congressmen. It had ignored its own political history. The Jana Sangh/BJP's meteoric rise began after the Congress was first damaged by non-BJP regional formations: The Janata Party in 1977 (Jayaprakash Narayan), V.P. Singh in 1989, and the rise of Samajwadi Party, Bahujan Samaj Party (BSP) and Rashtriya Janata Dal (RJD) following the Mandal agitations. The Mandal agitation damaged Congress's traditional support base. A bruised Congress then ceded substantial space to an industrious BJP which stepped up on aggressive majoritarianism using the Ram Mandir agitation and the Shah Bano judgement to further cripple the slumbering centrist party.

For the larger RSS family, the Sangh parivar, the Shah Bano controversy came at an opportune time. Already facing heat from Muslim conservatives, the Rajiv Gandhi government now faced heat from Hindutva groups as well. The increasingly militant Hindutva groups got a shot in the arm in February when the district court in Faizabad ordered the disputed site to be unlocked and allowed the public to pray at the spot. This seemingly small concession was to prove expensive in the future.[23]

TMC's new outreach, which was curated by Prashant Kishor, was the biggest challenge Congress faced because of a serious internal erosion since 1989. TMC had an ambitious destination: to become the second largest political party (propelling Didi to become prime minister in a hung Parliament situation). Discerning observers would have noticed that it had already checkmated the BJP by doing a reverse migration of leaders back to the TMC after their hurricane sweep in the assembly elections of 2022. At stake is 42 Lok Sabha (LS) seats in Bengal; the Congress has 52 LS seats pan-India.[24] If the TMC swept Bengal and the Congress stagnated or dipped, anything was possible. *The Economist* (it has endorsed Congress in practically every general election) said, 'The next general elections is about three years away. It is not too late for Congress to become a big-tent national party capable of representing all Indians, as its founders intended.'

Kishor may have made one fatal miscalculation in his Operation Mamata: his assumption that the Congress would just wither away, succumbing meekly to his grandiose designs. He had on the contrary awakened the sleepy, somnolent giant. Two developments gave a hint of an unusually combative Congress. Firstly, the Congress promptly reassembled its traditional allies like DMK, National Conference and CPI(M), in a quick bid to nip the TMC enterprise in the bud. Most importantly, joining them were also both NCP and Shiv Sena, who had momentarily buoyed TMC hearts. Realpolitik is never linear. Congress President Sonia Gandhi's decision to not invite TMC even as a perfunctory gesture for a dinner meeting at her home was a declaration of war. Secondly, Rahul Gandhi threw a curveball at the BJP, by belatedly biting the bullet on the Hinduism vs Hindutva debate. It is the elephant in the room that the Congress has imprudently dodged with disastrous results for too long. It showed a rare pragmatic risk-taking by the young Gandhi scion. Judging by initial reactions from the Sangh Parivar, the BJP appeared threatened, at least temporarily. Rahul was still the only Opposition leader who made the BJP squirm.

Although the assembly elections of early 2022 in UP, Punjab, Goa, Manipur and Uttarakhand led to a further decimation of the Congress, it did not mean that TMC would find replacing the grand old party as main Opposition voice, a slam-dunk operation. On the contrary, Kishor had inadvertently rekindled the Congress. The TMC's Goa experiment was a complete fiasco, and with that brief flirtation with a pan-India power pitch, it abandoned its national aspirations, sticking to the more familiar Northeastern states. The BJP benefitted from the split votes. The Congress lost again, but the party's ability to still hold on to 24 per cent of the votes and get 11 seats in the 40 seats state assembly left no one in doubt as to who the real Congress was, warts and all.[25] Rip Van Winkle had woken up at last.

I did not call Pawan Verma back. I don't think he expected me to.

9

THE LONG-DISTANCE RUNNER

*'Many things there are, weird and wonderful, none more so than
man. He sails beyond the seas, lashed white by winter wind,
piercing the waters roaring round ... In all things he
finds him a way.'*

—*Sophocles*

M Y FIRST MEMORIES of Ghulam Nabi Azad were seeing him
on Doordarshan, breaking down, sobbing uncontrollably as
he returned to the Delhi railway station to attend the funeral of
his friend Rajiv Gandhi in May 1991. When I met him, I realized
what 'warm hospitality' really meant. Courteous and caring, Ghulam
Nabi is a delightful company with a treasure-chest of stories that he
recaps in his inimitable entertaining way. A raconteur par excellence,
Azad shared an instant rapport with me; he was the senior mentor
who had traversed the treacherous terrain of politics adroitly and
commanded respect with his experience and demeanour, I was a
newbie whose disruptive, almost iconoclastic views sometimes, he
found worth ruminating on. We clicked. Azad personified the gritty
loyalists of the 1980s' Congress, a turbulent decade that would be

decisive in the party's political autobiography. In 2022, he sprung a surprise.

There were many who appeared gobsmacked by the stalwart's resignation from the Congress party on 26 August 2022. The timing was characteristically picture-perfect; the grand old party, somnambulating for the most part since 2014, had been showing some signs of resuscitation with the announcement of the Bharat Jodo Yatra at the Udaipur Chintan Shivir, which followed just a week after Azad's diatribe. That's what smart politicians do; they ensure amplification of their messaging. Azad had ensured that his earth-shattering resignation had at least temporarily hijacked, if not somewhat smeared, Congress's call of a national rebirth, a second freedom struggle of sorts against the authoritarian predispositions and sectarian manifestations of the BJP-led NDA government. The majority of Congress members treated Azad's resignation as an act of exaggerated self-importance by an ageing lion-hearted general in the December of his political career. The Congress's reluctance or refusal to see the writing on the wall was unusual. Azad was not a Jaiveer Shergill. One should treat every resignation seriously; do a biopsy of it.

The notorious word 'coterie', referring to a cabal of dubious lieutenants in the 1970s, was back in circulation, because the grand old party had become an anachronism even as India had moved ahead. There is a popular adage that is often used in the corporate world: a company becomes like its leader. It is no different for a political organization. Ever since the lethal knockout in the 2014 general election, the Congress has been dilapidating at a galloping rate. It needed an inspirational leader, someone who motivates cadres, engages energetically with seniors and leaders across tiers, and encourages a political culture of candid conversations. That's what internal democracy is about. Instead, Rahul Gandhi, abruptly thrust in the forefront in 2013, went into a cocoon. He literally disappeared, surfacing sporadically during state assembly elections as a star campaigner. His *Suit Boot Ki Sarkar* and *Fair and Lovely* sound bites were masterstroke, but the consistency evaporated after a transient flirtation with sabre-rattling. I tried meeting Rahul myself with a detailed PPT presentation about the 2019 LS elections but was stalled by his obdurate gatekeepers. Ideation was replaced by genuflecting adulation. A leader, hugely fortified by Special Protection Group (SPG) security, can often be given a visa to hallucination island by self-serving parasites. It is this caucus that got Azad, Anand Sharma and even Jaiveer Shergill hopping mad.[1] The buck stops at the top, and Rahul, who is genuinely well-intentioned, must take the blame for barricading himself from his own party colleagues. Whatever Rahul's compulsions, his self-imposed isolation, when the party frantically reached out for him, did not help either the Congress or himself.

One of the illustrious members of this coterie put forth his nonsensical theory to me, 'The Congress must strictly avoid TV shows. Once the Congress vs BJP slugfest is off the menu card, their TV ratings will drop. And we will not be subjected to unwarranted prejudices of TV anchors.' His advice clearly worked because following the 2019 LS defeat, the party boycotted TV channels for an extended period. I spoke fervently against the counterintuitive idea, arguing that mainstream media was a vehicle for public outreach, especially for an Opposition party needing to be heard, no matter their clamorous partisanship. Abandoning the platform altogether was committing hara-kiri, I insisted. A miffed member of Rahul's team subtly conveyed to me: 'Lay off, or there will be consequences.' Six months later, a suitably chastised Congress was back in the TV studios. There are innumerable such instances that perhaps Azad and Sharma can cite which had them feeling that the ship was meandering aimlessly in a turbulent ocean.

Despite the several setbacks and the continuing headwinds, the Congress remained the true inheritor of the fast vaporizing Idea of India. A week is a long time in politics. A rejuvenated Congress could still upset the arrogant BJP's applecart in several state elections till December 2023 where the two parties are in a head-to-head contest in Rajasthan, Madhya Pradesh, Telangana, Chhattisgarh and Mizoram. The part still remained the last big hope to resuscitate a dwindling democracy. The timing of the Bharat Jodo Yatra could not have been better. It came in the form of the fifty-two-year-old, great grandson of Jawaharlal Nehru.

The country looked fatigued with the cacophony of animus. Inflation, unemployment, rural distress, sectarian tensions and unprecedented inequality was being worsened by dogmatism, intimidation and authoritarianism. India needed to see a push-back to the rising crescendo of a single-party, one individual leader narrative. Gandhi's Bharat Jodo Yatra (BJY) would become akin to a nationwide movement, both a social mobilization and a political assembly, whose impact could be felt in other parts of the country. It was a resurrection of the collective conscience of a country, split on multiple fault-lines, principally religion, right down its middle. It reminded one of Shaheen Bagh, although that was stationary and on a smaller scale. But it was a peaceful, democratic uprising, nevertheless.

Shaheen Bagh, a suburb in southern Delhi, became the epicentre of the anti-CAA protests, a social movement that expressed not just opposition to a prejudiced law but offered an alternative vision for India, a fairer, more inclusive country, less masculine and less predatory. It became a space where Muslim women, of all age groups, levels of education and social backgrounds discovered their political voice and found an accommodating space. Young mothers brought tiny babies, the elderly sat fearlessly among their friends and strangers, some women came in veils, others in jeans, and around the edges were people of all faiths and classes who quickly became enveloped in the warm embrace of Shaheen Bagh.[2]

The Bharat Jodo Yatra had a Gandhian aura in the Age of 5G and post-truth.

The 3,500-kilometre-long march which started on 7 September 2022 in Kanyakumari, Tamil Nadu, was an intrepid step by the much maligned and frequently disparaged former Congress president. In all fairness, Gandhi has been a lightning rod, absorbing a lot of the incendiary heat emanating from the party's onerous historical baggage. The BJP had successfully branded him as 'Pappu' for long, but Gandhi was demonstrating chutzpah; bring it on, he seemed to be saying. Rahul Gandhi was beginning to look like Forrest Gump—that insanely-obsessed runner, the eccentric superhero without fancy headgear played by Tom Hanks in the movie that made a hurricane sweep of the Oscars. Aamir Khan's Bollywood remake may have received a lukewarm reception, but Gandhi was stubbornly at it, and it was evident that the voluntary public participation in the Congress' long walk to unity was staggering. Gandhi had arrived. So, were we seeing the Congress' imminent national renaissance, or was this a mere strategy for burnishing, reimagining the damaged brand of Rahul Gandhi? Time alone will answer that.

The BJP tried several dirty tricks to stigmatize Rahul's journey, from questioning the credentials of people who joined Rahul during his walk, to actually writing to Gandhi to stop his yatra because of a potential surge in new Covid cases, even as all BJP politicians, including Modi himself, were continuing with their public appearances, maskless.[3] Gandhi's meeting with a catholic priest George Ponnaiah in Tamil Nadu was made unnecessarily controversial over a remark which was distorted.[4] It reached a bizarre level when the price of Gandhi's polo-shirt became a BJP press conference item.[5]

In a nutshell, as the padyatra rolled ahead with several celebrities, political alliance partners, and people from all walks of life joining in (Raghuram Rajan, Swara Bhasker, Sushant Singh, Amol Palekar, Riya Sen, former RAW chief A.S. Dulat, Pooja Bhatt, Aditya Thackeray etc.), it was obvious that it would be imprudent to judge the impact of the Bharat Jodo Yatra in the short term (Rahul Gandhi did not campaign at all in the state elections; he left Himachal Pradesh to Priyanka Gandhi and made one brief appearance in Gujarat). It is the eighteenth general election of 2024 that Rahul Gandhi was working towards. While provincial elections are equally important (the Congress' lackadaisical predisposition towards winning elections in the past was baffling), it was obvious that 2024 was the litmus test. The yatra's raison d'etre was to unite a fractured society, where inter-faith conflict was being deviously instigated to splinter communities, to engineer an electoral windfall for the BJP. The yatra brought back into political discussions the nearly shredded Idea of India.

A state-based ethnic, religious, racial, or national conflict between 'us' and 'them' can hardly remain stable for long. And yes, even if fascism could remain a stable state, would it be a good political community, a decent country within which children can be socialized to become empathetic human beings? Children can be certainly taught to hate, but to affirm hatred as a dimension of socialization has unintended consequences. Does anyone really want their children's sense of identity to be based on a legacy of marginalization of others?[6]

The Us versus Them binary was India's careless, malicious adventurism with the lives of innocent people.

Would polarization continue to be a bulletproof piece of ammunition in the BJP war chest, effortlessly overwhelming the fundamental issues of raging inequality, poor governance, high unemployment, volatile agrarian unrest, communal tensions, institutional paralysis and democratic deconsolidation? Would the trifecta of Ram Mandir, Article 370 and the Uniform Civil Code determine the saffron wave? The BJP definitely thought so. Yet it was nervous. There were two visible expressions of the ruling party's worries. Firstly, Union Home Minister Amit Shah's unabashed attempt, during the Gujarat election, at rebirthing the ghosts of 2002 by talking about how minorities who took part in rioting at the time of the Gujarat pogrom were 'taught a lesson'[7] was a new loathsome page in the BJP modus operandi. One could expect the party to become more flagrant in its execution of majoritarian populism. Secondly, why would BJP's Assam Chief Minister Himanta Biswa Sarma compare Gandhi's appearance with that of Iraqi dictator Saddam Hussein?[8] The vacuous traducing was to draw parallels with Muslims. Both Shah and Sarma betrayed panic, and that should have delighted the Congress.

The ball was now in Rahul's court. Instead of merely intermittently, perfunctorily addressing the Hindutva vs Hinduism debate himself, he needed to leverage the institutionalized communication of the party and multiple voices. Congress needed to reclaim its principal centrist, secular, big tent party credentials. Ignoring BJP's populist extremism was a certain kiss of death for the Congress. The young rookie politician of 2004, maligned as a spoilt dynast and ridiculed as a bumbling blabbermouth, had come of age. Walking from Kanyakumari to Kashmir had transformed the man whom Newsweek magazine once called, 'India's Quiet Revolutionary.'

'In war you can only be killed once, but in politics many times,' said Winston Churchill.[9] If anyone fits the aphorism perfectly, it is Rahul Gandhi. I met Rahul even before he had won his first parliamentary election from the family bastion of Amethi in Uttar Pradesh. It was late February 2004, and if opinion polls were truly prophetic, the party that was once India's default political operating system would face its third successive general election defeat to the Atal Bihari Vajpayee-led National Democratic Alliance (NDA) within a short span of six years. Doomsday beckoned, according to most. Clad in a light beige cotton trouser and a white T-shirt, a smiling Rahul introduced himself, slightly awkwardly, but extremely aware of the treacherous battlefield ahead. Despite a family history of brutal assassinations, including those of his grandmother and father, which can create damaging, permanent scars in one's head, Rahul was bravely crossing the Rubicon. I applauded his intrepidity. Not easy. Not easy at all. Further, he was voluntarily participating in an electoral battle when the Congress party was facing hurricane-like headwinds. Rahul was pushing the envelope, getting outside of his comfort zone. I have always felt that he has never been credited enough for that early fiery baptism.

But looking at him speaking through the falling snow in Srinagar, a picture of resoluteness and conviction, an image of a man on a mission, I knew that he was probably coming to terms with India's eerily transformed existential truism. And his own.

'No single political leader can end a democracy; no single leader can rescue one, either. Democracy is a shared enterprise. Its fate depends on all of us.'[10] Rahul was holding national centre stage attention on his own footing at last and not because he was just a silver-spooned, entitled dynast of the Gandhi family. His speech was impassioned, honest, sans the jingoistic rodomontade we are used to these days. He made a constructive call for rebuilding India through a secular transfusion in its bloodstream.

The Bharat Jodo Yatra concluded on 30 January 2023 in Srinagar. It crossed seventy-five districts across twelve states and two Union territories. It appears to have been transformational for both the Congress and Rahul. Would a resuscitated Rahul Gandhi political brand (and by natural extension, a charged up Congress cadre) herald a pharaonic shift in Indian politics? Or would it end up being like the bedazzling first half before a disappointing climax in a Bollywood potboiler?

With the palpable renaissance of the Congress giving the party a new lifeline, it was imperative that Rahul Gandhi took pole position in the leadership of the Opposition's coalition arrangements. This was easier said than done. Regional satraps were seeing an emerging vacuum, and some had even renamed themselves in a pan-India pitch (Telangana Rashtra Samithi of K. Chandrashekar Rao is now called Bharat Rashtra Samithi). Mamata Banerjee's TMC was planning a similar repositioning. Akhilesh Yadav correctly believes that in Uttar Pradesh, Samajwadi Party is the last man standing to stop the BJP's take-no-prisoners domination. Instead of adopting a confrontationist attitude towards their New Delhi ambitions, the Congress needs to create a collaborative, trustworthy and strategic coalition to handle these restless leaders looking for pan-India spotlight. This will require excellent zero-ego interlocutors, savvy number-crunchers and skilful negotiators, all rolled into one.

The Congress also needs to immediately stop organizational leakage of talent; the BJP has ruthlessly exploited the grand old party's laidback, almost half-hearted approach here. I remember as the party's spokesperson, I repeatedly hammered away at the woeful talent-deficit in the BJP. In a country where political opportunism overwhelms ideological fidelity, one needs alert gatekeepers. Without good people, a political party is like a book without words. Organizational reforms that encourage meritocracy and a 24x7 grassroots mobilization of supporters (the *Haath Se Haath Jodo* campaign was a step in the right direction) at the booth level could make the Congress recapture its earlier dynamism.

Following the end of his pathbreaking yatra, Rahul travelled to the UK to have a series of candid conversations with overseas media, young students, British parliamentarians, think tanks and the Indian diaspora. After his speech was over at the Royal Institute of International Affairs at Chatham House in London, a dignified lady, fearless and earnest, spoke up. Her name was Malini Mehra. She did not hold back in expressing her anguish and said that she was 'feeling wretched about the state of my country'. But what got BJP sympathizers, Twitter trolls and the saffron cognoscenti infuriated was that Malini's late father had been an RSS member. 'My father was an RSS man, proudly. He would not recognize the country (today), bless his soul.'[11] Her forthright rejection of the politics of bigotry and religious chauvinism led to an avalanche of hate messages.

'It's been quite appalling. This is not what one should expect in a self-confident country, which is able to face criticism from independent-minded Indian citizens,' said Mehra,[12] as the world saw Modi's India in its true colours—intolerant, angry and pregnant with prejudice. To say that India seemed to be cruising on its way to becoming a Hindu Rashtra as imagined by the RSS and the Hindu Mahasabha would not have been an exaggeration.

Let's get this straight: there's no Godot coming to our rescue. Secularism and Muslims are considered lost causes and increasingly a political liability even by avowedly liberal mainstream parties. They're vying with each other to demonstrate their Hinduness—a sign that the Indian political landscape has changed for good. There's a new normal and as the English philosopher Alan Watts famously said, 'The only way to make sense of change is to plunge into it, move with it.'[13]

Rahul was refreshingly enough speaking of classical secularism, not the Hindutva-lite that Congress had been accused of flirting with of late.

A few weeks later, Rahul Gandhi would end up getting disqualified as a member of Parliament due to a foxy case of defamation, lose his 12, Tughlaq Lane residence and have the Damocles sword of being electorally disenfranchised hanging over him. And yet, his call for compassion, tolerance and love resonated loud across India: *Nafrat ke bazaar mein, hum mohabbat ki dukaan kholenge.*

10

HIS MASTERS' MEGAPHONE

*'The darkest places in hell are reserved for those who maintain
their neutrality in times of moral crisis.'*

—*Dante Alighieri*

I JOINED TWITTER in 2009 and have since maintained fidelity to
the social media platform. Frankly, I have never been a Facebook
aficionado, albeit I reluctantly opened an account there because
there was this phase when many thought that if I did not increase
Mark Zuckerberg's market capitalization, I was an anachronism in
the Age of Big Tech. It was the cool thing to do; I remember going
to parties frequented mostly by those with a visible hangover of a
midlife crisis who brightened up when saying: 'Let's connect on
Facebook.' That same seemingly innocuous Facebook has now
become an uncontrollable Frankenstein, a gargantuan monster
that is capable of slaying democracies, upending social behaviour,
destroying fragile minds and creating a toxic addiction to screen
time. Netflix's documentary, *The Social Dilemma*, tried to capture
the madness that has, mostly surreptitiously, overwhelmed humanity.
Incidentally, the Facebook (Meta) CEO is among the richest in the
world (in August 2023, he was the tenth richest with a net worth of

USD 110 billion)[1] in the company of Bill Gates, Elon Musk, Larry Ellison and Jeff Bezos. Zuckerberg is clearly doing something right. And some things calculatingly wrong.

When the American presidential elections were happening in November 2020 between a blustering President Donald Trump (the high profile Covid-denier who eventually got infected) and a sombre former Vice President Joe Biden, Facebook was back on prime-time headlines. In 2016, it was public knowledge that the social media leviathan (it also owns the instant messaging service WhatsApp and Instagram which have since become default apps for the millennial-zillennial generations) had a suspicious role in propagating Russian-sponsored advertisements which unethically maligned Democrat candidate Hillary Clinton with vicious mendacities. Many Americans genuinely believed that the New York senator was clandestinely running a child prostitution racket. Such outlandish vulgarity was finding popularity in various Trump supporter chat groups. Clinton was demolished by the organized chaos that was amplified on Facebook pages; the data mining services were exploited using the services of Cambridge Analytica. Since Facebook algorithms permit localized targeting of vulnerable audiences, it is interesting to know that despite getting 2.8 million votes more than Trump, Clinton lost a sure-shot presidency by a mere 78,000 votes in the key swing states of Pennsylvania, Michigan and Wisconsin.[2] The Democrats had underestimated Facebook's monumental impact on human psychology at their own risk. Conspiracy theories worked wonders on impressionable minds. 'A series of investigative reports being rolled out by the *Wall Street Journal* is putting a spotlight on the behind-the-scenes actions of Facebook. Ranging from rule exemptions for high-profile users to Instagram's toll on teens' mental health, the *Journal's* "Facebook Files" expose internal Facebook research that appears to show just how knowledgeable the company was of the platform's "ill-effects",' according to Time.[3]

The Right-wing strategy works better on Facebook because it has no compunctions in twisting facts to suit its political messaging, which is impregnated with negative emotions: fear, insecurity, anger, threat, danger, enemy, hate, etc. It appeals to one's basic instincts, our core susceptibilities. Secular, liberal fundamentalists are comparatively boring; their playbook is benign. Facebook has created a Zuckerbergfication of political communication; anything works, and the more outrageous the better. Free speech is the excuse to create social polarization. And fake news.

Zuckerberg is a megalomaniac; he has one obsessive objective: to dominate the planet. The thirty-nine-year old already has close to 4 billion active users (nearly one half of humanity) on multiple Meta platforms; it has become a vanity project for him. It is hard to even imagine the absolute power he commands through his social network. He can be the kingmaker on the political chessboard of democracies. Ankhi Das, the former public policy head of Facebook, went on record stating to her Indian employees, 'punishing violations from Mr Modi's party would damage the company's business prospects in the country'.[4] It was a loaded confession, a double whammy; one, the draconian environment created by a repressive political organization in power, and the second, the immoral social media giant's compromise for big bucks. Unsuspecting users were being covertly manipulated. Basically, it was a public acknowledgement that the red flags were down, and inflammatory material went uncensored into voter segments. Facebook courts governments: if a Democrat wins, Facebook will chaperone what Trump calls 'radical left loonies'. If BJP loses in 2024, Facebook and Congress will do a slow dance, cheek by jowl. That is Zuckerberg's business model—government schmoozing. That's why when the Telangana BJP leader T. Raja Singh attacked India's Muslims using undisguised loathing, Facebook looked the other way.[5] The fact that it took some brave Facebook employees to speak to WSJ was a manifestation of the company's compromised ethical commitment in maintaining neutral platforms. Facebook clearly had no intention to deodorize the combustible messages.[6] Raja Singh was finally forcibly banned under Facebook's 'dangerous individuals and organizations policy'. In the absence of a global kerfuffle over the issue, that would not have happened. The world needs to worry. More than any other country: India.

> Netflix's CEO Reed Hastings famously said his biggest competitor is sleep. This is the context in which modern political journalism is produced and absorbed: an all-out war for the time of an audience that has more choices than at any point in history. The digital revolution offered access to unimaginably vast vistas of information, but just as important, it offered access to unimaginably more choice. And that explosion of choice widened that interested-uninterested divide. Greater choices lets the junkies learn more and the disinterested know less.[7]

This helped proliferate polarization. And fake news

The fake news industry has prospered in leaps and bounds in India thanks to the tutelage of the ruling party. No one was spared, not even Congress leader Priyanka Gandhi Vadra. Priyanka lived in her Lodhi colony residence under full SPG security. But with a vindictive government, this abode was always going to be a vulnerable acreage. She was asked to vacate the premises during the pandemic. Even as the war of words between the Congress and the BJP intensified, a news report emerged out of the blue: 'PM Modi allows Priyanka Gandhi's request to stay on in Lutyens' bungalow for some time.' This was promptly challenged by Priyanka who shot off an angry tweet, 'This is FAKE NEWS. I have not made any such request to the government. As per the eviction later handed to me on the 1st of July, I will be vacating the government accommodation at 35, Lodhi Estate by 1st of August.'[8] She did.

It was another oppressive day, adding to the unending misery that became the second wave around early March 2021. On 19 May, India logged 4,522 deaths, the highest single day casualty since the beginning of the devastating pandemic in any country.[9] In a normal world, that alarming figure would be the country's headline story. In a parallel universe, something else stole the banner slug. The BJP launched an all-out fusillade against the Congress led by its irrepressible spokesperson Sambit Patra. The pitch deck was predictably out of the BJP manuscript: The Congress was trying to destroy Prime Minister Narendra Modi's impeccable reputation by shamelessly exploiting the health tragedy for political gains. Questioning the incompetent government was taboo. Senior government ministers promptly jumped in to trend #CongressToolkitExposed;[10] conspiracy theories floated like flotsam. But the BJP, in its frantic effort to salvage a rapidly crashing image for the inept handling of Covid, made a few grave miscalculations.

Rajeev Gowda, former Rajya Sabha MP who heads AICC Research and has been a dear friend, is a thoroughbred academician. He is the kind of a man who will carry an umbrella on a sunny day because there is a 0.3 per cent probability of a sudden shower. It was most unlikely that the innocuous professor would be authoring a shady political thriller that would annihilate PM Modi's Teflon imagery. Or that he would be delegating the assignment to a relative newbie. Secondly, even if that were to be true, the BJP's giveaway was the communal twist it gave the fabricated documen~ They alleged that the Congress asked its social media ~ to focus on the 'super-spreader Maha Kumbh' ' the holy dip in the Ganga between 14 Januar~ even as Covid surged) and soft-pedal the Ram.

by 'not commenting on Eid gatherings'. This was the core pitch of the twisted toolkit—introduce the Hindu-Muslim divide angle, which is the archetypal magic potion for the BJP. They may have been subsequently acquitted by the courts, but the Tablighi Jamaat congregation in March 2020 was successfully positioned as #CoronaJihad by Hindutva trolls, making India's principal minority community appear like the deadly virus. For BJP, this malicious strategy has mostly delivered. But this time (like in West Bengal), it boomeranged. The Congress, showing alacrity that it's not been particularly famous for, lodged an FIR against the BJP leaders. Fake news busting sites established that the original letterheads were morphed (in the age of fake RT-PCR tests this was a kindergarten plaything). And a day later Twitter flagged Patra and several BJP titans with a badge of mortification, the tag of 'Manipulated News'.[11] All political parties are guilty of occasionally propagating fake news, but the BJP has disinformation its core political strategy. Immediately thereafter, the government began using its muscular power to get Twitter to pardon its transgressions. Google, Facebook, Twitter, Instagram and YouTube are repeatedly told to take down posts that rile the government.

The Muzaffarnagar riots of 2013 were triggered by fictitious Facebook posts. Lynching deaths have occurred due to the circulation of WhatsApp forwards warning of cow slaughter. The Benghazi attack on the US embassy in Libya happened because of an inflammatory religious post on YouTube. Donald Trump's relentless questioning of Barack Obama's birth certificate had over 50 per cent of the Republicans believe that he was a Muslim.[12] And white supremacists in America's rust belt are convinced that Hillary Clinton still runs a child prostitution racket, apropos #PizzaGate.[13] Fox News claimed that Joe Biden planned to ban hamburgers.[14] Bottomline: politicians are not just abusing social media, they mock country's collective intelligence. BJP led the political pack in India in spurious misinformation and disinformation. Super-spreaders of fake news are the greatest danger to democracies worldwide. Twitter and Facebook could ban President Trump in the US, but none had the guts to take on an autocratic regime in New Delhi. The Indian government was crushing truth and dissent like a feral monster on the prowl. Additionally, it was indoctrinating people with a concocted theory of politics, through what is jocularly referred to as WhatsApp University. I experienced it firsthand in 2021 in the city where I live.

An evening walk by the seaside in Mumbai is always rejuvenating. The feeling of the strong breeze swirling against your face is liberating, emetic, matching the euphoria of sighting a mirage in a never-ending desert on a sweltering summer day perhaps. Some time ago as I sought to deeply inhale the Arabian sea air as the twilight hour set in, the sight of a familiar face, of someone who is at most just a benign acquaintance, stopped me on my tracks.

'Can I walk with you today?' he asked.

Since that was not really an objectionable request (although I love my solitary odyssey) I reluctantly acquiesced to it. We had walked barely 10 metres, when he broke my state of joie de vivre, 'So what do you think about Afghanistan?'

Once people see you as a political personality, they mistakenly assume that you are a treasure chest of knowledge; they think you have all the answers. I could not therefore disappoint him, partly helped by the fact that I am a student of political history and find foreign policy fascinating, often disoriented by how one stupid leader can easily lead millions to ruins and devastation.

I gave him a boilerplate response: America's myopic worldview, the lessons they have not learnt despite Iraq, Vietnam and Cambodia, why the airlifting of US citizens in armoured helicopters from Kabul embassy was akin to the Saigon rescue operations in 1975, and why it portended danger for India now that the Pakistan-sponsored militant organization, the Taliban had access to both better physical infrastructure and sophisticated arms left behind by the US forces.

Frankly, I thought I gave him a measured thoughtful response, which would be termed 'holistic'. But I don't think he heard me or cared to. He probably thought my analysis was pregnant with drivel.

'That's why I think India must become a Hindu Rashtra,' he said matter-of-factly. I was nonplussed, even if these days I half expect my dog to also campaign for the Right wing. 'I didn't understand,' I queried, playing dumb, an act that I think I have mastered over years of making television appearances. 'See, the Taliban is so rabidly Islamist. The only answer to them is that Hindus must also become communal,' he said, clearly convinced that his spectacular political prescription was the best protection for preserving our porous borders. 'I agree that Taliban is a real danger. But you think the BJP is not communal?' I deliberately instigated him, by now confidently cognizant of his political predilections.

'Of course, the BJP is communal,' the gentleman countered back, a trifle exasperated, I thought. 'And they should be. Otherwise, India will become Islamic and the Muslim population will overtake ours.'

'But Sir,' I said, pretending not to hide my rising annoyance at his laughable treatise. 'Between 1947 and 2014, India became the toast of global investors and created a buoyant prosperous middle class. We were seen as a respected democratic liberal republic while being a secular state for sixty-seven years. And Hindus are 79 per cent of our population, while the Muslims are 14 per cent (I did not explain their diminishing fertility rate etc. as I thought that was too technical a subject). Why should we become a Hindu Rashtra now? On a serious note, what tangible achievements have really happened in the past seven years of the current government? Can you list me even one?'

After a pregnant pause that lasted till eternity, I thought I heard him mumble something that sounded like toilets. His cheeks were perceptibly flushed. Almost apologetically, he said he had to hurry home, probably to a 4BHK on the fifteenth floor in the country's sexiest residential address, Malabar Hill.

I took a deep breath, filling my lungs with as much air as I could, and began to walk briskly home, grateful that at least some Indians were not yet brainwashed. Once fascism takes root, it is like a psychological detergent which cleanses one of reason, logic, truth and rational argumentation. It is impossible to argue with irrational emotional tropes, which is exactly what conspiracy theorists augment. But India's descent into a partially-free country was not going away unnoticed.

> The old line on local reporting was: 'If it bleeds, it leads.' For political reporting, the principle is: 'If it outrages, it leads.' And outrage is deeply connected to identity—we are outraged when members of other groups threaten our group and violate our values. As such, polarized media doesn't emphasize commonalities, it weaponizes differences; it doesn't focus on the best of the other side, it threatens you with the worst.[15]

Feeding the media with inflammable fodder was the BJP and its voluble leaders.

During the Karnataka elections held in April 2023, in which the hot-button issue was corruption, Modi spent considerable time promoting a commercial, fictional film called *The Kerala Story*. It appeared as odd as US President Joe Biden promoting Tom Cruise's *Mission Impossible*. Written by Sudipto Sen, Suryapal Singh and Vipul Amrutlal Shah, *The Kerala Story* (disclosure, I have not seen it) is a story of a malevolent conspiracy hatched by diabolical Muslim men to boondoggle innocent Hindu and Christian women of Kerala into a dubious relationship with them, brainwashing them and then convincing or cajoling them to join ISIS in Syria. Essentially, it is a picture about forced radicalization.

The promotional campaign for the film highlighted that '32,000' women from Kerala had been conned into joining ISIS.[16] When the number was fact-checked, the producers, fearing a defamation suit or negative publicity, immediately plummeted the count to '3'. The hyper-exaggeration reflected the ideological motive behind the cinematic enterprise. Why would a prime minister dive deep into a fictional story allegedly inspired by some true events as his main campaign pitch when his party was being demolished as a '40 per cent commission Sarkar', the most corrupt government in Karnataka's history? If anyone needed further proof of how demonizing Muslims as terrorists, or accusing them of practising surreptitious underworld human trafficking which undermined society was the main plank of the BJP, there it was. It was an abysmal low even by India's already rancid political parleys.

> Krista Tippett, host of the humane and wise public radio show On Being, once told me the media often looks to her like 'a conspiracy to surface the loudest voices.' She's right, but it's no conspiracy. It's more like the reason the food and restaurant industries pack products with salt and fat and sugar: that's what the market demands. And market demand in media has become a more powerful and more precise force.[17]

A desperate media and a motivated BJP found in each other romantic soulmates. Vitriol circulated 24x7.

It was clear that *The Kerala Story* was invigorated by the stupendous success of *The Kashmir Files*, one of the blockbuster hits of 2022. The latter film's director, an obstreperous but sharp Vivek Agnihotri, has been Modi's most boisterous cheerleaders in the BJP's Bollywood project. Modi reciprocated in full measure by almost appearing as the film's brand ambassador and getting the rank and file of his party to support the controversial film. Gujarat and Uttar Pradesh chief ministers gave the film tax exemptions, government staff were given time off to see the film during work hours and special screenings of the film were held for party workers. Modi lauded the fictional story, as if it was a historical commentary, castigating an 'ecosystem' for propagating lies about the exodus of Kashmiri Pandits from the Kashmir valley in 1990. The truth is that the film peddled blatant lies, among them that Rajiv Gandhi was responsible for the mass migrations following militancy breakout in 1989. While it is true that there was trouble brewing for a while, the fact is that the exodus happened when the governor of Jammu and Kashmir was Jagmohan. He was appointed by Prime Minister V.P. Singh, whose Janata Dal-led coalition was fully supported by the BJP itself. Why did the BJP welcome the man (Jagmohan) who many believe triggered the Kashmiri crisis into their party in 1996?

> The emotional appeal of a conspiracy theory is in its simplicity. It explains away complex phenomena, accounts for chance and accidents, offers the believer the satisfying sense of having special, privileged access to the truth. For those who become the one-party state's gatekeepers, the repetition of these conspiracy theories also brings another reward: power.[18]

The Muslims were vilified as the ugly perpetrators of a social divide, with little respect for the historical context of that unfortunate conflict. The film went on to become one of the year's biggest money-spinners. The truth about the film finally surfaced, paradoxically enough, at a government-sponsored event, the annual International Film Festival of India (IFFI) 2022 held in Goa.

A well-own Israeli filmmaker Nadav Lapid, who headed the festival's jury, said: 'That (*The Kashmir Files*) felt to us like a propaganda, vulgar movie, inappropriate for an artistic competitive section of such a prestigious film festival.'[19] He would go on to say later, as the BJP, suitably publicly punctured, let loose its PR cannonballs for damage control, that he had been shocked by the 'transparent combination between propaganda and fascism and vulgarity. In countries where people are increasingly losing the ability to speak your mind … someone needs to speak.' Within days, if not hours, Lapid was abused, attacked and threatened by Right-wing fringe mobs all over social media. He even had a police complaint lodged against him. But instead of getting spooked by the hateful crowds and pushing the panic buttons, as most would do, Lapid doubled down. He eventually had the last laugh.

The Reporters Without Borders report showed India sliding down in World Press Freedom rankings to 160 out of 180 countries in 2023,[20] its lowest ever ranking during Modi's reign. During the Lok Sabha elections in 2019, there were complaints from Ladakh in Jammu and Kashmir of journalists being bribed to write in support of the BJP. It was initially widely reported, but the natural exponential outrage that it ought to have caused never happened. It was promptly blacked out by a pliant media not bold enough to escalate it into the gigantic scam that it really was. What was particularly distressing was that the BJP was treating journalistic ethics as a garage sale item, a purchasable commodity with a price tag.

In January 2023, the BBC released a two-part documentary called *The Modi Question*, in which it concluded that Modi was squarely responsible for the Gujarat riots, mostly through deliberate inaction.[21] I saw the documentary, and although there was nothing dramatically revelatory in it that one did not know, the part where Babu Bajrangi, the Bajrang Dal member who was convicted for many murders, talked openly on camera about being given bail by a judge on instructions from the chief minister was a complete shocker. For Modi, in the year of India assuming the G20 presidency, it was a public relations turkey. The government moved swiftly to ensure that the video of the programme was taken off social media like Twitter and YouTube immediately, by invoking emergency powers.[22] Not surprisingly, a few weeks later, the Income Tax Department conducted what they called a survey operation for a tax evasion case on the BBC offices in Delhi and Mumbai.[23] A BJP spokesperson even called the London-headquartered news organization 'the most corrupt in the world' and insinuated that it was working at the Congress party's behest.[24] The party was remarkably hypersensitive to criticism, disinclined to have a democratic exchange, and its sole mission was to protect Narendra Modi's 'image'. To that latter end, the party would go to any length. Even without seeing the documentary, the verbose external affairs ministry described the documentary as 'a propaganda piece designed to push a particular discredited narrative'.[25]

The entire BBC brouhaha, created largely by the nervy BJP and the clumsy external affairs spokespersons, only ended up bringing to centre stage once again the Gujarat riots and the role of Modi. The government's conduct was nothing short of totalitarian.

The government has also ensured that other media entities don't crop up in the country through the use of regulatory mechanisms. Raghav Bahl, the earlier owner of Network 18, which was taken over by Mukesh Ambani's Reliance Industries Limited in 2014, had applied for a news TV channel licence in collaboration with US data and media company Bloomberg. His application was rejected by the country's I&B ministry, citing security reports.

Tiranga TV, using the name Harvest TV, which went on air on 26 January 2019, had to close down within a year of starting operations due to financial reasons. The channel, which was propped up by Congress leader Kapil Sibal, collapsed immediately after the election results in May 2019, citing a lack of funds, as the BJP's massive electoral victory was announced.[26]

TV channels were so reluctant to question Narendra Modi, Amit Shah and the BJP that it reached a point of utter hilarity. I do not remember even a handful of programmes over ten years that dared to focus on even a few of Modi's innumerable failures or Amit Shah's vituperative tirades. While some TV channels had a clear political prejudice or were seduced by the dollops of easy money coming through government advertisements, there were others who had a few anchors who tried valiantly to adhere to a more impartial dialogue. Some looked distraught at the unconcealed nastiness from BJP loudmouths and the one-sided nature of the TV debates happening right under their nose but could not stop the sham from being showcased as a news programme. They tried hard to give the slanted debates a veneer of normalcy, difficult as it was. Often they were accused by BJP spokespersons (who presented themselves with the cool confidence of a large equity shareholder of the enterprise), of being a Congress mouthpiece. Since most spent considerable time on channels that gave them unlimited, uninterrupted time and had TV anchors functioning like their private counsel, they were easily peeved when confronted by a neutral inquisitor. Their annoyance perceptible, they would get restless to prove their point, often interrupting the Opposition speaker impertinently or just berating the anchor itself. One could see that the anchor, feeling both rebuffed and rebuked by the petulant character, was angry, but they smothered their gnawing frustration. It was not easy to be neutral and ask probing questions of the ruling party, as BJP spokespersons were easily upset by questions which revealed that they had either no defence or at best could muster a pallid counterargument. But the anchors are themselves to blame for allowing the quality of debates to degenerate into a parody. For one, they allowed whataboutery to divert serious issues into a brick wall, resulting in meaningless meandering tropes masquerading as serious conversations. If the BJP was asked a question on the arrest of a journalist in Manipur for a Facebook post, the retort would be predictable: 'But the Congress imposed the Emergency in 1975 and suspended civil liberties.' Yes, that was factually true, but how did that answer the question of the illegal detention of a journalist who was within his fundamental rights to question the government? It was akin to blaming FDR for the 2008 mortgage crisis post-Lehman Brothers because of the lingering effects of the Great Depression. It was a joke. The usual trope deployed by the BJP when cornered was 'this is a legacy issue, inherited by us from the vile, corrupt, incompetent UPA that has been reduced to 44 seats, and has been rejected by the people'. This was repeated ad nauseam by most of them, particularly when they had no substantive content. One of them would invariably call the Congress a regional party and dismiss it with contemptuous indifference. Besides whataboutery, which was a convenient strategy to dodge tough questions, most anchors allowed a flawed application of the law of equivalency which allowed the BJP to get away scot-free. Under the façade of holding a fair debate, even serious subjects were hijacked towards a frivolous distraction. For instance, when discussing a venomous statement by BJP leader Anantkumar Hegde on Muslims ('There will be no peace in the world as long as Islam is there,' he said in March 2016)[27] the anchor would grill the Opposition for a polemical comment made by someone years ago. They would compare apples and oranges. For instance, Modi's '*Hum paanch hamare pacchis*' comment (portraying Muslims as child-producing factories) would be juxtaposed against Rahul Gandhi calling Modi a 'chor' by saying, '*Chowkidar chor hai.*' It was an asinine comparison, but it helped the BJP, nevertheless. When discussing the death of

Pehlu Khan, lynched in Rajasthan, a laughable intrusion by many was, 'Is Congress politicizing it for minority appeasement?' It made no sense. Shouldn't any normal entity or individual with even an iota of moral conscience rise against the hideous savagery of an Indian by an inflamed mob of killers? When an individual or political party has erred, they must offer an explanation; the law of equivalency was used as an unctuous curveball to circumvent the deeper malaise of poor governance which never really got investigated? The BJP disliked being interrogated with tough questions. On being asked about the women wrestlers protesting against a BJP leader accused of sexual harassment, one of BJP's most aggressive voices on television, Meenakshi Lekhi, bolted, in what looked like a comical escape, as she was being chased by a bunch of panting hacks gingerly carrying their microphones as they followed her into the car park.[28] Lekhi drove off in a wild frenzy, liberated from what was clearly a sprint that she could have done without. Modi and the BJP got a gratuitous gate pass to freedom.

As for Modi, the media was at his beck and call. Being elliptical was never Modi's style. Once he was before the camera, he milked it. All TV channels would interrupt their shows to focus on some boring bromide that he was dishing out. This was a quasi-dictatorship. No one dared to not cover the supreme leader. It was a baroque capitulation, unbearably craven. Indian media was getting an F grade for failing to protect Indian democracy even as it was being beaten black and blue. It was a Judas-like act with the people of India. They were letting democracy down.

Everything under Modi was about a sparling headline. The truth was harsher. While the government went into an enthusiastic overdrive on India becoming the fifth largest economy in the world (a cumulative increase over a period of time would have happened even if India performed modestly), the government froze when it was reminded that it was the poorest of the G20 countries. Or when told that Bangladesh's per capita worldwide ranking was higher than India's. Or that the per capita GDP of UK was USD 43K while India was barely at USD 2,000. Or that the per capita GDP of India's most populous state of Uttar Pradesh where BJP had been winning consistently was lower than that of Nepal and Tanzania.[29] On the Human Development Index, a balanced representation of individual access to basic services, India ranked a lowly 132/191. On the Global Hunger Index, it was at a sorry 101/116. Of course, the government tried to scuttle and shoot the messenger, but these statistics burst the gas balloons of the BJP, showing them for what the big BJP spin was—burlesque.

It was rumoured among journalists, that there was a structured secret outfit which monitored television content and critical social media conversations from well-known Twitter handles and made a daily summary of media throughput to a senior cabinet minister who was given the title of 'Bureau Chief' (literally meaning someone who controlled information dissemination). Well-known journalists Abhisar Sharma and Punya Prasun Vajpayee lost their jobs in ABP News because the Bureau Chief was terribly unhappy with their critical reportage.[30] Ravish Kumar of NDTV India received death threats for challenging the government in his inimitable chatty, caustic style.[31] And Karan Thapar, India's Hard Talk man, was stripped of his signature show on India Today.[32] The list of casualties was as long as Rapunzel's hair. India's press freedom, as described by many, was misunderstood by the Modi government as 'pressing of the freedom'. The SC busted the Modi government's standard artifice to bulldoze India by using 'national security' as their trump card.[33] In the Malayalam channel Media One's case which had been banned, it said, 'The State is using the plea of national security to deny rights of citizens. This is incompatible with Rule of Law. National security claims cannot be made out of thin air.'[34]

The BJP IT cell was indulging, without an iota of conscience, in a deliberate policy of agitprop. Damaging reputations, spreading lies, quoting incorrect data, spinning yarns and defending the indefensible with whataboutery which focused on distorted facts was their political strategy. It helped that they got the maximum airtime. Deep fake videos were in circulation, too. Rahul Gandhi was repeatedly assaulted with morphed videos on social media.

The predatory takeover of NDTV, the Dr Prannoy Roy-founded pioneering private TV news channel, by the Adani Group was a marker of India's broken democracy. BJP spokespersons had boycotted the channel for years because it was perhaps the only one which consistently questioned them probingly, relentlessly, instead of the superficial inquisition that was being done by 'North Korean' channels. The electronic media capture was now meticulously effectuated. Modi regime's wherewithal to influence public opinion was further emboldened. The political disquisition was ridiculously one-sided. The fourth pillar of democracy was not just wobbly, it was falling apart. And it was taking Indian democracy down with it.

11

REWRITING THE PAST

'Those who control the present, control the past and those who control the past control the future.'

—*George Orwell*

POLITICIANS ARE AN extremely insecure bunch. Please do not be fooled by their rugged appearances or fiery speeches. They live their entire lives worrying about what people think about them, an understandable quagmire in a democracy, where it is the popular opinion alone that can provide them a sustainable future. But for some of India's leading national superstar leaders, it borders on paranoia. They are like those adolescent somethings frantically monitoring their 'likes' on Instagram after posting a selfie. A politician's narcissism can be deleterious.

Prime Minister Narendra Modi dramatically tweeted on 6 August 2021, 'I have been getting many requests from citizens across India to name the Khel Ratna Award after Major Dhyan Chand. I thank them for their views. Respecting their sentiment, the Khel Ratna Award will hereby be called the Major Dhyan Chand Khel Ratna Award. Jai Hind!'[1] The award was formerly called the Rajiv Gandhi Khel Ratna Award. It was an illustration of an orchestrated

BJP programme to gradually obliterate the Gandhi family name from national events of import and several infrastructure projects that adorn their surname. In the run up to 2024 general elections, expect more of such headline-grabbing tableaux as it suits the BJP narrative of targeting the Congress party as a private, family fiefdom which had conveniently monopolized the branding of state institutions and public-owned assets in their favour. There is, of course, partial merit in the argument but that is only part of the concocted communication.

It is true that the Congress went berserk naming every conceivable concrete structure and soft power gala (ranging from expressways, international airports and educational institutions to state-funded programmes, festivals and national events) after the Gandhi family, in the foolish belief that they were assured of permanent power. This pattern became particularly problematic when the culture of sycophancy within the Congress reached sky-high levels, landing on Mars without a space capsule. It was a genuflection that the party of Mahatma Gandhi and Jawaharlal Nehru could have done without. The fact that a disproportionate number of high-profile projects have been appropriated by the Congress leaders had riled the BJP, which has a pathological hostility towards Nehru in particular and his political lineage. However, the fact also is that the Congress has governed India, directly/indirectly for fifty-five of the seventy-six years since Independence, and every ruling dispensation would logically have a bias for their own leaders. Modern India, at its core, is a Congress construct, forcing Modi to continuously talk about his grand vision of a 'New India' (basically it was Hindutva Undiluted) which is nothing but hollow grandstanding as nobody knows what that means other than RSS and BJP acolytes. Altering history and changing names was integral to the master plan.

Modi thought that he was killing two birds with one stone

in renaming the iconic awards after the legendary hockey great
Dhyan Chand (he won three Olympic gold medals). Besides
bankrupting the Gandhi name, it would sound churlish if the
Congress opposed it on the day when the Indian men's hockey team
won a bronze medal after a gap of forty-one years in a remarkable
comeback match against the German team. Thankfully, Congress
did not succumb to Modi's calculated gambit. It welcomed the
renaming. The Congress hit back with a comprehensive riposte:
But then it raised a pertinent question: Would Modi kindly get
his name removed from the recently constructed Motera cricket
stadium (where Modi hosted former US President Donald Trump
in February 2020 when the pandemic had already established
footholds on Indian soil)? Why did the BJP rename the Feroz Shah
Kotla cricket stadium in Delhi after their late leader Arun Jaitley,
who in any case was mired in several corruption scandals, if World
Cup winning player Kirti Azad is to be believed? Would the BJP be
generous enough to disengage the names of its RSS veterans and
other party stalwarts, like Syama Prasad Mukherjee, Deen Dayal
Upadhyaya, Sushma Swaraj, Manohar Parrikar, etc., from several
institutions that demanded independence from political branding? If
the BJP agreed to this rational and fair proposition, they were both
within their fundamental right and moral custodianship to remove
the names of Congress leaders since 1947, was the Congress's
comeback. The BJP was speechless. They were equally guilty of
abusing power to promote their favourites using public resources.

It was odd that the name of a brutally assassinated former prime
minister, who died a valiant martyr for his country, was removed
from a prestigious award, while the living PM arranged a monolithic
stadium in his name, reminiscent of the pre-World War fascist era
of personality cult politics. Incidentally, the National Stadium in
Delhi and several hockey stadiums already carried the glorious
legacy of the legendary Dhyan Chand. A better idea would have

been to give Dhyan Chand the Bharat Ratna or name a new special award for Olympic medal-winners under his name. But then as Dr Shashi Tharoor correctly said, 'Mr Modi's government is not a game-changing but a name-changing one.'[2] As many as nineteen Modi government schemes were UPA programmes, which were simply rechristened.[3]

'When it does not simply invent a past to weaponize the emotions of nostalgia, fascist politics cherry-picks the past, avoiding anything that would diminish unreflective adulation of the nations' glory.'[4] Alamgir Aurangzeb, the sixth emperor of the Mughal dynasty was the favourite dartboard of the Sangh Parivar. Aurangzeb Road in Delhi was renamed after former President and nuclear scientist Dr A.P.J. Abdul Kalam. Aurangzeb was liberally reviled in BJP leaders' political speeches, in an unambiguous design to disgrace the Muslim community. Modi loved looking backwards, gingerly exacerbating imaginary wounds. In Aurangzeb, he found an oilfield worthy of endless extraction; the brutal ruler had demolished Hindu temples and imposed discriminatory taxes. Aurangzeb was a potent instrument for the BJP for disparaging Muslims whenever they wanted to. As was Tipu Sultan.

The names of several cities was changed, like Allahabad became Prayagraj and Aurangabad was called Chhatrapati Sambhaji Nagar. The famous Mughalsarai station, a legendary terminus, was renamed to Pandit Deen Dayal Upadhyaya junction. The honourable Muslim freedom fighter Maulana Abul Kalam Azad found his name missing or vastly reduced in NCERT textbooks, which saw a huge deletion of references to the period of Mughal rule in India's history.[5] The iconic Nehru Memorial Museum Library was recast as Prime Ministers Memorial Museum and Library. The new textbooks in political science had also excluded the fact that Jammu and Kashmir had acceded to India on the specific condition that the state would remain autonomous.

The distortion of history often moved from the sublime to the ridiculous. In 1952, PM Jawaharlal Nehru, India's most farsighted and visionary leader, laid the foundation of India's first IIT at Kharagpur. Nehru was blessed with an understanding of scientific temper; it led to India's celebrated space research programme, among others. Decades later, one of his successors believed that India was the pioneer of plastic surgery from the time of Lord Ganesha. History lessons now came with outlandish, bizarre twists. Astrology is the biggest science, uttered a BJP minister. One minister believed that the Vedic theory was greater than the theory of relativity, while a former police commissioner turned BJP leader considered Charles Darwin's theory of evolution to be humbug; Had anyone seen an ape turn into a human being? he worriedly asked.

The BJP and the RSS don't just have contempt for Gandhi, they abominate him with unparalleled vigour. Trivializing Gandhi and belittling his greatness was their pivotal preoccupation. The well-known Gita Press, which published religious texts and mythological magazines, always had a sympathetic leaning towards the Hindutva cause, prior to Independence. The Hindu Mahasabha, RSS, Jana Sangh and the BJP were closely associated with its rocketing growth. Their editorial pronouncements toed the hardline expressions of the BJP.[6] The Gita Press called for violence against Muslims in 1946, lampooned Dr Ambedkar for shepherding the Hindu Code Bill and believed that 'Christians and Muslims would enter our (Hindu) homes, marry our daughter, beef would be cooked in our homes.'[7] The 'love jihad' goblin was not a new phenomenon. After Gandhi was assassinated, among the 25,000 people who were arrested for questioning was Hanuman Prasad Poddar, the founder of the Gita Press. In June of 2023, the Gita Press was anointed with the Gandhi Peace Prize on the occasion of Gandhi's 125th birth anniversary.[8] Nathuram Godse, Gandhi's assassin was probably chuckling away somewhere. But it was the Covid vaccination certificate that took the cake and the factory.

Modi's face was plastered on all Covid vaccination certificates— millions of them. It was morally reprehensible, and a complete travesty of fairness. India officially lost over half a million people due to the virus (unofficial figures are several times higher). For the BJP, it became an opportunity for running a marketing campaign at government cost; the personal branding of Modi, positioned him as the great saviour. It was deeply personalized, like a digital wallet item. The ethical decomposition was for all to see. The world's largest cricket stadium, which had been called Narendra Modi stadium, had two bowling ends: the Adani End and the Ambani End. It was surreal, that the names of two of the richest men in India, symbols of its brazen plutocracy and crony capitalism, were brandishing their proximity to the prime minister in such an ostentatious manner. It became the butt of a billon memes. But Modi was not going to give up on his megalomaniacal fetish with one gigantic cricket stadium. He had a spectacular architectural structure in mind. It was called the Central Vista project.

According to his numerous cheerleaders, Modi was creating an alternate Indian version of Washington DC's iconic National Mall or the grandiose Champs-Élysées in Paris. Called the Central Vista project, one must look at it without jaundiced eyes though, and certainly beyond its proposed architectural aestheticism and tourist footfall. A chagrined Opposition was calling it a concrete monstrosity, a monument to an individual's (PM Modi's) extravagant self-indulgence, his I Me Myself project. Modi dismissed this as Congress's and the Opposition's characteristic pettifogging. The project would fructify in 2023, showboating a modern parliamentary infrastructure in Modi's New India. BJP's political business model has always been to alter India gradually but finally in gigantic magnitude. The proposed new Parliament annexe was part of that scheme. But maybe many were missing the woods for the trees here.

The Vista's real significance lies in something that hasn't yet captured public imagination: The future of representative democracy in India. It has an underlying message of grave import. Without worrying about mathematical exactitude, former President Pranab Mukherjee had once said that India needed 1,000 Lok Sabha members of Parliament.[9] There was a reason why the late commander-in-chief talked of ballooning the LS to twice its current size of 543.

In 2014 Manish Tewari, current Lok Sabha MP, casually asked me if I was interested in contesting the general elections. Although I didn't say no to him upfront, my mind was already made up; I was not going to. I had my reasons. There's an intrinsic fault-line in India's electoral ecosystem. For one, being brought up by an unassuming professor with humble middle-class values—which meant frugal pocket money—ruled me out for using the parallel economy (hard cash-based) to fund my campaign expenditure. I was told that for a Lok Sabha contest one needed a minimum of Rs 15– 25 crores depending upon the nature and size of the parliamentary constituency.[10] The legally permitted expenditure is capped at Rs 75–90 lakhs. The variance is atrociously skewed. Everyone violates the statutory limits in broad daylight with little to no consequence, and they also submit written affidavits confirming that they have adhered to the stipulated requirements. Proxy accounts, in-kind favours, third party tie-ups, and pure cash and coins takes care of the usually unlimited access to black money. It is a complete farce. The EC is a toothless paper tiger. I was convinced that this was hardly the route I wished to take to live out my fantasy of cleansing Indian politics of the muck. Secondly, the sheer gargantuan size of a parliamentary constituency makes an elected representative's task a Herculean one. For instance, a British House of Commons MP has an average constituency of 72,000 people (they have 650 MPs for a 68 million population). By contrast, his average Indian Lok Sabha counterpart has a staggering 20–25 lakh people per constituency, almost 35 times more. It is preposterous, and the disproportionate load makes an MP, at best, a glorified tourist on his home turf.

Now, whether one loves fish and chips or paneer paratha, human beings have the same time-space bandwidth, preordained to some extent by the gods. Even the US House of Representatives peaks in constituency size at 5 lakh. Since 1952, India's average constituency size has ballooned four times. If voters are usually discontented and disillusioned with their Lok Sabha MPs, it's therefore hardly surprising. That's why the frequent lamentation: 'We never see our MP after they win.' An MP has to attend Parliament sessions, pay obeisance to the royal excellency in the Delhi darbar, travel as a star campaigner to other states, etc. Besides, they also have lives of their own. Constituency time, anyone? No wonder anti-incumbency is an intrinsic character of Indian elections, unless one is a charismatic personality like Modi, Pawar, Kamal Nath, or a popular dynastic brand name like the Gandhis.

The Opposition was right in questioning the opaque selection criteria behind choosing the Central Vista construction company or the project's likely environmental costs. Or its humongous budgetary allocations at a time of enormous human misery following the devastating coronavirus. India's cultural connoisseurs felt, understandably, cheated too, but the bull-headed BJP dismissed it as their habitual propensity to get their knickers in a twist. Unknown to many, Modi was once again assiduously biting the bullet on an oceanic transformation of Indian politics.

Modi was likely to push for the much-delayed delimitation exercise, pending since 1971. Besides creating a historical marker that will far outlive him and give his New India a state-of-the-art physical infrastructure, it would also be a permanent testimony of the entrenched penetration of Modi's legacy. It would literally be deep in the soil of India's capital city, once ruled by Mughal emperors and the British Raj. The Hindu Hriday Samrat would have ensured the correction which his historically wounded vote bank craved for. Just as post-1947 became the Nehruvian era that Congress eulogized, BJP would have the Modi narrative for future generations. Most in the Opposition had not quite understood the obvious end goal of the prime minister. Modi's penchant for risk-taking, as opposed to Congress's guarded incrementalism, was turning out to be a political masterstroke. A new aspirational India prefers bold decision makers; nothing else can explain why Indians tolerated gigantic goof-ups such as demonetization, GST execution, lockdown, unemployment, etc. and continued to trust the strongman leader. But the Central Vista project it had to be admitted was the right call, given the need for an expanded Parliament in the foreseeable future.

Opposition parties who are flummoxed by Modi's cult-creating fetish may find this an unplayable googly. Modi will justify it as pro-democracy, a citizen empowerment story backed by a constitutional mandate. Rapidly increasing constituency size has consequences such as sub-standard local governance, poor voter turnout, anti-incumbency and grossly inadequate servicing of constituency imperatives. A correction is required, and it is already inordinately delayed. The voter deserves better from their elected representatives. Politically, too, it gives Modi a secret weapon: he can crucially turn around the genuine trepidations about India's illiberal democracy. The internet shutdowns, Twitter blockades, relentless targeting of journalists, arrests of stand-up comic artistes, ED raids on news portals, the arrest of young Disha Ravi, harassment of Opposition leaders, religious persecution, rigged institutions, etc. have diminished Modi's carefully cultivated global reputational capital massively. The delimitation exercise can boost his flagging ratings on the democracy scale while giving him an enduring edifice of the Central Vista to accommodate 888 LS and 384 RS MPs.

India will have to increase the size of the Lok Sabha either by 2029 or 2034 general elections to approximately 848, according to researchers Milan Vaishav and Jamie Hintson.[11] Since the scientific barometer for seats-per-state has to be the population, it's very likely that UP, Bihar, Maharashtra, Rajasthan, West Bengal will see big jumps. But ironically, southern states that have been both socially emancipated and economically advanced will remain frozen at current levels. Based on current trends, this will advantage BJP. While there is an inherent anomaly in a political representation paradigm that rewards poor performance while penalizing super-achievers and it has the potential for a major north-south faceoff, prima facie, it appears to be advantage BJP, given its pre-eminent suzerainty in mainland India.

Nothing that Modi does isn't carefully structured towards definitive electoral impact. The much-excoriated vanity project is Modi's trump card in the December of his political career. Modi has often ridiculed Edward Lutyens denizens who have lived in the opulent luxury of its sprawling bungalows. The Central Vista is his way of bearding the arrogant lion in its own stately den. It was a farsighted, well thought out political plan, but one that needed sensitive handling, given the justifiable apprehensions of the southern states. The BJP's policy of divide and rule was unlikely to work when it came to delimitation though, given the complex enumeration of the bifurcation and gerrymandering of parliamentary constituencies.

In his brilliant book, *South vs North: India's Great Divide*, R.S. Nilakanthan nails the delicate challenge before the next government.

This success of the southern states, though, is under increasing pressure. The Indian Union, buoyed by the politics of nationalism, has sought to centralize policymaking. The declining significance of the southern states in national politics has coincided with the rise in prosperity in those regions. South India's concerns, to start with, are often orthogonal to those of north India, given the different stages of development they are in. South India also forms a demographically smaller section of the country.

The rise of nationalism as the dominant political ideology in northern India does not look at diversity in polity and policymaking as desirable. The demographic divergence between the north and south, which was already skewed in favour of the more populated north, has been made worse by a further skew in population growth that favours the north. All this makes south India a junior partner in the zero-sum game called electoral politics, diminishing its influence in decision-making. The successes of south India have led to a really paradoxical situation: success in areas of health, education and economic growth is being met with a policy regime that penalizes it; success in population control will be met with a likely loss of political representation in 2026. How will the region cope with such an assault?[12]

For Modi, the path to accomplishing a fair acceptable model for all states would be far from easy. If the preceding ten years were any indication, the road ahead was ragged, uneven. India's history was in tatters, disputed, and distorted systematically to create a new reality, while its future remained clouded in uncertainty.

12

THE DIFFICULTY OF BEING
THE 'OTHER'

'The whole aim of practical politics is to keep the populace
alarmed (and hence clamorous to be led to safety) and menacing it
with an endless series of hobgoblins, all of them imaginary.'
—*H.L. Mencken*

IIT: PRACTICALLY EVERY Indian knows the expanded form of the popular acronym. The Indian Institutes of Technology have been the glittering jewels in India's soft power fable. Approximately 2.2 million students compete for 16,000 seats in the prestigious institutions.[1] While they may not possess the star power of superstar Shah Rukh Khan's outstretched arms for the Indian diaspora, they are crucial stakeholders in Nasdaq market valuations of some of the prominent Big Tech firms. Silicon Valley, I am sure, has an active IIT alumnus, and some of them are celebrity CEOs. The big names include Sundar Pichai, CEO of Alphabet, Satya Narayana Nadella of Microsoft, former CEO of Twitter Parag Agrawal, IBM CEO Arvind Krishna, Adobe CEO Shantanu Narayen and George Kurian of NetApp. But in India, another IITian from Hyderabad overshadowed his astral senior counterparts in the month of October 2021. His name was Ram Nagesh Srinivas Akubathini. Akubathini, a twenty-three-year-old software engineer, had been working with a prominent food delivery app in Bengaluru until a month before he rose to the limelight. He had quit his job to prepare for a master's degree in the USA. Why was this IIT student making headlines? The young man was arrested because he had issued rape threats to actor Anushka Sharma and cricketer Virat Kohli's nine-month-old daughter. There could be nothing more terrifying, perverted and devilish than that. But why did the IIT student behave in such a depraved manner? His reason was one man, one of India's best fast bowlers in international cricket, Mohammed Shami.

Terribly foul comments appeared on social media after India's comprehensive defeat to Pakistan in a T20 World Cup match in Dubai on 24 October 2021. The main target was Shami because he conceded valuable runs at a crucial stage of the match. But in the eyes of rogue fundamentalists, Shami had deliberately lost out on those precious runs. They saw him as a willing saboteur of India's chances. This was a sinister allusion; it was being openly shared that Shami, being a Muslim, was a traitor. Most Indian captains, TV commentators and newspaper columnists were too lily-livered to comment on the sensitive subject. But Virat Kohli chose to be a man. He counter-attacked the hatemongers.

'Attacking someone over their religion is the most pathetic thing one can do as a human. That is a very sacred and personal thing. People take out their frustration because they have no understanding of what we do,' Virat Kohli told news reporters.[2] All hell broke loose. The twenty-three-year-old IIT graduate was incensed.

Akubathini had been slowly sucked into the dark underside of conspiracy theories and Right-wing extremism via the internet, where trolls dominated social media, often buttressed by the IT

Cell of the ruling party, the BJP. He was not an isolated example. India's dewy-eyed young appeared consumed by the fantastical propaganda of the giant PR machine, which had seduced many through its scientific persuasion algorithm. Bad-mouthing Muslims was an integral part of the script. It had started much earlier, mostly after India's Independence itself.

> The BJP's identity is crucially dependent on the presence of the Muslims as the enemy. Other. Christians are part of its demonology, but its historical grievance is centred on the Muslim conquest. Its nationalism is premised on Hinduism beleaguered by Islam. It is a sheepdog chauvinism where the BJP is the sheepdog, trying to keep a Hindu flock together, protecting the strays from Muslim and Christian wolves. If there were no wolves, there would be nothing for the BJP to do. It is a nationalism that like so many of its type in Europe, slips easily into chauvinist intolerance and bigotry. It isn't a coincidence that Golwalkar in the Thirties wrote in admiration of Hitler's way with Jews and the lessons to be learnt from this by Hindus faced with intransigent minorities.[3]

India after 2014 has become an angry nation, frothing with hate, brimming with uncontrollable rage at most times. On social media, a one-and-a-half-minute long video, which showed a photographer jumping menacingly on a man lying unconscious on the ground, went viral. It looked savage, weird, repugnant. There was a clear intent to ensure that the wounded man became permanently motionless. It was macabre, an exhibition of choleric infuriation. Worse, the guardians of law and order, India's policemen stood by, quietly watching the grotesque spectacle. Several of them even thrashed the inanimate body with their powerful batons themselves, not wanting to miss the violent confetti. Thankfully, someone posted the horrific video, otherwise Indians would have never known about the brutality in the fields of Sipajhar village in Assam's Darrang on 23 September 2021. While responsible sections of the mainstream media and online portals did recommend viewer discretion when watching the reel, maybe India needed to look in the mirror. Societies often go through slow-motion disintegration, revolting at the core, but imperceptible to most. But the degenerative collapse is for real. The anger has metastasized into a Frankenstein's monster where taking the life of a fellow citizen (in riots, lynching, mob violence, etc.) seems proforma. The pornography of hate is now the new normal. The veil of collegialism was off. When hate becomes quotidian, people usually don't think much before practising it. There is little remorse or guilt. In fact, it soon became fashionable to be anti-Muslim, as if it was prerequisite for being a true nationalist.

On Twitter, expectedly, the trends of the Assam ugliness had a communal colour. The dead man was reportedly one Moinul Haque, allegedly one of the people protesting forced eviction of their land by the Assam government (the court case is still pending a final judgement). His parents had crumbled in grief. Haque was a father of three children, aged seven, five and two. Their emotional laceration would haunt them forever. Soon their father would become another statistic among those who had an unnatural death. In the video Haque was seen chasing a press photographer with a lathi, supposedly prompting the cops to shoot him in the chest (pictures showed a red blot on his upper abdomen). The police said that he was killed in self-defence. In India, the victim often miraculously becomes the accused. The new national pastime is the glorification of violence from those responsible for law and order. It is institutionalized. It reveals a deeper resentment. But it was not something novel; it had a historical foundation. Minority Muslims were the soft target of systematically executed barbarity.

Sardar Vallabhbhai Patel warned against the danger that nationalism posed to a newly independent India. In a speech in Madras in 1949 that would resonate with many in India today, he said: We in the Government have been dealing with the RSS movement. They want that Hindu Rajya or Hindu culture should be imposed by force. No government can tolerate this. There are almost as many Muslims in this country as in the part that has been partitioned away. We are not going to drive them away. It would be an evil day we started that game.[4]

The online trolling by internet fanatics reached vulgarity levels which was unimaginably sickening. A fake auction site was created where Muslim women in public life (activists, journalists, film actor, etc.) were listed for trading, like commercial prostitutes up for sale. The Bulli Bai App and the Sulli Deals App were created by young boys in their early twenties, who had bought into the Right-wing's hatemongering and had now become an independent militia online, like cow vigilantes on the ground. If Virat Kohli's child was threatened by an IIT student, these trolls included MBAs and many working in multinational firms. Education and bigotry can be in a happy union, if properly manipulated. The Muslims seemed to be the predominant object of this anger, albeit the Dalits were equally frequently attacked. Disturbingly, many quietly acceded or reconciled themselves to gradual social segregation.

I have Muslim friends who are frightful of what lies ahead for them in the country where their forefathers have lived for centuries. They are repeatedly asked to corroborate their patriotic credentials. In the New Age of identity politics, they stand little chance when the ruling dispensation encourages the hot-headed nativist to repeatedly call them cross-border traitors. Tribalism is in vogue and accelerating in both swank urban homes and thatched huts in the rural interiors of India. Hate is pervasive and often increases exponentially when people find politicians indifferent to human suffering. The hate memorandum is usually dispatched from the top. The mainstream media obfuscates open and shut cases of gross violence through whataboutery. The latter creates a false equivalence, almost giving the perpetrators a license to violence in the name of historical score-settling. The culprits get away, on account of both a compromised criminal justice system and state-sponsored benevolence. Death is soon forgotten. India moves on. Violence to vent frustrations and often to seek revenge for the real and imagined sins of the past gradually becomes kosher.

At Jantar Mantar in Delhi (and in Haridwar in Uttarakhand), there was an infernal call for teaching Muslims a lesson. An open call for genocide was made amidst other incendiary, provocative slogans at the political event organized by a BJP member and former spokesperson, Ashwini Upadhyay, against 'colonial-era laws'.[5] The inflammatory outpourings were made, ironically enough, at an event organized by the 'Bharat Jodo Movement'. It sounded familiar. Hate speeches were the norm, not the exception.

> Early in April 1979, Bala Saheb Deoras, head of the Rashtriya Swayamsevak Sangh (RSS), a Hindu fundamentalist organization, visited Jameshedpur and exhorted Hindus to assert their rights in a Hindu country. Ten days later the city went up in flames, reducing entire localities to ashes and leaving scores of innocent men, women and children dead.[6]

The Supreme Court in the Shaheen Abdulla vs Union of India & Ors case mandated that all state police forces were to suo moto register FIRs in hate speech cases attracting offences under Section 153A, 153B, 295A and 505 of the Indian Penal Code (IPC), 1860, etc., even if no complaints were forthcoming.[7] If they failed to do so, it would place the officers concerned in contempt of court. While the SC step appeared at face value to be a belated correction needed to stem social polarization which was being ruthlessly implemented as a political tool, it had serious collateral risks. One of them was deliberate abuse by the men in khaki, under orders from their political masters to harass and threaten opponents, activists and critics alike by lodging fabricated cases against them.

Is the state impotent? These were the discomforting words of frustration and anguish of the SC on the hate speeches given in the dharam sansads.[8] The BJP, of course, appeared to be more annoyed than worried at the reprimand.

India under the BJP has become an angry nation; the manifestations were visible in multiple forums; WhatsApp groups of school batchmates, television debates, family conversations over the dinner table, social media trolling, inflammatory hate speeches, it was happening everywhere. The dog whistle of those BJP politicians who said 'Kabristan-Shamshan, 80:20, perpetrators of riots can be judged by the colour of their clothes, and Abba Jaan' added fuel to fire. Vinayak Damodar Savarkar, whom Modi lionized as a true patriot, would have been pleased.

> Savarkar became president of a party called the Hindu Mahasabha in 1937, and busied himself with reconverting non-Hindus to Hinduism. He again offered his co-operation to the British as the latter imprisoned Gandhi in 1942. 'The essential thing,' he said, 'is for Hinduism and Great Britain to be friends and the old antagonism was no longer necessary.' Lacking a mass base, Hindu nationalist leaders had from the 1920s onwards opposed Gandhi and courted the British in an attempt to bring an anti-Muslim Hindu nationalism into Indian politics through the back door.[9]

One of the most effective ways to ghettoize minorities is to put embargoes on what people should eat. And those who sell the food. Gujarat chose to lead the way, when the Ahmedabad Municipal Corporation (AMC) passed strictures that prevented street hawkers and vendors from selling non-vegetarian food.[10] The discrimination was not blurred. Food vigilantism was in vogue. An RSS-affiliated organization wanted the IITs to serve only vegetarian food.[11]

In several cities of Gujarat, the sale of non-vegetarian meals itself, was being withdrawn. Beef was always not on the menu, now it included chicken, fish and mutton too. The non-veg food proscriptions were dictated by religious politics. Gujarat, the home turf of BJP's two most powerful leaders, Modi and Amit Shah, was to go to polls at the end of 2022. In the 2017 elections, the Congress nearly upset their unshakeable applecart. Sectarianism and communal polarization is to BJP what serve and volley and single-handed backhand was to Roger Federer. They consistently deliver. Why else would not just Ahmedabad, but even other BJP-controlled cities, such as Vadodara, Rajkot, Bhavnagar and Junagadh, pass similar restrictive orders?[12] Almost uncannily, after decades of commercial sale, non-vegetarian food became 'offensive' and obstructed proper hygiene standards. Aggrieved politicians were also apprehensive that eating meat could negatively impact the minds of young children. The official fiat also stated that hawkers would not be allowed to peddle their protein-heavy delicacies within a radius of 100 metres from schools, colleges and religious places.[13] It was astounding that the BJP would try and destroy the livelihoods of those living on daily wages, especially after Modi's enormous catastrophe called demonetization had pulverized the informal sector. The Gujarat ban orders was adding insult to injury.

Politicians alone were not the heavyweight champions of fractionalizing society. Joining the bandwagon of social schism propagators (intentionally or otherwise) were even the august men in black robes. The controversial statement by Jammu, Kashmir and Ladakh High Court Chief Justice Pankaj Mithal that secularism had lowered India's 'spiritual image'[14] would have come as an open-mouthed shocker had it been uttered prior to 2014. Since then of course it is a rare day when secularism is not jeered at, dismissed as nothing more than a constitutional accoutrement. Several BJP leaders have publicly called for deleting the inclusive term from the Preamble (PM Indira Gandhi introduced secularism in 1975 in the Constitution). Chief Justice Mithal's observations were, however, conspicuous for two reasons; he was a senior member of India's judicial ecosystem, and secondly, the state of Jammu and Kashmir is a hypersensitive state, placed precariously in the political roadmap, given its convoluted past. But one must not forget that the political discourse on the subject of secularism was given a vertical trajectory by a man who is ninety-four years today.

Ever since BJP's Marg Darshak Mandal mega-leader L.K. Advani used 'pseudo-secular' to describe communal harmony with his trademark acerbic cynicism, secularism has been receiving brickbats. Advani, the original mastermind behind the current Hindutva hegemony in India, was an attractive blend of a street fighter, dog whistler (his Rath Yatra was probably the biggest game changer in the complicated electoral arithmetic of the late 1980s) and a political philosopher (his charitable disposition towards Mohammad Ali Jinnah would later trigger his political obsolescence). But in stigmatizing secularism as meretricious, fake almost, Advani emboldened the Right-wing skeptics and pushed the Hindutva franchise into fresh territories with new believers slowly trickling in. It took time, but today BJP gets 37 per cent of the popular vote (as in the 2019 general election) and over 40 per cent of the majority community votes.[15] The BJP saw a celestial resurrection, going from 2 LS seats in 1984 (even Atal Bihari Vajpayee lost) to being the largest political party with 182 seats in 1999, forming the government in the process. This was entirely due to Advani's modus operandi of barefaced polarization. While BJP had an extraordinary ascendancy, India slumped into an oppressive, dark period of suspicion, hate, violence and bigotry. The destruction of the Babri Masjid in December 1992 was followed by nationwide communal conflagrations. Mumbai, India's cosmopolitan lodestar, became a new hotspot of pernicious power-play, with religion becoming as important as Reliance shares on Dalal Street. Dawood Ibrahim retaliated with malicious mayhem in March 1993, unleashing serial terror attacks on a city that appeared completely paralyzed, dumbstruck by the bloody destruction. Mumbai has never been the same again. And neither has India.

The grand old party, the Congress, unfortunately, both on account of intellectual arrogance and political miscalculation, failed to vigorously defend secularism. Perhaps its lackadaisical response was influenced by the BJP's complete annihilation at the hustings in 1984. It did not take Advani seriously. It would have grievous consequences. Advani had launched populist nationalism long before the Hindu Rashtra crescendo became the leitmotif after 2014. The targeting of the Other had been artfully articulated. 'Minority appeasement' was the new buzzword, albeit statistical data on employment, subsidies, education, health and other parameters of government funding did not undergird that claim.

The Sachar Committee did an excellent job of marshalling data from different government sources and came to the following conclusions about India's largest minority:

- It had abysmal literacy figures, much lower than the n‸⋅˙
  average, and 25 per cent Muslim childrer ˈ
  and 14 were not at school.

- Muslims constitute only 3 per cent in the Indian Administrative Service (IAS), 1.8 per cent in the Indian Foreign Service (IFS), 4 per cent in the Indian Police Service (IPS), 4.5 per cent in Railways (98.7 per cent of the 4.5 per cent at lower levels), 6 per cent of police constables, 4 per cent in health and 6.5 per cent in transport.

- The average amount of bank loans disbursed to Muslims is 2/3rd of that disbursed to others.

- Muslim Other Backward Classes (OBCs) are worse off than Hindu OBCs.

- The school attainment levels of Muslims are close to Scheduled Caste/Scheduled Tribe (SC/ST) and much lower than them in rural areas.

- The share of Muslims in all recruitment by State Public Service Commissions is about 2.1 per cent whereas the population is about 14 per cent, leaving a conspicuous deficit.

- There is negligible representation of Muslims in the judiciary (7.8 per cent).

- And many other similar factual findings give lie to the irresponsible charge of appeasement of Muslims by the Congress or Congress-led Governments.[16]

The Congress was sacrificing Hindu community interests for obtaining crucial 14 per cent Muslim votes which tilted electoral battles in their favour it was alleged, as Muslims traditionally voted en masse. The Shah Bano case had been a luminous showpiece of Congress's pusillanimity, timidly pandering to conservative Muslim clergy's rigidity to change, ignoring the modern India that Rajiv Gandhi intrinsically stood for. The BJP exploited the constitutional amendment which overruled the Supreme Court verdict to the hilt. Even today, after thirty-four years, BJP spokespersons ad nauseam use that about-turn by the Congress to hang it from the tallest tree by the thinnest thread. Banning Salman Rushdie's *The Satanic Verses* added fuel to fire (The book was banned in India on 5 October 1988). The Congress still appears gobsmacked, stuttering and incoherent, when addressing them. That is the problem.

The years 1984 and 2002 saw how vulnerable India's minorities were; Sikhs were butchered in cold blood in Delhi and mostly Muslims were brutally exterminated in Gujarat. Both Rajiv Gandhi and Narendra Modi, who were at the helm of affairs, went on to win elections. Both also became prime ministers. For many ideological hardliners, it was divine retribution, a justifiable carnage. They blamed the Sabarmati Express compartment burning of fifty-seven kar sevaks in Godhra, Gujarat and Indira Gandhi's assassination at the hands of her Sikh bodyguards as the validation for the bloody massacres that followed. But secularism was being pilloried.

Beef bans, mob lynching, 'love jihad', anti-Romeo squads, ghar wapsi, vicious physical intimidation of Muslim small traders etc. have become de rigueur. None of it creates breaking news anymore like they once did. Even 'Abba Jaan' an affectionate reference to a solicitous father is converted to combustible material. India is struggling as a nation. Hinduism was being redefined.

'It is remarkable, for instance, that the only country on earth where the Jewish people have lived for centuries and never experienced a single episode of anti-Semitism is India. That is the Hinduism in which I gladly take pride.'[17] A spiritual country does not kill its own. It does not tape the video of that gruesome perpetration. It does not circulate murder on social media. Its leaders do not garland the nihilists accused of lynching. If India abandons secularism (in practice at least, it seems headed in that direction), it will give up on its own civilizational values. Tragically, even the chief justice of a high court did not know that. The subcontinent was bedeviled by a similar malaise.

In April 2000, I travelled to Dhaka with a formidable battery of talented lieutenants from my internet venture, CricketNext. com. The occasion was indeed historic. The International Cricket Council (ICC) had curated an extraordinary contest: the world's first Asia XI versus Rest of World XI ODI. The Kargil betrayal was indeed afresh in most minds, but in an unparalleled tiding, Pakistani and Indian players, were playing on the same side. The world's wiliest left-arm genius Wasim Akram was the captain of Asia XI, and playing under him were India's legends, such as Sachin Tendulkar, Sourav Ganguly, Anil Kumble and Ajay Jadeja. As someone said to me, 'It is incredible seeing the two neighbours who had a nasty military conflict less than a year earlier play like a bunch of school-mates, as one collective unit.' Dhaka appeared like any capital city in South Asia, brimming with staggering aplomb, its tilted demography favouring strapping youngsters who vociferously screamed for Tendulkar, its main street a crowded marmalade, reflecting a country in a chaotic state of profligate frenzy. They welcomed us with bounteous love. They loved their cricket. They clearly idolized their Big Brother to their west, the one that had valiantly, in the war of 1971 against Pakistan, helped give them their unique identity. Thus, when I saw the deadly attacks on Hindus being perpetrated in an organized manner, I was perturbed. Something had clearly changed. After all, it was almost two decades since that public bonhomie and the political birth of a nation.

There were over half a dozen Hindus killed in a violent case of religious targeting in October 2021 in Bangladesh.[18] The International Society for Krishna Consciousness (ISKCON) was singled out too. As is the usual communal template, the inferno happened at the time of an annual religious festival; this time it was the Durga Puja. The trigger for the violent aggression was a social media post, which apparently ridiculed the Quran. Many Hindu temples were vandalized by violent goondas. The fact that cannot be denied is the flash point in which several societies exist today, especially those in India's neighbourhood. In India itself, in West Bengal and Bihar, Ram Navami, once a day of joyous celebration, has now become a periodic if not permanent powder keg because of competitive religious contestations. All it takes is one WhatsApp instigation to create social unrest and bloodletting. Years of peaceful camaraderie can be incinerated in minutes.

Hindus are a small minority of 10 per cent in Bangladesh, which had been experiencing the rise of Islamic fundamentalism, as the former East Pakistan grappled with local extremism. In the age of social media, it takes little to influence brittle minds. While Prime Minister Sheikh Hasina reacted promptly, thus demonstrating her commitment to a secular composition, it is quite likely that the aftermath of the mayhem will linger much longer. The BJP has a vulture-like propensity to sweep down and low when it sees a communal carcass.

On a TV show, the BJP spokesperson screamed loudly about why the Opposition parties were playing minority-appeasement politics in opposing the Citizenship Amendment Act passed by the Modi government in 2019 by using the Bangladesh episodes as their lethal political AK-47. It was obvious that the BJP would once again raise the 'outside infiltrators' story as crucial state elections in Uttar Pradesh and Uttarakhand drew closer in early 2022. One expected the 'termites' aspersion to return to the mainstream. Until the coronavirus pathogen, which suddenly hit India in March 2020, the country was witnessing an unheard of, nationwide spontaneous uprising against the brazenly discriminatory CAA law, which disallowed Muslims refugees persecuted in their home countries (Pakistan, Afghanistan or Bangladesh) from being given sanctuary in India. Coupled with the nationwide Nation Register of Citizens (NRC) and the National Population Register (NPR), it formed a deadly triumvirate that could disenfranchise India's largest minority population.[19] The apprehensions were genuine. Detention centres for illegal migrants were going to be the next big infrastructure project. Polarized politics is BJP's coveted meal menu. It has worked magically at the hustings for them, mostly. Bangladesh appeared to be following the same political model. Both sides feasted on religious extremism.

As the highly reprehensible attacks on Hindus showed, Bangladesh was following the recent global trend of rising majoritarian populism. A few years earlier, *The Economist*, considered a free-market torchbearer, had shortlisted Bangladesh among the countries of the year for its booming exports, trade liberalization, improved transparency in government administration and poverty alleviation measures.[20] Bangladesh is the world's second largest garment merchandise exporter. For four years in a row pre-2020, its GDP growth exceeded 7 per cent, helping it to outperform its two bigger and more senior benchmarks, Pakistan and India. On crucial Human Development Indices such as education access, infant mortality, primary healthcare and women's participation in the workforce. Bangladesh has registered a robust turnaround. It has a higher per capital income than India. Thus, if PM Sheikh Hasina were to allow sectarianism to spread, it would come at a huge social consequence and economic cost. No country can get away with manufactured social disunity for short-term political aggrandizement. India's GDP growth was sub-par, the pandemic notwithstanding, (averaging below 4 per cent since 2019) because social tensions and economic growth are directly related.

Radicalism is the bane of fragile democracies which are also battling economic inequalities and social upheavals. Nativism is retrograde even if in the short-term it pays handsome electoral dividends for Right-wing populist parties. Bangladesh and India needed to be watchful here. When Sheikh Mujibur Rahman became president in 1971, he had inspired millions with his sincere message of a secular Bangladesh. His daughter now needed to walk the talk. But for the BJP, Bangladesh was a godsend, as it was eyeing the border state of West Bengal. Bengal was like the last frontier of the east which had to be captured willy-nilly. Bangladesh suited their plotline. Cross-border violence against minority Hindu populations gave the BJP the ammunition it was looking for.

Salman Khurshid, former external affairs minister, and one of the finest gentlemen around, wrote a book, *Sunrise over Ayodhya: Nationhood in our Times*. There was a furore over one line in the book: 'a robust version of Hindutva [is] by all standards a political version similar to the jihadist Islamic groups like ISIS and Boko Haram of recent years.'[21] One is known for beheading its prisoners while shooting video images, while the other mutilates the genitals of women in an abhorrent cowardly act of morbid misogyny. The BJP promptly used its giant megaphones to publicize the affront by Khurshid. This was in the Age of Modi, giving the BJP a carte blanche to run down the Congress as a party which, it believed, was anti-majority community. Khurshid is a rare public intellectual in Indian politics, but India had changed right under his nose. Nuanced debate was an oxymoron. Khurshid unfortunately demonstrated a baffling misjudgement in expecting a reasoned conversation around his book, which only exacerbated Congress's woes in UP, where an election was due. He had played into the saffron party's playbook. Promptly, FIRs were filed in a few places against Khurshid, and soon India's cumbersome legal process would adjudicate on Khurshid's treatise. Some nihilistic miscreants even tried to burn down his Nainital home. Ugliness enveloped India from all sides.

The secularists had to adopt better ways to take on the BJP and the RSS. Congress needed to address BJP's Hindutva campaign by asking fundamental questions that raise public consciousness on a sensitive subject which BJP had monopolized with its own narrative. Khurshid could have focused on the hard-line extremism that has pervaded India since Narendra Modi became prime minister in 2014.

> Make no mistake. Emphasizing its Hindu credentials, and in the process stoking resentment against Muslims and 'secular' political parties which also cater to Muslims, has helped the BJP. In this quest, the party is willing to deliberately use tools of deception. It is willing to disrupt social harmony. It is willing to stoke low-intensity conflict and even riots.[22]

Hinduism is an eclectic 4,000-year-old religion, all-encompassing, seminally embracing all. Swami Vivekananda said, 'Hinduism stands for both tolerance and universal acceptance.'[23] Hinduism has an intrinsic inclusiveness, which is its inherent beauty. Hinduism is distinctly different from the political mobilization of Hindutva (coined by Savarkar in 1923), which is used by the BJP as an exclusionary instrument to make India's largest minority population feel like second-rate citizens in their own country. BJP, in its political practice, violates secularism, which is part of the basic structure of India's Constitution.

The Congress also had to stop being apologetic about protecting minority human rights.

> The RSS blames Nehru for promoting Muslim communalism for votes in the garb of Muslim appeasement. If Nehru can be faulted for this, then Gandhi should be called the originator of the idea of Muslim appeasement. Because it was Gandhi who openly supported the Khilafat movement in India in 1919 and later on as well, but his endeavour was to unite Hindus and Muslims, bridge the gap between both the communities and to foil the British policy of divide and rule.[24]

For instance, it made its biggest monumental blunder eons ago when it allowed L.K. Advani to christen it as 'pseudo-secular'. That distorted dig went uncontested. How could a party which governed India for fifty-four years since Independence and won ten out of seventeen general elections have done so without majority Hindu votes? It was patently dorky. The Congress allowed BJP's communal polarization spin to bludgeon it and thus gave a carte blanch to the 'minority appeasement' tag. It got stuck. Ignoring it has not worked in the age of social media, fake news, dog whistles and a malleable mainstream media keeping the Hindu-Muslim binary alive.

> This is an artificial, and false, division. The BJP is both. It is a Hindu party. Its leaders and support base harbour deep resentment against Muslims. It does not hesitate to sharpen the Hindu-Muslim divide in the pursuit of political power. And it also believes that infrastructure, investment and the modern economy are essential to catapult India to the global high table.[25]

In short, the BJP speaks with a forked tongue, and tries to be a modernist (economically liberal), obscurantist (socially regressive) party. It has found buyers for this political business model.

The Congress needed to sell its political ideology while batting on the front foot—not squeamishly. The time for languid pussyfooting was long over. In an enlightened society, the majority population protects its more vulnerable minorities. That has been part of India's civilizational ethos. Congress has epitomized secularism ideologically, despite a chequered political practice of the same. It needed to look no further than Pandit Jawaharlal Nehru for inspiration. Nehru said to a riotous mob planning a deadly massacre, 'If you harm one single hair on the head of one Muslim, I will send in a tank and blast you to bits.' Nehru did not lose any Hindu votes for displaying genuine compassion and sterling statesmanship. India's current crisis is not of the rising Hindu-Muslim divide alone being engineered by poisonous zealots. It is mostly about its inability to reclaim humanity. Khurshid was on the right side of the cause, but on the wrong side of political articulation. The entire Opposition needed a strategic pushback to BJP's Us vs Them leitmotif.

At the Rashtriya Manch meeting in Delhi in June 2021, hosted by political heavyweights Sharad Pawar and Yashwant Sinha at the NCP supremo's residence, the mood was both sombre and sanguine; contradictions can coexist. There was understandable apprehension about the future of our wobbly democracy, battered and bruised, and requiring frequent judicial interventions to keep itself afloat. At the same time, there was hope that the country had reached a tipping point, and that there would be an equally resolute fightback against the rising authoritarian culture, both by civil society and Opposition parties, the two bulwarks as it were. During the deliberations, one erudite individual raised a pertinent issue: Is ideology going to be the final arbiter of India's destiny in 2024? Was a country of nearly 140 crore people hypnotized by one individual largely because they knew what he stood for? That it had nothing to do with moral grandstanding, rhetorical promises, oratorical flourish, campaigning style, image management, etc.? Who cares for a V-shaped economy and transparent governance? All they wanted was a leader who walks the talk. They may not agree with him, they may even dislike him, but there are no hidden surprises. To borrow from computer geeks, what you see is what you get. This was one question that got everybody thinking. It was a germane issue that would perhaps determine the future of Opposition unity and fightback; what does one stand for? The choice, in reality, was clear. The expression of it, was however, problematic.

The central challenge of India is the challenge of accommodating the aspirations of different groups in the national dream. The ethos of Hinduism—inclusionist, flexible, agglomerative-helped the nation meet this challenge. The doctrine of Hindutva prefers uniformity to accommodation. The battle for India's soul will be between two Hinduisms, the 'secularist' Indianism of the nationalist movement and the particularist fanaticism of the Ayodhya mob.[26]

The BJP has however adroitly made a reductionist argument to explain its political ideology: are you pro-Hindu or pro-Muslim? It is an uncomplicated binary. It is easily understood, and more importantly, felt. The communication strategy of the party has always been the simplification of political idioms, which are then deep fried with emotional fervour to inflame passions. The BJP addresses the hoi polloi in a language that they do not just understand but identify with. That is the key to identity politics. At the hustings, the impact has been hurricane like. It is an electoral pattern that delivers results consistently for the BJP, which beggars the question: Why has the Opposition (Congress, in particular) not figured out a robust response? There are two reasons for this.

The first, is fear. The Congress has ducked and dodged the Hindutva vs Hinduism debate, listening to the unwise counsel of conservative, calcified leaders in their midst who prefer the status quo. They have convinced the leadership that doing a deep dive into the delicate religious debate will boomerang against the party. The result is that the BJP gets a free pass; it remains totally uncontested, unchallenged. The saffron narrative gets a huge tailwind as the principal Opposition party avoids asking the tough questions: Isn't Hindutva just a vote mobilization strategy? Who has appointed the RSS/BJP as the custodians of such an eclectic, tolerant and ecumenical religion as Hinduism? If minority appeasement was indeed true, would Muslims truly be as worse off as they are today? Can India truly psychologically ghettoize and socially marginalize a population of 200 million Muslims, the third largest population anywhere in the world? These and innumerable related questions challenging the BJP's bigoted politics have not been consistently and aggressively raised by the Opposition. The Congress has meekly surrendered to being branded a pseudo-secular party; the BJP leadership, its blabbermouth spokespersons and evidently partisan TV anchors, have feasted on it. The Opposition parties, as a result, have become collateral damage to Congress's limitless waffling. In politics, inaction is not a good thing.

The second reason is leadership. Even PM Narendra Modi's bitterest critics will agree that Modi has never been uncomfortable with being called the Hindu Hriday Samrat. The prime minister has refused to honour the traditional practice of attending Iftaar parties at the Rashtrapati Bhavan. He has brazenly deployed communal calisthenics during election campaigns. Lynchings have been condemned in a synthetic manner, if at all. Several of the rabid motor-mouths in the BJP want to delete 'secularism' from the Indian Constitution. Several institutions have been gradually taken over by religious affiliates of the Sangh Parivar. Whether it is Article 370 or the Ram Mandir, the BJP has stuck to its manifesto commitment. The discerning know that a Hindu Rashtra has already been imperceptibly established in India, sans ceremonial fanfare. Thus, to take the bull by the horns, the Opposition needs a leader who encapsulates vigour, self-belief, passion, communication skills and a genuine ideological commitment to secularism. The janeu-dhari Hindutva-lite approach plays into the BJP playbook. Paradoxically, it is the BJP that plays 'majoritarian politics' (Hindus are 80 per cent and therefore the bigger political market segment), but no one in the Opposition has ever pointed that out.

Mamata Banerjee was called a Muslim-sympathizer, an ally of Bangladesh, and accused of being discomfited with the chant of Jai Shri Ram. The BJP deployed a massive Big Media push, social media barrage, door-to-door knocks by the RSS, massive rallies by the PM and its huge financial resources into West Bengal. But come April 2021, the TMC still won handsomely, routing the BJP and winning the bulk of both Hindu and Muslim votes in the process. The TMC won 215 seats, increasing its tally by 4 seats, and garnered nearly 48 per cent of the aggregate votes, although the BJP did corner an impactful 37 per cent of the vote share. Secularism survived a litmus test, giving the Opposition parties a winnable model. To defeat the BJP, one had to wear the secular badge proudly and genuinely carry everyone along, without parochial considerations driven by short termism of election wins. It also needs leaders who battle on fearlessly and enjoy the big fight, as Didi smartly demonstrated. Didi oh Didi, as she was jeered at by Modi, had the last laugh.

On a panel discussion on a TV channel, BJP spokesperson Nupur Sharma, often prone to vitriolic outbursts and vicious slanging matches with panellists opposed to her, crossed the red line on the evening of 27 May 2022. She made a sacrilegious observation on the Prophet that bordered on unadulterated vulgarity. The head of the BJP media cell Navin Jindal also contributed to the religious slur. The result was a diplomatic crisis which ricocheted across the entire Middle East and the Arabian Peninsula. There were calls to boycott India-made products in the whole region. Saudi Arabia, Qatar, Kuwait, Iran, etc. summoned the Indian envoys amid widespread outrage of social media. The Organisation of Islamic Cooperation (OIC), based in the Saudi city of Jeddah, also condemned the remarks. While Sharma and Jindal were later suspended by the BJP, which offered the usual diplomatic bromide to diffuse a volatile situation, the damage had been done. The anti-Muslim tirades were becoming a global talking point and a diplomatic mortification.

Back at home, a massive, motorized machine used in road construction was gravely destroying the country's already frangible social structure, bulldozers. It is this monstrous bulldozer which is normally seen near real estate projects which was the popular buzzword in Indian politics. According to political analysts, the brand of being called Bulldozer Baba helped the UP Chief Minister Yogi Adityananth to successfully defend the anti-incumbency that was accumulating against him in the Uttar Pradesh assembly elections where the BJP, as predicted by most exit polls, made a triumphant return to power with 258 seats in 2022.

The bulldozer imagery and the operation were simple: If anybody dared to allegedly take law into their hands in the perception of the government, the state would order the JCB bone-crushers to drive into their ramshackle homes and bring them down; destroy them into fine dust particles. The fear of a cold, ruthless authority was supposed to have a domino effect, scaring the daylights out of mischief mongers, hardened criminals and petty thieves. It seems the people of Uttar Pradesh gave this unique BJP model of governance a thumbs up. Expectedly, most BJP-ruled states have gleefully adopted the bulldozer model as their unique solution for law-and-order problems. Despite a USD 3.5 trillion economy and being a member of G20, India resembled a feudal kingdom where the rule of law was only notional; the writ of a popular czar is what mattered. The czar was the state. The state could do as it wished, sometimes even dissing the country's highest court, the Supreme Court of India's cautionary advice with disdain. Was adequate notice given for the planned wreckage? Were the demolitions retaliatory? Was it in accordance with the law? Was it just a punitive action for protesting against the government? Why were Muslims households mostly the principal targets? BJP-ruled states like Karnataka and Madhya Pradesh were quick to implement the bulldozer model in their states as well. It was all about winning elections by targeting one community as unreliable, lawless and against the majoritarian interest. Besides the bulldozer, one saw hijab, halal, azaan, beef and meat bans, love jihad, ghar wapsi, threat to doing business near majority community dwellings, and of course, lynching, dominating airwaves. India was seeing the naked countenance of religious loathing. Communist Party of India (Marxist) (CPM) leader Brinda Karat stood out for being valiant, when the bulldozer continued its razing down operation in Jahangirpuri despite a Supreme Court prohibiting it, on the pretext that the municipal body had not received the SC order on 'paper'. It was cockamamie, a lumpen expression of BJP's fascism; the SC would have been circumvented. Karat carried the copy of the SC order physically; it was unconscionable and exhibited India's dive into darkness at daytime.

> When social rankings and divisions solidify, fear fills in for understanding between groups. Any progress for a minority group stokes feelings of victimhood among the dominant population. Law and order politics has mass appeal, casting 'us' as lawful citizens and 'them' by contrast, as lawless criminals whose behaviour poses an existential threat to the manhood of the nation.[27]

In the case of razing down people's homes, Muslims were being positioned as intrinsically criminals who occupied land illegally. The vilification project was far from nuanced.

It appeared like one was watching director Anurag Kashyap's *Gangs of Wasseypur* redux. On live television, a dreaded gangster called Aatiq Ahmed was gunned down by three hoodlums masquerading as news reporters in Prayagraj in April 2023.[28] Ahmed was a former parliamentarian. His brother Ashraf Ahmed, who like him was handcuffed, was also shot at close range in the head. Incidentally, they were under police protection, and were being taken to a local hospital for a medical check-up. What was Aatiq Ahmed's bio?

He presents himself as a politician, contractor, builder, property dealer and farmer by occupation. What is missing in this extensive profile is that he is also an accused in a number of grave crimes and has been arrested more than once on serious allegations ranging from kidnapping to extortion to murder. Once the undisputed strongman of Allahabad-now Prayagraj-Ateeq Ahmed has, of late, become something of a political untouchable. Parties that had once done business with him are now keeping their distance. Perhaps he has outlived the purpose he served for them, or maybe his own clout in the city and neighbouring areas is a thing of the past.[29]

In what was clearly a planned assassination, the messaging was crystal-clear: non-state actors were the new militia. Officially, Uttar Pradesh saw 180 deaths in encounter killings.[30] The perpetrators of the cold-blooded extrajudicial killing of the Ahmed brothers shouted Jai Shri Ram after their deed was done. Everything played out faultlessly to a predictable script. Across India, Right-wingers were thrilled at the shootout. Violence was the shortest route to criminal justice.

Stone-pelting incidents were captured live on social media in many parts of the country on Ram Navami, held on 10 April in 2022. it was obvious that these were not a spontaneous outburst of anger. The unhinged history of communal riots in India shows that religious fanatics on both sides of the fence anxiously await these exploitable moments (25 per cent riots have happened during religious congregations). All it takes is one stone, a loud abuse meant to instigate, an isolated instance of eve-teasing, a WhatsApp rumour, an insulting act before a place of worship, etc., for the situation to become uncontrollably ignitable. Instead of religious harmony and collective celebrations of a festival, Indians see staged outbursts and a scary confrontation. That's how a communal riot is born. According to the government's own submission in the Lok Sabha, there were 3,400 riots (reported) during 2016–20 in India; perhaps many never made it to the official records.[31] 'Low-intensity but widespread communal disturbances,' appeared to be BJP's gameplan. The 1984 anti-Sikh riots, the aftermath of the Babri Masjid demolition that led to nationwide riots in 1992, Gujarat genocide of 2002, Muzaffarnagar communal deaths of 2013 and the Delhi riots of 2020 cannot be replicated frequently because of the massive reach of cable television and social media. The horrific images would be unpalatable for the moderate Indian to swallow; more importantly, the culprits could be caught red-handed on camera. A denial may not work. Hence, the new tactical strategy was to keep the hate campaign on in full swing, but like a new weekly or monthly episode in a streaming service. The idea was to keep the divisive pot on a perpetual boil, simmering at the top, whirling feverishly beneath. A restless society, forever living precariously on the precipice, arouses distrust, uneasiness, fear and discomfort, which is a toxic panoply for manufacturing rage that can then be effortlessly mobilized at short notice. BJP was creating an ecosystem of real-time instant delivery of hatemongers. That is how India was suddenly experiencing a nuclear cloudburst of daily anti-Muslim rhetoric, promoting their defenestration all over the country.

Hate had become a fashionable retail product in India. Quite literally, as Fabindia, the popular fashion brand of ethnic clothes and furnishings discovered to its surprise. To celebrate the hugely popular Hindu festival of Diwali, they came up with a lively watchable campaign which was however titled using evocative Urdu terminology, Jashn-e-Riwaaz, which translates into, a 'celebration of tradition'. Instantly, a furore erupted on social media as Right-wing trolls took a deep personal affront at the use of Urdu language to describe the Hindu festival of lights.[32] The ad was instantly withdrawn, but Gandhi's India was clearly moving in the direction of his assassins. The religious chasm was increasing; the '*Hindu khatre me hai*' catchphrase was finding fluttering wings, although no one asked the simple question: How can 14 per cent of people be a threat to 80 per cent of the majority? The numbers were illogically skewed. But there were enough takers for the mendacity that was marinated with venom.

Parvesh Verma, a BJP MP, said, 'We must totally boycott the Muslims. We can teach them a lesson in 24 hours.'[33] With such conspicuous hate in display, it was hardly a surprise that among 200 million Muslims in India, BJP did not have a single Muslim MP in Parliament. The Jim Crowism of the BJP was unmistakable. Hate speeches flourished periodically, getting progressively odious. The new normal accepted that without much of a protest.

Two men's charred bodies were found in Haryana's Bhiwani in March 2023. They belonged to the state of Rajasthan. Their names were Nasir and Junaid, victims of the new pastime of Hindu cow vigilantes: hunting down Muslims for alleged cattle-trading, kidnapping them and then thrashing them to death even in the absence of zero evidence. It was visceral bloodlust. The principal accused in the FIR in the case was a miscreant called Monu Manesar, a member of the Bajrang Dal, who roamed around freely, completely unaffected, as if certain of police protection. What kind of message was being given to the minority population of India? Things were so out of hand that there was a sedition case against a Karnataka high school for staging a drama which was against the CAA/NRC legislation. The state had become a laboratory for communal experimentation.

Social harmony was being ridiculed regularly. Even individuals holding Constitutional positions were having a field day;

Maharashtra Governor Bhagat Singh Koshyari was jeering at it, 'Have you suddenly become secular?' Koshyari was attacking the former CM of Maharashtra, Uddhav Thackeray, for not opening Hindu temples quickly enough during the lockdown.

There was not a single parliamentarian (Lok Sabha and Rajya Sabha) and a state legislator (assemblies in states and Union Territories) who was a Muslim, among 4,908 such seats aggregated together, representing the BJP after mid-2022. Every slogan of the Modi government was nothing more than a fallacious gimmick; 'Sab ka saath sab ka vikas', a term that all spokespersons were trained to mouth religiously on TV panel discussions, sounded not just inaccurate, but completely dishonest.

> Majority communalism is in fact an extreme form of separatism, because it seeks to separate other Indians, integral parts of our country, from India itself. I am proud of those Hindus who recognize that the saffron and the green both belong equally on the Indian flag. The reduction of non-Hindus to second-class status in their own homeland is unthinkable. As I have pointed out here, and in my other writings, it would be a second partition: and a partition in the Indian soul would be as bad as a partition in the Indian soil.[34]

It was not a strange coincidence perhaps, that the last five big communal bonfires over the last three decades, involved the BJP and the Sangh Parivar at the center of it all. Babri Masjid riots (1992–93), Gujarat riots of 2002, Muzaffarnagar riots (2013), Delhi riots (2020) and Manipur (2023). The BJP was sending a clear message to India's citizens: they believed an election victory meant a mandate to do as they pleased. The absence of a sturdy Opposition which could galvanize voters had made BJP believe they were insuperable. They were thus pulping the Idea of India, a Nehruvian construct which celebrated social fusion, constitutional democracy and fundamental rights of every citizen, sans discrimination. The New India of Narendra Modi which was being created, would thus rise from the rubbles of a bulldozed democracy of a great nation that once was.

> If lawyers had followed the norm of no execution without trial, if doctors had accepted the rule of no surgery without consent, if businessmen had endorsed the prohibition of slavery, if bureaucrats had refused to handle paperwork involving murder, then the Nazi regime would have been much harder pressed to carry out the atrocities by which we remember it.[35]

Democracy is a shared endeavour, a collective enterprise. Every citizen is a stakeholder. Every neighbour, every friend, every stranger, irrespective of caste, religion, ethnicity, language, sexual orientation, language, gender, or race is a co-builder of a nation. The failure to stand up and defend them when they are being persecuted is what weakens society, emaciates its soul. Self-preservation or perpetuation at the cost of others is a myth. That's what history teaches us.

> First they came for the Communists
> And I did not speak out Because I was not a Communist
> Then they came for the Socialists
> And I did not speak out Because I was not a Socialist
> Then they came for the trade unionists
> And I did not speak out Because I was not a trade unionist
> Then they came for the Jews

And I did not speak out
Because I was not a Jew
Then they came for me
And there was no one left
To speak out for me.
—Martin Niemöller, German pastor, 6 January 1946

Niemoller's forewarning though fell on deaf ears, mostly. The Muslims were being methodically marginalized, pushed quietly to the periphery of India.

13

THE SHAME OF MANIPUR

'If I seem to take part in politics, it is only because politics encircles
us today like the coil of a snake from which one cannot
get out, no matter how much one tries. I wish therefore
to wrestle with the snake.'
—*Mahatma Gandhi*

FRANKLY, NO ONE noticed it. At least, not enough. The Northeast always gets treated like a third cousin twice removed by India's mainstream media.

It was barely discussed on prime-time television, other than a sporadic mention. For many, it was just another social imbroglio in a distant state with its convoluted history of ethnic conflict which appeared like a byzantine mess. There was a more entertaining spectacle being played out, which was at least less complicated: the state assembly elections in Karnataka. With a 'double-engine' sarkar in Manipur, even if there was an alarming development, the Vishwa Guru (as Modi was constantly referred to by his toady acolytes) would use his magic wand and reassuring dialogue to solve the crisis pronto. Even as Modi did his road shows at the crammed junctions of Bengaluru with several bright techies and CEOs of start-ups in India's Silicon Valley serenading him, two women were being paraded naked by an angry mob in the 'mother of democracy'. Apparently, nobody knew. But on 20 July 2023, every Indian did.

The riots commenced on 3 May 2023 after a protest march by a tribal union opposed to the recent Manipur High Court order, which had mandated the Manipur government to send a recommendation to the centre regarding the demand to include the majority Meitei community (53 per cent of Manipur's population) in the Scheduled Tribes (STs) list. On 4 May, the Centre invoked Article 355 of the Constitution, as the state entered a dangerously uncontrolled state of affairs. Both sides hurled allegations and counterattacks at each other, listing among them, poppy cultivation, illegal migration of Myanmar refugees, the alleged deforestation, war on drug cartels, freedom to buy land in the hill areas, etc.

The Supreme Court's observations were extremely terse, made on 17 May 2023 against the Manipur High Court's direction to the state government to consider the inclusion of the Meitei community in the ST list, which turned out to be the flashpoint for the conflagration. 'I think we have to stay the order of the High Court. We have given Justice Muralidharan time to correct himself but he did not. I mean it's very clear what to do if High Court doesn't follow constitution judge benches,' CJI Chandrachud remarked, orally, as reported by LiveLaw.[1]

I think Modi-Shah (the duo practically run the country together) probably thought that the country, always guilty of ignoring its far east, would treat the violence there as a regular local conflict issue. The video proved to be a curveball, a smoking gun, which ensured that Modi broke his silence, even if it took him seventy-eight long days. When he did speak, he took all of thirty-six seconds only to make a passing reference to it. It was clear that he did not want to talk about the Manipur massacre because his government had failed, both in the state and at the centre. Modi appeared indignant, as he spoke prior to the commencement of the monsoon session of Parliament on 20 July 2023. Modi said, his heart was 'full of pain and anger', and that the ghastly incident was 'shameful'. He vowed prompt action, while adding that Rajasthan and Chhattisgarh (ruled by the Congress) also had sexual crimes and that chief ministers ought to 'protect mothers and sisters'. It was imbued with ballyhoo and his words appeared as synthetic as a fairness cream. For nearly three months, Modi had studiously ignored Manipur. In the interim, he had campaigned vigorously in Karnataka, made a visit to the United States as an official state guest, travelled to see Emmanuel Macron in France and also shaken hands with the rulers in the UAE. He had tweeted several times in between, but Imphal had vanished from his radar screen. The deplorable Manipur carnage was conspicuous by its absence in his mentions. It was baffling. Because several political commentators had by then surmised that the conflagration in Imphal was no ordinary happenchance. It was ugly and horrendous, which is why Modi's deafening silence left India unsettled. The hypocrisy would soon unravel.

Modi's fulminations sounded frivolous. His braggadocio that the culprits would not be spared is the kind that invites cynical sniggers, similar to the Bollywood dialogue: *'Kanoon ke haath lambe hai'*. And like the poor Bollywood policemen, the BJP was arriving languorously late to the killing fields, long after death and destruction had ripped the social fabric of Manipur's society. Why was Modi silent until that wretched video became a viral tornado on Twitter and social media? Would he have spoken at all if that had not happened, keeping India wilfully in darkness? Incidentally, until then 160 people were killed in a deadly bloodbath by revanchist mobs, and over 60,000 were displaced. As many as 249 churches had been burnt down.[2] It beggared the question: Why did Modi have to be triggered into belated action only when the national outrage had reached sky-high levels? Why wasn't the massacre and humanitarian crisis in Manipur not known adequately to New Delhi? Why did he appear so blissfully indifferent to the death of his own people?

In India, since 2014, Modi has made questioning his ability to keep law and order satisfactory, protect India's territorial sovereignty and contain violent extremism, an act of effrontery, nearly blasphemous. How could anyone question Modi's muscular patriotism or his prime obsession, national security? One had to be an anti-national to even insinuate that Modi was incompetent or worse, was playing with dangerous embers in pursuit of his political gameplan. Protected by a kowtowing mainstream media, Modi's strategy was straightforward: first, ignore a brewing crisis altogether, and if it were to however escalate, bludgeon it with his ruthless propaganda machine. Thus, Manipur hardly bothered him as he was convinced that no one would have the guts to interrogate his failure in allowing the searing wounds of Manipur to fester. That is, until the video of the gangraped women began to circulate. He panicked. But the politician in him is irrepressible. Humanity's suffering could wait.

Modi converted what should have been a head-hanging shameful moment of remorse and regret into a dog-whistling carnival; without batting an eyelid, and with minimum tumultuousness in his moral depository, he brought in cases of sexual violence in Rajasthan and Chhattisgarh (both governed by the Congress) to the fore, drawing a false equivalence to the dastardly madness in Manipur. It was a moment that was stunning in its taradiddle, even as it also scraped the bottom of the barrel where political ethics was concerned. There was none. The truth is that had both the central and state governments acted swiftly, arrested the perpetrators, and had not allowed anarchist mobs to strip women publicly, and gangrape one of them, the worsening situation could have been halted. But they did not. Honestly, that India's prime minister could indulge in such vulgar point-scoring whataboutery at a time when the country stood outraged, tells us where and how India has fallen off the grid. Even a nonpartisan columnist commanding universal reverence like Pratap Bhanu Mehta had to call out the cunningness using nuclear terms. 'And for us, unless we throw out from power this morally callous regime that peddles absurdities and revels in atrocity, our expressions of shame will be just empty hand-waving.'[3] It would be.

I remember meeting former Finance Minister Yashwant Sinha at the book launch of his autobiography, *Relentless*, in Mumbai in 2019. His most wrenching lament was that 'Indians have forgotten to protest'. He was so right. To take just two examples: George Floyd's cold-blooded murder by US policemen evoked nationwide horror, and cutting across racial divides, the #BlackLivesMatter movement began. In fact, the courts passed a lawsuit giving a massive compensation of USD 13 million to protestors in New York.[4] Creating public consciousness against state-sponsored discrimination requires all stakeholders to be kinetic participants. Secondly, Paris erupted over the death of seventeen-year-old Nahel M. who was a victim of targeted racial shooting. As his mother said, the policemen who shot him 'saw an Arab face, a little kid and wanted to take his life'. His crime: to drive his car during a regular police traffic check. The French President had to promptly, publicly state that the police highhandedness was 'inexcusable'. By comparison, it appeared, that most Indians had left the heavy lifting to Opposition parties, brave social media influencers running their YouTube news shows, and some NGOs. It was a phlegmatic, enfeebling response.

A sliver of hope remained in the Supreme Court of India, especially under D.Y. Chandrachud, the chief justice himself. The Supreme Court took suo motto notice of the gut-wrenching video and using strong words, literally lampooned the impotent government, both at the centre and the state. 'What matters is that this is just simply unacceptable … This is the grossest of constitutional and human rights violations … We are expressing our deep concern … We will give the government a little time to take action or we will take action,' the chief justice said, while upbraiding the BJP-run state and centre.[5] 'The court is deeply disturbed by the visuals which have appeared in the media since yesterday depicting the perpetration of sexual assault and violence on women in Manipur,' the three-judge Bench headed by the CJI added. Nothing more needed to be said.

The political executive had been a failure, prompting the SC to step in. The SC observations were to say the least, damning. 'Investigation is so lethargic. FIRs registered after two months. Arrests not made. Statements recorded after a long lapse of time. This gives us the impression that from the beginning of May till the end of July there was no law. There was absolute breakdown of machinery that you could not even register FIR. State police is incapable of investigation. They have lost control. There is absolutely no law and order.'[6] Modi had won 2014 on his rallying cry of 'maximum governance'. This was nothing short of a complete sham.

Easy access to megaphones and their ability to manipulate misinformation and disinformation had made the BJP leaders thick-skinned. They knew that they could insouciantly control the narrative or thrust a red herring, even at a time of the greatest national shame, even if the press conference was egregiously fabricated. Like senior minister Ravi Shankar Prasad claiming that the 'timing' of the leaked video that shamed India globally, could have been a political conspiracy curated by a desperate Opposition to embarrass the Modi government before the start of the parliamentary session. It was a mockery of the public discourse. Essentially, according to him, the Opposition was using the ghastly humiliation of India's women as an instrument for filibustering in Parliament. This was vile, given the sensitivity of the case and the circumstances. But that did not matter in a country that had blithely assimilated a political culture of deliberate falsehoods. Fake news and post-truth was common practice. It was now part of communications strategy. Prasad should have been answering the following questions which every Indian was thinking: How come the Manipur administration (read Chief Minister Biren Singh) was not aware of such violent manifestations which had happened in a state with a population of just 3 million, until the horrific video surfaced? Since Singh had stated to a TV channel that there were 'hundreds of such cases', what had he done about the gangrapes which had not been captured on video and circulated? Why did it take the victims over a fortnight to get an FIR registered on 18 May 2023? Why was it a Zero FIR when the faces of several rogues were easily decipherable? Why was it that only on 22 June 2023 was a complete FIR filed? Since central forces had moved in on 4 May 2023 itself and India's Union Home Minister Amit Shah had visited the state on 29 May (twenty-six long days after the ethnic conflict broke out), was he apprised of the dastardly incident by the CM or was he not? Both ways, did anything justify the radio silence thereafter by both of them? Was this not wilful deception on the part of the BJP to obfuscate and bury an ugly truth under the pretext of internet shutdowns and national security? Is it not true that the CM said on 20 June, right in the middle of the ethnic conflict which many have dubbed as a civil war, 'These acts must stop. Mainly the SOO (Suspension of Operations) kuki militants should stop it, otherwise they will face the consequences. I also appeal to Meitei people, who are with arms, not to do anything illegal.'[7] Was this not a case of biased messaging, using the powerful bully pulpit for playing a prejudiced politics? Is it not true that in another speech, he had alluded to 'terrorists' in Manipur? Who was he referring to? How is it that over several days, several thousands of arms, ammunition and bullets were stolen right from under the nose of the Manipur police (state police estimate above 3,500 weapons and 5,00,000 bullets)? How was that possible without wilful collusion between both the guardians of law and order and the torchbearers of hate? It is a grocery list of questions to which the BJP had obviously no answers. But topping it all remained the billion-dollar question that a frightened media dared not to ask of Modi: Why had he chosen to be mummified at a time of such incendiary madness? Why had Modi behaved like the prime minister of the BJP instead of acting like the prime minister of India? To understand that better, one has to understand the nitty-gritties of fascist leadership.

Modi represents the archetypal 'strongman leader' profile who have sprouted across Turkey (President Recipp Erdoğan), Hungary (PM Viktor Orban), PM Benjamin Netanyahu (Israel) and others such as former President Bolsonaro of Brazil, Roger Duterte (Philippines), and of course, Donald Trump, former president of USA. The common thread unifying authoritarian demagogues is their attempts to perennially appear in command in the cockpit. Any acceptance of non-performance, awful decisions that may have backfired, or a failure to deliver on an announced commitment, has to be handled deftly. Of course, all politicians dodge an underwhelming delivery, but muscular despots worry themselves sick about their 'image'. They can never afford to look weak, indecisive and clueless. They must continuously be projected to be in control. It is a pathological prerequisite for maintaining the dominant leadership syndrome. Cracks must be hidden; craters must be camouflaged. The last and most convenient option was to blame somebody else, either within the party or the Opposition, mainly. The supreme leader was infallible, a fountainhead of immaculate perfection who could never go wrong. Invariably, at a moment of grave crisis, they would be missing in action. The playlist played to perfection. Always. Modi was not seen or heard at all during the second Covid wave in April 2021 which had left India literally breathless, and dead, in astronomical numbers. As hapless migrants trudged tarred roads under a scorching summer sun, many dying along the way, the PM, who had made frequent televised appearances, was unavailable to offer them even words of sympathy. When the farmers were on the roads for months begging to be heard, the prime minister refused to be visible when it came to addressing their grievances. Thus, as Manipur faced one of its worst ethnic clashes, Modi was everywhere but in Manipur. But he had carried the Ignore-till-it-is dead policy to ludicrous lengths. Not one word. Not one tweet. Nothing. Even his most passionate toadies, I am sure, were left wondering if the textbook adherence to the strongman stereotype would boomerang. It did. The feet of clay was more like the red sand of Roland Garros. But for the people of Manipur, the cataclysmic damage could be seriously irreparable. Modi's pet project is infrastructural investment; what he forgot was that societies need to build bridges between communities. Making highways, impressive flyovers and long concrete bridges is no guarantee of a syncretic society that India needed.

The BJP, a past master at the blame game, was already deflecting the issue towards the state's troubled legacy. But while the diversionary tactics could provide the wily party with ephemeral relief, the entire Northeast ran the grave threat of becoming a dangerous timebomb. The immediate ramification was first felt in the neighbouring state of Mizoram.

Several people belonging to the Meitei community were frantically trying to leave Mizoram, where the local Mizos share a deep historical bond with the Kuki–Zomis of Manipur. Mizoram was understandably restless, riled at the outrageous assault happening across the state's borders. Panic-stricken Kukis took the long, torturous seventeen-hour drive to Mizoram airport to leave for safer havens. Flying through the Imphal airport, a mere forty-five minutes away, was a security risk. This is how precariously were innocent lives placed, even as the prime minister campaigned in Rajasthan. Given the strategy of dogged obstinacy to be transparent on the Manipur crisis, it was hardly a surprise that parliamentary gridlock became inevitable. Indian democracy had been reduced to a travesty.

The Parliament is supposed to be the most sacrosanct embodiment of a country's political heft. It is here that deliberations happen, debates get heated up, and constructive discussions transpire in the hour of a national emergency. Mostly, a consensus is reached on matters such as Manipur. Manipur was an explosive subject; in the state, bloodshed and violence was rampant, and the state government had proved to be a disastrous administrator. It was imperative that India's CEO would step up to assure the stunned nation and the grieving people of Manipur, that calm would be restored under any circumstances at the earliest, and that no more lives would be lost. Everyone was safe, because that's the first essential obligation of an elected government. But that was not to be. India's supreme leader has a fragile ego, and a macho-man image to protect. The government stonewalled Opposition demands for a full-fledged discussion on Manipur, with the prime minister in attendance. According to them, Amit Shah, India's most undistinguished, incompetent home minister (the Delhi riots happened under his watch) would be present. This was outrageous and defied logic. It was evident that the BJP was ringfencing their key electoral asset from looking like a miserable failure. Modi, clearly, had no compunctions about his dereliction of parliamentary responsibilities. The 'mother of democracy' had been gangraped in broad daylight, but that self-congratulatory slogan on giant billboards welcoming G20 delegates was a higher priority of the government.

Even as the world stood stunned, disgusted, watching the Manipur tapes, the government brutally let loose its authoritarian tentacles. Aam Aadmi Party leader Sanjay Singh was suspended for the entire session. The Opposition demand to have discussions under Sec 267 (which allows for unlimited time, and a resolution can even be voted upon) was rejected; in an hour of human tragedy, the BJP-led NDA seemed disinterested in permitting conversation. That people were expected to feel elated and satisfied just because Modi 'spoke', (after seventy-eight days for thirty-six seconds), was scoffing at Manipur's trauma. But then that was standard operating procedure of Modi. It had worked for him politically in the past; why would he change his winning strategy?

Over nine long years, the prime minister of the world's largest democracy had not held a single press conference. Using a controlled mix of state broadcasts (his radio show Mann Ki Baat had Joseph Goebbels written all over it; for instance, even TV channels which are a visual format were forced to play out just the audio). Being supine had been made into a sublime experience. Choreographed interviews with craven journalists, teleprompter driven histrionics, sponsored op-eds, tweets and photo-ops, huge front-page advertisements in daily newspapers, etc. had Indians insulated against the need for interrogative journalism. No questions were asked of Modi. As with everything else, this anomaly was normalized. Indians were just happy that he spoke. Actions taken to ameliorate matters, whatever they maybe, was inconsequential. It was a fascist cult power on fast forward.

The Supreme Court had once observed (April 2004) in a scalding indictment in the Best Bakery case during the Gujarat pogrom of 2002, 'The modern-day Neros were looking elsewhere when Best Bakery and innocent children and helpless women were burning and were probably deliberating how the perpetrators of the crime can be protected.'[8] It was quite apparent as to where and whom did the needle of suspicion pointed towards. As several political commentators noted, Manipur was being subjected to the same iron-hearted, merciless abuse. The true face of the Gujarat model was there for all to see. Modi had himself survived a public rebuke of his sectarian politicking in a press conference by then prime minister, Atal Bihari Vajpayee, who had reminded him of his raj dharma. Was it any surprise therefore that Modi was stubbornly refusing to engage in any confabulation on Manipur, both inside and outside Parliament? Did he even possess the moral wherewithal to sack the bungling chief minister, Biren Singh, who had created a serious challenge for the Indian republic itself? Would Modi, for a change, take political accountability for Manipur's uncontrollable chaos and inexcusable blunders? That was wishful thinking. The politician in Modi always overshadowed his faux nationalism.

Even as Opposition parties legitimately protested, asking for Modi to participate in a televised session in Parliament, the latter was firing salvos full of contemptible lowbrow language at them, calling them Indian Mujahideen and East India Company. It was clear that Modi had decided to steadfastly follow the BJP programme: brazen out the attack and convert it instead into an anti-national rant. That the BJP and Modi believed in the Nazi, fascist propaganda machine model was beyond doubt; converting a grave national crisis on account of astounding incompetence into a conspiracy theory hatched by disgruntled opponents was therefore hardly surprising. The Opposition had seen that before.

The ordinary Manipuri, whether a Kuki, Meitei or a Naga, was in the meantime struggling amidst the oppressive strain of fear, suspicion and uncertainty. There were disturbing stories of inconceivable horror. An eighty-year-old woman, the wife of a freedom fighter, was set on fire in her own home. Her late husband was a freedom fighter, who had been decorated by former President A.P.J. Abdul Kalam. On the day the two women were subjected to inhuman sexual abuse, the father and brother of one of the women was murdered for trying to intervene. It was dastardly, and unimaginably hateful. There were innumerable incidents of bloodletting in over 6,000 FIRs. It made for a dismal tale of a state's abdication of its duties. While the political slugfest escalated, India had abandoned democracy, it seemed. For the people of Manipur, there was no light at the end of a dark tunnel.

The BJP, past masters at passing the buck to the Opposition and never ever taking responsibility for their own disastrous snafus, were cornered, because their own leaders were spilling the beans on the sordid developments. The Bharatiya Janata Party's Mizoram Vice President R. Vanramchhuanga resigned from his post as well as the party, accusing the Centre of indifference towards the Christian community. Vanramchhuanga said in his resignation letter to Mizoram BJP chief Vanlalhmuaka that he was deeply hurt by 'anti-Christian activities' in the neighbouring state. He alleged that the Meitei militants had burnt down '357 Christian churches, pastor quarters and office buildings belonging to different churches'.[9] This was damning and frightening. There were other lawmakers from the besieged state of Manipur who had chosen to call a spade a spade. One of them was Manipur BJP MLA Paolienlal Haokip. He alleged 'complicity of the state' in the ethnic violence as one of the reasons why it took time to be contained.[10] Haokip is one of the ten tribal legislators of the Northeastern state who wrote to Chief Minister N. Biren Singh in May 2023 itself, demanding a separate administration for the Kuki-dominated districts in the state. He was speaking to Newslaundry. 'Proof of state complicity can clearly be discerned from the fact that what started out as a purely ethnic-communal violence was later on attempted to be portrayed by the chief minister as the state's war on "narco terrorists",' Haokip wrote in an opinion article for *India Today*.[11] There were many such disconcerting expressions of anguish being made by the deeply worried people of the Northeast as they felt as ostracized from mainland India as their geographical distance from its capital city.

To refer to Indian politics as a theatre of the absurd is being highly charitable. It was downright farcical in its political mudslinging even as Manipur continued to simmer, the violence refusing to abate. Thousands were enduring a wretched ordeal in relief camps, even as fear enveloped their habitation. But a conversation about their rehabilitation in New Delhi was turning out to be nearly impossible. The stubborn denial to answer Parliament by the prime minister was a shocking neglect of political responsibility.

The Opposition led by the newly formed Indian National Developmental Inclusive Alliance (INDIA) had a reasonable and legitimate expectation: Modi had to break his silence on the floor of the house. They were expectedly barricaded by the belligerent BJP. Eventually, a frustrated Opposition was compelled to utilize their last card: a no-confidence motion against the government. The prime minister would now have no option but to defend his government in the Lok Sabha, in what should have been under normal circumstances, par for the course. Political parties were no longer just ideological or field opponents; they were arch enemies. This bitterness and distrust does not augur well for India's democratic future.

Democratic accountability had been reduced to just an academic phrase. It was pre-destined that the no-confidence motion would pose no threat to the NDA; at 353 LS seats, the NDA outnumbered the Opposition comfortably. But it was an ignominious embarrassment for the Modi government that it was being forced, through the adroit use of valid legislative provisions, to be answerable to the 140 crore people of India. Sometimes you win even if you lose, appeared to be INDIA's motto. The Manipur imbroglio indeed had raised several questions. And among the most perturbing developments was the arms that were looted by rioting mobs right under the nose of the police. Was the Manipur internal conflict now a full-blown civil war? It appeared to be. Estimates varied, but the number of sophisticated AK-47s, rifles, etc. that were missing was in the range of 3,000–4,000 according to media reports.[12] These were rampantly looted from police armouries, and according to several FIRs filed, it had been done in broad daylight, with some allegedly even promising to return them over a period, in what seemed like a peacefully collaborative project.[13] The breakdown in law and order was full-blown.

The BJP's discomfiture worsened with the arrival of Rahul Gandhi in Manipur. While the PM was guilty of perplexing silence over months, his arch nemesis had bravely stepped into the embers of virulent hate hanging ominously over the state's skies.[14] Even Modi's hatchet man Amit Shah had reached Imphal only weeks afterwards. His efforts at troubleshooting had been a monumental failure. The madness had continued unabated. In the BJP-scripted modern political encyclopaedia, whataboutery was weaponized and treasury benches used it for deflecting and diverting from subjects that caused heartburn.

Sexual violence against women in India has only worsened with the passage of time. The Nirbhaya case had stunned the country into a much-needed deep introspection, but that moral uprising had since been extinguished. Sexual molestations had returned with inexorable vengeance; no deterrent, even the prospect of capital punishment was a disincentive to carnal power. Across India, across states, women were vulnerable, an easy prey to lascivious monsters. Thus, for Modi and his team to talk about such cases in only non-BJP ruled states to score brownie points at a time when the nation was still recovering from the hellish video from Manipur, was a bottomless fall. It made a mockery of the emotional trauma and the physical degradation that several women from all communities had suffered in Manipur. Using the prowess of powerful propaganda machines, the lines between sexual crimes against women and the communal targeting of women by organized mobs driven by an insatiable ethnic hatred was being made nebulous. It was barefaced in being disingenuous. Of course, the perpetrators in both cases must face the most stringent penalty, but understanding the underlying cause was of seminal importance. Manipur was not an isolated example of rogue behaviour by perverted minds. It was proof of inter-ethnic rivalry that had been malevolently pursued and converted into a religious divide. The women were victims of political chieftains fully aware of the consequences of their cunning moves. The violence against women in communal bloodbaths of the past is a warning of what one can expect in the future as well.

> When we think of the Nazi Holocaust of the Jews, we imagine Auschwitz and mechanized impersonal death. This was a convenient way for Germans to remember the Holocaust since they could claim that few of them had known exactly what had happened behind those gates. In fact, the Holocaust began not in the death facilities, but over shooting pits in eastern Europe.[15]

Brij Bhushan Singh, the discredited, controversial and rape-accused leader in the infamous wrestlers' case, was chosen by the BJP, to be its principal microphone to address the Manipur crisis. It was an act of incandescent effrontery; the party was basically sneering at the critics and liberals whom it labelled as political conspirators to defame Modi. The BJP alleged that the champion women wrestlers were part of a cabal that ran a motivated campaign of sexual harassment to taint the reputation of the former president of the Wrestling Federation of India. Singh had got bail from the Delhi High Court, despite the Delhi Police chargesheet literally lampooning his earlier denials. But according to the BJP, Singh was as pure as bottled water. It was being blasé. Indian politics was scraping the bottom of the barrel.

India's premier video news agency, ANI, in an act that was shockingly fissiparous, casually put out a newsflash that one of the culprits behind the gruesome gangrape was a Muslim.[16] Given the tenuous social environment in India, this could have led to a volatile situation, exposing the minority community to untold danger. Although that fictitious news was subsequently deleted, it had been given substantial firepower to circulate on WhatsApp and other social media platforms, providing hatemongers an opportunity to further divide and sub-divide India. The political mission had been successfully accomplished. Indian media was failing India. An Orwellian nightmare was now a daylight reality. Amidst all this, children were being born in the relief camps in Imphal. Manipur remained in an internet clampdown. The parallel with Jammu and Kashmir up in the north was unmistakable, especially the blanket ban on information that followed the abrogation of Article 370.

> Far away from the deafening celebrations in various parts of the country, amplified jarringly by the electronic media, as the political and geographical fate of 13.6 million people was being decided in New Delhi through an Act of Parliament that remains challenged in the Supreme Court, Kashmiris were confined in their homes, trapped inside like mice in mousetraps. The landscape of spools of razor wires, barricades and soldiers outside turned homes into tiny prisons in which movements of the inmates were frozen. And pin-drop silence, eerie in its resonance, was imposed by blocking all communication channels, including internet, mobile phones and even landline phones.[17]

In fact, as the events of the summer of 2023 concluded, India's social polarization was nearly complete. Despite the in-the-face-horror of Manipur, there was no political answerability. When

PM Modi was at the White House during his US visit in June 2023, former President Barack Obama gave a frank assessment of where he thought India was in an interview to CNN's Christiane Amanpour. Amanpour called Modi an illiberal democrat. 'If I had a conversation with Mr Modi—who I know well—part of my argument would be that if you do not protect the rights of ethnic minorities in India, then there is a strong possibility India at some point starts pulling apart.'[18]

Obama was attacked by BJP leaders and ministers who rose like a pack of wolves to protect their supremo. It was funny, because in 2015 they boasted loudly of a bromance between Obama and Modi. But a lot has changed since then. As Manipur showed, Obama's words were prescient. India was indeed pulling apart.

14

INDIA: THE MOMENT OF TRUTH

'Even if you are a minority of one, the truth is the truth.'
—*Mahatma Gandhi*

T O UNDERSTAND INDIA, one must visit traffic junctions near local railway stations. Lawlessness prevails. Although the traffic signals maybe working, few respect its timings, recklessly breaking them, even at great risk of personal injury or a traffic ticket, given that many urban cities have CCTV cameras. But that is usually a frivolous deterrent for most. For no apparent reason, people honk at those in front of them, as if to remind them to be alert when the signal turns green. Everyone appears tense, impatient. Often, it determines survival itself. The wailing siren of an ivory-white ambulance carrying a critical patient stuck in a man-made traffic jam is symptomatic of a country in crisis. There is the urgent compulsion to get ahead in the serpentine queue. If unfortunately, the vehicle stalls in front, colourful expletives fly liberally. Sometimes that can lead to road rage. And in rare cases, even death. Joining the disorderly festivity are cows, water buffaloes, goats and their shepherds who walk in slow motion, monopolizing roads with casual disdain. BMW SUVs obediently crawl behind them, till the cows condescend to change direction and make way. I have never understood why traffic policemen (at least in Mumbai) insist on intervening in the normal functioning of the electronic-controlled signal system. They cause further confusion. Public transport buses, usually the most menacing vehicles on the road, bully everyone down by breathing down their necks, the driver enjoying his first among equals status; mirroring a national character trait. Two-wheelers with three people sitting on them, none wearing a crash helmet, do a zigzag through the line of vehicles in front of them and disappear from sight with everyone looking suitably impressed. The police van, of course, is the one for whom the traffic rules don't apply. They stop, change lanes, take a U-turn, and break traffic lights with the imperiousness of monarchs. No one complains. 'We are like this only,' say most, as they inhale poisonous chemicals, burn fuel and await their long and tortuous journey home. India is a bedlam on wheels.

The pomp and pageantry of hosting the G20 Summit in September 2023 New Delhi notwithstanding, the road ahead appears long and hard. The chronic obsession with GDP growth figures had India's political leadership feeling smug; but it was a case of erroneous aplomb. In India, when you fail to deliver, all you need to do is to create new goalposts, mostly another deceptive mirage, which temporarily delivers the main purpose: keep everyone living in a fool's paradise. It helps to keep the bad news in the background; the broken promises remain uncontested. All highfalutin, authoritarian leaders keep changing the storyline. Modi's pompous-sounding prediction, 'India will become a USD 5 trillion economy during my next reign, within 3 years', made in August 2023 deserves an examination to explain its vacuousness.

According to the finance minister Nirmala Sitharaman, India had registered a GDP of USD 3.75 trillion by March 2023.[1] Assuming that to be the correct figure, to reach USD 5 trillion in three years,

India has to perform at just 10 per cent nominal growth (which is a combination of real growth coupled with inflation). In short, even a disappointing 6 per cent GDP growth and a modest to high 4 per cent inflation would effortlessly deliver the USD 5 trillion objective on a compounded growth basis. To put it bluntly, unless the PM announced another economic kooky, like the occultist demonetization to disrupt and destroy growth, India is in an autopilot to reach the USD 5 trillion mark, without breaking a sweat. Theoretically, Modi was killing two birds with one stone: preparing for a modest growth in economic performance while bamboozling people into believing that a huge milestone had been achieved. Economic data can be easily cherry-picked by confident tricksters or manipulated. Even popular TV business channels and pink papers debated the humbug behind this facile headline as if it was a watershed accomplishment on the way. Politically, Modi had once again successfully navigated away from the negative developments of high inflation and record unemployment, among other pressing failures, through the powers of the BJP's information engine. While the print media was more analytical, in the age of WhatsApp University, they faced tsunami-like headwinds.

Modi's Amrit Kaal, another gigantic googly, a shining chimera of boundless sunshine which would have made cricketer Anil Kumble proud, could not hide the truth of real economic prosperity. During NDA's 2014–23 period, India's average GDP growth rounded off to 5.7 per cent.[2] Comparatively, the Congress-led UPA coalition put up a significantly better show at 7 per cent between 2004 and 2014. This was normally challenged by government mouthpieces as ignoring the 'black swan moment' of the Covid pandemic of 2020. A fair enough argument, one would concede. But what's sauce for the goose is sauce for the gander, right? In that case, did not the UPA face the unprecedented 'Great Recession of 2008' following the mortgage crisis in US home loans which overnight upended the global financial system? What about the fact that global crude oil prices had reached a high of USD 149 a barrel during the period? Amrit Kaal was, in short, another calculated ruse, just a creative blue-ribbon spin. Under the NDA, statistics were just that; numbers that were either massaged (India's GDP had been cushioned up by 2.5 per cent, according to the former Chief Economic Advisor Arvind Subramanian)[3] or broadcast by cherry-picking what appeared to be of sales value. Politicians are, of course, forgiven these regular peccadillos because it is dismissed as the nature of the beast. But a country pays dearly over the long-term for mislaid faith. India was a classic example of a nation that had developed a tolerance for the execrable failures of its government because the packaging was golden, even if the carton inside was empty. But things were far from bleak for Big Business, and especially those who lived in the big boys' club, a charmed circle. Kleptocracy was firing on all cylinders; after an epic stock market meltdown, the news breaking business group of Adani was on the prowl again for fresh buyouts.

Just when the Adani-Modi government malefaction story had begun to ratchet down from public memory, what with the latter business group back to making controversial acquisitions like the Dharavi slum redevelopment plan, cement manufacturing company Sanghi Cements, etc., came another seismic disruption in the form of Organized Crime And Corruption Reporting Project (OCCRP). The OCCRP is an international group of investigative journalists tracking corruption scandals in different parts of the world. On 31 August 2023, the report findings of OCCRP were published in two foreign dailies in the UK: *The Financial Times* and *The Guardian*.[4] No Indian mainline newspaper would have acceded to being a co-collaborator in this material divulgence. It would be too risky for their business survival given the swift comeuppance from New Delhi.

The OCCRP quintessentially corroborated the Hindenburg report of January 2023 which had resulted in the Adani group's meltdown. Through a detailed probe it was established that overseas shell companies had been actively trading in Adani group companies.[5] The ownership of various Mauritius-based investment funds was hidden behind multiple layers to conceal the ultimate beneficiary, but there was one common thread running through the smokes and mirrors transactions: the role of Vinod Adani, Gautam Adani's elder brother.[6] In simple language, the brother was a frontman in a dark trench coat who was rigging the stock prices of various group firms, pushing the share prices to dizzying levels. It was made easy meat, because along with two other shady characters, Nasser Ali Shaban Ahli from UAE and Chang Chung-Ling from Taiwan, it appeared that the Adanis controlled more than the prescribed limit of 75 per cent of stocks which are permitted by the capital markets regulator. This is a serious contravention of the law. But SEBI had chosen to blindfold itself. Why? That's a mystery wrapped in an enigma and served as a riddle. Or is it?

The OCCRP report exposed that the Director of Revenue Intelligence (DRI) had written to the SEBI chief in January 2014 about a potential foreign exchange scam by Adani companies and a subsequent round-tripping of funds through over-invoicing of coal imports. What it said is a bombshell: 'there are indications that a part of the siphoned-off money may have found its way to stock markets in India as investment and disinvestment in the Adani group'.[7] In any other country, the Adani Group would have been under 24x7 warlike surveillance thereafter. In India, the reverse happened. Because by May 2014, Modi had become the prime minister.

SEBI, in fact, amended listing rules in 2018 which made it difficult to discover a promoter and close-cronies trail. This was incomprehensible to most. There is a reason why white crime flourishes rampant in India; few understand complex financial engineering in government (CAG's 2G notional loss of Rs 1,76,000 crores was complete baloney); and secondly, so-called independent regulators usually perform dutifully as a janitor as opposed to a responsible sentinel.

The Expert Committee appointed by the Supreme Court of India to report on the Adani scam had no investigative powers, and barring making some commonplace observations, they appeared to be toothless tigers. They were depending on SEBI, which in turn, seemed to be awaiting instructions from New Delhi. The conflict of interest was stunning; SEBI had appointed Cyril Shroff, a well-known corporate lawyer to its committee on corporate governance and insider trading (two charges against the business conglomerate); Shroff's daughter was married to Gautam Adani's son.[8] No leader of a free world who was accused of having blessed, promoted and then protected such an allegedly dubious financial lawbreaker would have survived. But Modi, shielded by the Big Media and effete institutions, can still get away, his brilliantly manufactured image of incorruptibility overpowering demonetization, Nirav Modi and Atul Choksi, Rafale, electoral bonds and even the supposed Himalayan misdemeanours of Adani.

Among the political leaders who had been questioning the Modi-Adani Group nexus loudly, was TMC MP Mahua Moitra. It helped that she was a former banker, and thus could comprehend the intricate web of complex financial subterfuge. But the government was adamant on stonewalling the growing chatter on business chauvinism, which favoured the Gujarat-based group. Moitra would soon find herself in a salacious gossip-strewn exposé, sponsored by a team that comprised a young billionaire businessman, a ruling party's member of Parliament who had many a face-off with Moitra and someone who Moitra termed as a 'jilted ex'.[9] A media trial ensued; the misogyny of India's male-dominated political culture was evident. Probing Adani's wrongdoings was forbidden territory. There could be unpalatable consequences.

One of India's most dangerous, continuing fault-lines is opaque, anonymous political funding. It is mired in cobwebs. It threatens its democratic resilience, as it makes the political system hostage to large, unscrupulous, self-serving donors. A by-product of this shady quid pro quo arrangement between industrialists and businessmen with political parties is what has been christened by the media as Operation Lotus. Nothing proved how the Indian political ecosystem had become like an electoral marketplace, a modern-day bazaar, where one could trade in buying and selling of elected lawmakers, as the crisis which engulfed the state of Maharashtra in June 2022 showed. The BJP, seething with rage that its one-time ideological Hindutva comrade-in-arms, the Uddhav Thackeray-led Shiv Sena, had dumped its powerful partner and formed a government with the NCP, and the Congress had been waiting to strike back, by hook or by crook. The latter option was relatively easier. Thus, one fine evening, an exodus of Shiv Sena MLAs began. The first port of call was Surat in Gujarat. It then moved to Guwahati, before culminating near the strikingly picturesque beaches of Goa. Operation Lotus, as it was charitably branded, as if a blossoming of divine acts of purity, soon took over. An unofficial stock exchange for MLA trading had been inaugurated.

Over the following weeks, a dumbfounded nation saw Indian democracy being crucified, reduced to a reprobate desi version of Game of Thrones being played out in real time. The BJP had successfully created a split in the Uddhav faction of the Shiv Sena, led by the party's reliable sheet-anchor turned Trojan horse, Eknath Shinde. Who funded the frequent chartered flights and the unlimited five-star hospitality provided to the defectors group? One saw obnoxious scenes of adult legislators being whisked away under armoured security to unknown destinations, their mobiles phones seized from them, to ensure that they were incommunicado with the outside world. This was state-sponsored kidnapping by mutual consent. There could not be a better example of the Stockholm Syndrome. In the new normal, TV anchors gushed with perceptible goosebumps, 'This was a masterstroke by the Chanakya of Indian politics: Amit Shah,' the putative Indian Machiavelli. If threatening MLAs with tax raids with the Damocles sword of cooling heels in a cold cellar or allegedly offering them dollops of black money was considered ingenious chessboard play, then Shah had mastered the art of *Saam, Daam, Dand, Bhed*, which was the Kautilya genius's forte. The lesser said about the role of the governor, Bhagat Singh Koshyari, the better. This constitutional position has been reduced to being a perfect puppet of the party at the centre, or a glorified courier service. The slushy melodrama ended with Shinde becoming the chief minister, with former CM Devendra Fadnavis, agreeing to play second fiddle, which was akin to swallowing personal humiliation to dethrone the real nemesis: Uddhav. 'Resort politics' was the popular new buzzword in India's political dictionary. Public immorality was on the mannequin; up for sale to the highest bidder. But the Maharashtra soap opera had still another twist.

In July 2023, Ajit Pawar, India's political football with a leather-thick texture, surprised his ageing uncle, the veteran craftsman of Indian politics, Sharad Pawar, by joining the Shiv Sena (Shinde)-BJP government in Mumbai. The sordid, stenchy game of backstabbing moved in a higher stratosphere. Ajit Pawar's early dawn swearing-in ceremony of 23 November 2019 was an unforgettable masterpiece in the obscene universe of post-2014 political skullduggery. The brazen treason, the shameless genuflection before the muscle-money combo, insulted the poor voter, whose choice on the EVM ballot had been transferred to another election symbol. Pawar had done it again. Just a week earlier, India's Prime Minister Modi, had lamented the oceanic Rs 70,000 crore irrigation scam for which Pawar was the principal accused, calling the NCP a 'Naturally Corrupt Party'.[10] A few days later, NCP was part of the Shinde government in Maharashtra.

Democracy's low point was reached on several occasions, but one of them was when the Supreme Court had to chide Rahul Narwekar, the speaker of the Maharashtra assembly, for dilly-dallying on resolving the Maharashtra political impasse. The SC warned of taking action unilaterally on its own, if Narwekar (who symbolized Maharashtra politics; he had switched from Shiv Sena to the NCP and then joined the BJP), did not pass a verdict before 31 December 2023. The speaker was evidently evading taking a decisions on the disqualification pleas filed by the opposing camps of the original Uddhav Thackeray-led Shiv Sena. Constitutionally, it could be postulated that he faced Hobson's choice; the government could face a serious crisis if the Eknath Shinde faction was deemed to have no tenable case for continuing in office along with fifteen other legislators. Alternatively, it could lead to another round of legal battles challenging the speaker's decision, which was already bound by SC strictures.

In late October 2023, about a dozen Apple iPhones in India received a dreaded message from the phone company: 'State-sponsored attackers maybe targeting your phone'. Among the receivers of this threat notification was Rahul Gandhi, Mahua Moitra, Shashi Tharoor, Sitaram Yechury, etc. Significantly, they were all Opposition leaders. Ever since the Pegasus spyware issue had come up in 2019, when WhatsApp video calls were allegedly intercepted by hackers, the fear of government surveillance remained. While Apple Inc. issued a caveat that it could be a false alarm, out of 12 million iPhone users in India, why would only a dozen political personalities be under watch? There was reason to be worried. *The New York Times* had investigated the Pegasus deal and concluded that it was indeed part of the USD 2 billion defence deal that India and Israel had struck in 2017. The Modi government, of course, had publicly chosen to be noncommittal. But why?

Operation Lotus (the new Age name for horse-trading) was not a novel experiment though; the BJP had tried it with immense success in Goa, Manipur, Arunachal Pradesh, Karnataka, Puducherry and Madhya Pradesh earlier. Toppling state governments using questionable methods meant that India's democracy was being overtly destabilized. There was a state of forced disequilibrium, which would lead to shabby governance, poor administrative functioning and usually, high levels of corruption. The people of India were being cheated, their faith in the democratic process was being mercilessly thrashed and openly ridiculed. The resistance, regrettably, was feeble. The media was a mute spectator, and the SC remained the only shield for judicial and constitutional safeguard. The public seemed confused with the whataboutery; didn't the Congress play the game of cloaks and daggers before too? This was therefore poetic justice, according to the loyalists of the BJP. Corruption in India's public life was no longer seen as a shameful betrayal of public trust; instead, it was being applauded as an act of adroit statecraft. The road ahead was a downhill drive. One man for sure was paying a huge political price for vocalizing the gradual corrosiveness of an already frail moral architecture: Rahul Gandhi.

Rahul Gandhi had become BJP's marathon, unending paranoia. He was targeted in what appeared to be prima facie, a nebulous case of defamation following his diatribe against the Modi-Adani nexus in Parliament. In a speech at Kolar in Karnataka on 19 April 2019, Rahul had said, 'Why do all the thieves, be it Nirav Modi, Lalit Modi or Narendra Modi, have Modi as the common surname?' Such sarcastic wordplay is garden variety rhetoric during an election campaign. But a BJP MLA from the state of Gujarat, by the name of Puresh Modi, filed a case against Rahul, alleging that he had hurt everyone belonging to the Modi community. What followed was mind-boggling. Gandhi was not just convicted by the Surat sessions court on 23 March 2023 for his ostensibly disparaging remarks but remarkably, punished with a two-year sentence. This is where the odd judgement became foxy; in the history of criminal defamation since the British era law had come into being, no one had ever been punished for such a long period—the maximum period applicable. But interestingly, under the Representation of People Act, 1951, the two-year imprisonment barred Rahul from political contestations for six years, with disqualification being immediately effected. The Lok Sabha Secretariat notified it with extraordinary alacrity on 24 March 2023 itself. On 22 April 2023 Gandhi was even forced to vacate his 12, Tughlaq Lane residence where he had lived since 2004. The Modi government seemed to be in a frantic hurry to disenfranchise Rahul. In July, the Gujarat High Court upheld the Surat court judgement, forcing Rahul to take recourse in the highest court of the land. A nation watched with breathless anticipation, the possibly uncertain future of a political leader who had just walked the Bharat Jodo Yatra and captured national imagination, facing potential circumscription. The Supreme Court would now be the final arbiter.

'Had [the] sentence been a day lesser, provisions would not have been attracted, particularly when an offence is non-cognizable, bailable and compoundable. The least the trial court judge expected was give some reasons to impose maximum sentence. Though appellate court and high court have spent voluminous pages rejecting stay on conviction, these aspects are not considered in their orders,' said the Supreme Court in its historic correction of the past anomalies in August 2023.[11]

After a hiatus of over four months due to brazen harassment, Gandhi was electorally rehabilitated. But a serious question had been raised: Were India's lower courts insulated from political manipulation? India's Supreme Court, its last surviving bastion of hope, was seized of one major amendment to criminal law, whose frequent applications by a powerful state put at risk the fundamental right to freedom of speech of every Indian citizen: sedition.

I was extremely disappointed that the Congress did not forcefully support one of its liberal lynchpins, Dr Shashi Tharoor, when he (along with several journalists) was accused of sedition for his tweet on the violence that took place during the 26 January 2021 Republic Day celebrations.[12] India's ramshackle democracy was like a car with four flat tyres; it was going nowhere. The accusation was heavy handed and borne out of clear malice against those who were supporters of the agitating farmers. The sedition charge was made under Section 124A of the IPC which the Congress had promised to abolish if it came to form the government in its 2019 election manifesto. The Congress manifestos are well-researched; they are not ideologically fly-by-night. While many in the commentariat think the Congress merely provides superficial lip-service to freedom of speech but starts to tergiversate at crunch time, the fact is that the party is a lot more liberal than it is given credit for. Its problem has been political communication; clarity in expression. For inspiration, it had to just look at Pandit Jawaharlal Nehru, who had said: 'The sooner we get rid of it [Sec 124] the better.'[13]

The Modi government came up with a new sedition law in India under the Bharatiya Nyaya Sanhita Bill, 2023, which was more draconian than the original Nazi formulation. The Supreme Court has held that sedition can only be invoked when there is a clear and imminent threat to public order or violence. The new law goes beyond this definition and criminalizes any dissenting opinion or criticism of the government. Second, it is vague and ambiguous in its definition of sedition, leaving it open to arbitrary and subjective interpretation by the police authorities. Terms such as secession, subversive activities and separatist activities are not clearly defined and can be used to target any individual or group that challenges the dominant narrative or ideology of the state, or political party in power. Third, it is disproportionate and excessive in its punishment, creating a chilling effect on the exercise of democratic rights and civil liberties. The bill does not provide any safeguard against misuse or abuse of power and does not prescribe any bail provisions for the accused. The bill is a clear attempt to stifle dissent and dissenters in India. It goes against the spirit of democracy and constitutionalism that India prides itself on. It is a step backwards from the progressive and liberal values that India aspires to uphold. The bill should be scrapped and replaced with a law that respects and protects the right of the citizens to express their views freely and peacefully. To understand how draconian a quasi-police state could be even without the harshest laws, one had to just see the plight of India's decorated women wrestlers.

It was a sight that reminded one of a documentary on despotic states where leather-booted policemen wearing military colours, looking like minatory stormtroopers, have a violent blowup. Delhi policepersons hammered India's national champion sportspeople with heavy batons in a hostile scuffle, for daring to protest against the central government. Actually, just a lone individual, a popular representative of the ruling party, the BJP, whom they accused of being a sexual predator. Someone who had on multiple occasions, molested them. They had evidence. They wanted justice. They demanded respect. They wished to protect their honour. They were women, whom the government had promised to protect and promote as part of their Beti Bachao, Beti Padhao campaign. That slogan sounded spurious; deceitful.

They were no ordinary people; these were sports stalwarts who had brought India handsome prestige in the most competitive international tournaments; they were Olympic champions. They were Commonwealth stars. They were Asian Games gold medalists.

Modi would invest substantial time to do photo shoots with them when they returned to India and would post the pictures on his Twitter account. But to protect Brij Bhushan Singh, the accused Wrestling Federation of India supremo, Modi seemed to go into hibernation, almost pretending that the wrestlers did not exist.[14] Taking the cue from him, many BJP leaders accused the suffering women wrestlers of being part of a political conspiracy to besmirch the Modi government.[15] A handpicked committee of eminent sportspeople including P.T. Usha and Mary Kom were asked to investigate the allegations of sexual harassment. Their report was not made public. It seemed strange. Ultimately, after months of protest, which began in the cold wintry days of a chilly New Delhi in January 2023 at Jantar Mantar, the wrestlers were forced to plead for justice before the Supreme Court, the last frontier of constitutional guarantees.[16] The disingenuous government could not prevent the investigations any further. The Delhi Police were forced to file an FIR. The chargesheet later corroborated the wrestlers' accusations. It said Singh was 'liable to be prosecuted and punished for offences of sexual harassment, molestation and stalking.'[17]

The public humiliation of Vinesh Phogat, Sakshi Malik, Bajrang Punia, Babita Phogat and several sportspeople was a pathetic low for India. In a country that has been called the most dangerous place for women in the world,[18] where on an average eighty-six rape cases are reported daily,[19] the Modi government had pushed self-made global assets of India's soft power triumph to the precipice of desperation and shame. The state behaved like a cold-blooded fiend which obviously had no empathy, no feelings. Everything was about measuring the likely political impact of sacking Singh. Singh is a parliamentarian from the constituency of Kaiserganj in the most crucial state of Uttar Pradesh, BJP's vote-catchment preserve. The entire drama ended in a sorry consequence, reducing the reputation of India to a pitiable nadir. With the government dilly-dallying on holding fresh elections to the Wrestling Federation of India, the country was officially derecognized by United World Wrestling federation. This meant that in all world championships, they could not officially belong to the Indian contingent. They would be clubbed in a group called Neutrals. No national anthem would be played for them at the podium. No Indian tricolour flag would represent them either. The irony was that BJP would continue with their rodomontade about being the authentic 'nationalist' party. India's moral degeneration looked irreversible. Even the scalded Manipur continued to simmer. And few seemed to care.

Large parts of Manipur remained under curfew even as September 2023 dawned on its tattered hinterland, its panoramic hills throbbing with both apprehension and abjectness, the valley, broken and bruised. After creating a national uproar over hate crime, communal killings, and a gruesome gangrape captured on a videotape, would the neglected Northeastern state quite simply fade away from public memory? India's new-found finesse in quickly 'moving on' from bloodcurdling tragedies was a post-Modi phenomenon. In political circles, it was jokingly called 'Godi media management'; the Big Media's efficacy in changing headlines at the drop of a hat. Or creating an alternative narrative (Modi burnt the candle at both ends after the Manipur carnage began, was an oft-repeated balderdash to neutralize the damage done to the prime minister's endless silence on the state). But in a world dominated by social media escalations, the exit door for Modi from the stigma of Manipur's ethnic conflict remained tightly shut. It was the global media that unrelentingly pursued the reality of Manipur's orchestrated annihilation of social kinship. It was politically motivated. Few dared to say so, but the reluctance of the BJP to sack the CM N. Biren Singh, who belonged to the majority Meitei community, spoke a million words. Thus, CM Singh, displaying unreservedly his fear and insecurity of being exposed to the whole world, stooped to playing the unsurprising gambit: attacking the messenger itself. The Manipur government filed an FIR against the Editors Guild of India for stoking divisions in Manipur, based on one photograph which was wrongly captioned.[20] It revealed the Modi government's mindset; truth was an unwelcome visitor. It had to be summarily shot down. But what could they do when the European Parliament issued a terse communique? The resolution told the recalcitrant Modi government to 'take all necessary measures and make the utmost effort to promptly halt the ongoing ethnic and religious violence, to protect all religious minorities, such as Manipur's Christian community, and to pre-empt any further escalation'.[21] The European Parliament went a step further in categorically stating who the possible culprits were. It said that the communal violence was provoked by 'politically motivated, divisive policies promoting Hindu majoritarianism', besides militant organizations on both sides. Unfortunately for the BJP, they could not file an FIR against the Strasbourg-based institution. But where they could, the government was quick to demonstrate that none who opposed them would be spared.

In his research paper published on 3 July 2023 at the well-known Ashoka University, professor Sabyasachi Das exposed an earth-shattering analysis of alleged electoral malpractice in India. Titled *Democratic Backsliding in the World's Largest Democracy*, the abstract said,

Democratic backsliding is a growing concern globally. This paper contributes to the discussion by documenting irregular patterns in 2019 general elections in India and identifying whether they are due to electoral manipulation or precise control, i.e.: incumbent party's ability to precisely predict and affect win margins through campaigning. I compile several new datasets and present evidence that is consistent with electoral manipulation in closely contested constituencies and is less supportive of the precise control hypothesis. Manipulation appears to take the form of targeted electoral discrimination against India's largest minority group—Muslims, partly facilitated by weak monitoring by election observers. The results present a worrying development for the future of democracy.[22]

In the concluding remarks of the investigative report, Sabyasachi came to some epoch-making discoveries: 'The results point to strategic and targeted discrimination against Muslims, in the form of deletion of names from voter-lists and suppression of their votes during election.'[23]

Ideally, Sabyasachi's astonishing revelations should have resulted in a parliamentary debate, and for sure, about whether the 'Othering' project of the BJP was now tactile. Was the disenfranchisement of India's largest minority group being engineered surreptitiously, step-by-step, by keeping it covered, resulting in their gradual irrelevance as a voting constituency in the political ecosystem? The paper created a huge social media hullaballoo with the Opposition finding a legitimate basis for its constant bugbears—the abuse of EVM machines which are prone to tampering and hacking, gerrymandering, deliberate voter suppression, the use of statistical data to isolate voting patterns and therefore threaten minority communities, and the pusillanimous conduct of the Election Commission, which had been reduced to being a handmaiden of the government. But not surprisingly, the reverse happened. Ashoka University was palpitating with fear of having got on the wrong side of a vindictive government that saw no limits when it came to requitals. Their consternation was understandable, given what had happened to other iconic academic institutions like the Jawaharlal Nehru University, Jamia Millia Ismalia and the Aligarh Muslim University. The easiest option to mollify the enraged bully from South Block was to disassociate itself from Das's findings. They did precisely that. Das's paper was called out for being his own personal passion project—one that did not have the official approbation of the Ashoka University. The latter had shrewdly distanced itself from the eye-popping unmasking of a potential fraud in India's elections. In a liberal democracy, Das would have been lionized as an outlier, a saviour of representative democracy; now, in a controlled environment where people even whispered gingerly and spoke only on WhatsApp calls for fear of being snooped upon, he had no chance whatsoever. Within weeks Das had resigned from his job, another victim of the Orwellian environment that India had become under Modi.[24] On 23 August 2023, members of the Intelligence Bureau landed up at the Ashoka University campus looking out for the marked research disciple.[25] Das had to set out to correct a glaring fault-line of Indian democracy; he had ended up being driven into a cocooned corner, deserted and forlorn, while the long uneven shadows of ominous jackboots drew perilously close. Das was not the only one staring blankly at shadows on the wall. The son of a popular chief minister was receiving death threats.

Udhayanidhi Stalin, a minister in the Tamil Nadu government and son of the chief minister and head of DMK party in Tamil Nadu, M.K. Stalin, suddenly became the breaking news item in early September 2023. Addressing a close audience of Tamil Nadu Progressive Writers and Artists Association, he talked of equality, social justice and the deleterious influences of the caste system. He went on the offensive, calling Sanatan Dharma, a term that is subject to various interpretations depending upon the philosophy or ideology which one practices, similar to diseases like 'dengue, malaria, and Covid-19,' which required to be exterminated.[26] All hell broke loose. The BJP leaders accused Stalin Jr of hate speech and a call for genocide. They quickly conflated the context of Tamil Nadu's social movements and political-ideological origins, inextricably intertwined with the preaching of Periyar Ramaswami and Ambedkar, to a pan-India controversy because it played into the majoritarian manuscript. A priest from Ayodhya, clearly enraged, called for Stalin's beheading and put up a reward of Rs 10 crores. No one asked how a religious priest could amass such a massive personal fortune or mobilize donations for such a violent act. Stalin was booked in different parts of the country and provided extra security, even as he reiterated that his call was for removing the caste system and was not intended to hurt religious sentiments. As elections appeared closer, Modi jumped into the fray, telling millions of his frenzied minions, through his office bearers, to give 'a befitting reply' to Stalin. India was spinning into a disturbing whirlwind to damnation. Jobs, inflation, health, education, skilling, everything else could wait. The communalization of India was moving into fifth gear. Would India's secular Opposition parties rise above their internecine squabbles and prevent Gandhi's India from mutating into a majoritarian bulldozer?

The Opposition parties in India had discovered, rather belatedly, that the BJP under the Modi-Shah duo had a clear mission: destroy each and every political party, each indistinguishable from the other. The modus operandi was straightforward—accuse them of dynastic domination, parochial ambitions, outright corruption, incompetent leadership and, when nothing else worked, there was always the silver bullet of 'being anti-national, anti-Hindu, pro-Pakistan and anti-development'. It was a concentrated cocktail, at once both cheap bluster and utter falsehood, but when headlined on every TV channel every day, it found millions of gullible takers.

While regional parties and the Congress had thwarted the BJP in several state elections (sixteen of the twenty-nine states were governed by them), which had provided a counterbalancing relief, the future looked uncertain and often frightening. All Opposition parties faced threats of imminent arrest, a buyout of supporting legislators and the prospect of being electorally destroyed. Jharkhand, Delhi, Maharashtra and Tamil Nadu (where BJP-appointed Governor R.N. Ravi violated all norms of constitutional proprietary by actually reading out an altered speech instead of the one given to him by CM Stalin's cabinet) were being subjected repeatedly to external tornadoes. Something had to give. It resulted in what would be called the Patna Summit.

A crisis brings odd balls together. An emergency can unify those with a bitter past. An existential crisis can coalesce even erstwhile sworn enemies. The Patna Summit (the Opposition meet deserves a dignified moniker), which had several of India's leading Opposition parties come together under the indefatigable stewardship of Bihar CM Nitish Kumar, was an extraordinary happenstance—make no mistake about it. Expectedly the BJP ridiculed it as a desperate measure for the survival of dynastic political parties, a shibboleth that has worked wonders for it in the past, but which may be now on tired legs. The BJP has a laundry list of powerful dynastic family members, and the world knows that internal democracy within it is at best a meretricious chimera. When was the last time one saw a genuine contest for the party president's position? Whether it was Nitin Gadkari, Rajnath Singh, Amit Shah or J.P. Nadda, they were anointed chiefs with much ceremonial fanfare, mostly by the big bosses sitting in the RSS office at Nagpur. The BJP appeared frazzled by the Patna Summit, and it was not unusual at all. If its political arrogance is so insuperable that it cannot read the obvious, it could be committing political hara-kiri. As for the Opposition, it was quite literally the throw of the last dice. They must make it count. There are five fundamental factors that they needed to ruminate on.

First, they need to define the big-ticket issues on which they can checkmate the BJP. There is no dearth of them—youth unemployment, stagnant real wages of the unorganized sector, a shrinking middle class, Adani's alleged contract grabs and the rent-seeking culture, the savage laceration of constitutional institutions, democratic deconsolidation and above all, the poisonous toxification of India's society. The list is long. If all the Opposition parties repeatedly hammer the same message to their electorate, their collective crescendo could overcome the silence of the largely lame-duck mainstream media. Their voice could catch the national public imagination, apropos Adani, Manipur, the wrestlers protest, etc., where they have punched above their weight.

Secondly, they needed to draw some red lines; under no circumstances should they indulge in ad hominem attacks on each other even inadvertently (Congress versus TMC, Congress versus AAP; they needed to stop their silly slugfests). But bad habits die hard, so this was easier said than done but it was a prerequisite for increasing public confidence. It gives the BJP an opportunity to tarnish them as opportunistic dealmakers who basically despise one another. Thorny issues among them had to be recognized but they could be amicably put on the backburner till 2024. The big prize was 2024; nothing should distract the Opposition from the main goal.

Third, the Opposition needed to have a clear strategic plan to address what is likely to be BJP's 2024 electoral pitch; for instance, welfare expenditure on the poor, digital revolution, Ram temple construction, infrastructure investments, and of course, its USP, the guardian angel of Hindutva anxieties. The government's failures were eye-popping—massive unemployment, rising income inequality, high incidence of borderline poverty, destruction of small and micro businesses, food inflation, large-scale corruption, crony capitalism, etc. In short, they need sharp rejoinders which are evidence-based but also communicated savvily. After the mammoth rout of the BJP in Karnataka and their disgraceful apathy in handling Manipur conflagration, the dubious double-engine bromide had probably derailed permanently for the BJP. For the Opposition, new doors have opened. Politics is fluid. Things change.

Fourth, while single-Opposition candidate per Lok Sabha seat was a great idea, it might turn out to be a utopian construct (vote transfers are not a linear by-product). Further, it might have two contrarian consequences. BJP and Modi could play the victim card and mobilize disaffected, nonchalant voters from all sides, by portraying themselves as being victims of 'collective targeting'. Secondly, rebel candidates (propped up by the cash-rich BJP) could end up demolishing the entire gameplan, by making it equivalent to a multi-party contest. A better idea could be for political parties to only contest if they have an authentic opportunity to win; the 'low-hanging fruits strategy'. Or else, not contest at all. But this should be left to their discretion. This will be the litmus test of political leadership in 2024.

Lastly, Hindutva is an emotive subject; it is vaccinated against rational economic arguments (jobless growth, high prices, poverty and destitution). It even overpowers intellectual conversations about institutional debilitation and governance failures, and abstruse paradigms such as the Idea of India, which many do not understand. None of these worked in 2019, as India was swept away by the hyper-majoritarian nationalist war cry. The Opposition needed to challenge BJP's faux nationalism, and de-hyphenate Hinduism from Hindutva. They must take the bull by the horns; they cannot ignore the elephant in the room, Hindutva. Modi needs just 40 per cent of the majority Hindu vote of 80 per cent (giving BJP 32 per cent of aggregate vote share) to be at the halfway mark. It would help if the Opposition realized that a vast section of the majority population is religious, but not communal. There is a need for dialogue and engagement with them. BJP has so far received a red-carpet free pass. It has got away with crummy claptrap using polarization politics, totally unchallenged by confused adversaries.

The Opposition alliance needed to respond and do so quickly and efficiently.

In summary, it was important that the Opposition recognized that defeating the BJP must not be treated as just an electoral objective, but a national responsibility given the visibly clear and present danger of authoritarian and divisive proclivities of this government. The road to Delhi could go through Patna, instead of Lucknow. If even the former US President Barack Obama, sitting thousands of miles away, publicly expressed solicitude about India disintegrating, it was time to start stitching up. Sometimes winning becomes a duty. The battle for the country's emaciated soul needed to be fought. But first, the Opposition alliance needed a name, the most defining common denominator of intent. In the Bengaluru Summit, the bedraggled assortment came up with a masterstroke: INDIA.

In calling the alliance of twenty-six political parties INDIA (the Indian National Developmental Inclusive Alliance), the Opposition stumped the BJP, leaving them knocked out, like a pugilistic punch from a heavyweight champion. What's in a name, goes the colloquial quip. Apparently, plenty. The BJP, riding lazily high on its easy capture of the hyper-nationalist narrative, was nonplussed. Attacking INDIA was impossible; completely shoehorned, they appeared tongue-tied and on the defensive. By the time the third summit ended at Mumbai on 1 September 2023, INDIA had quickly come up with a catchy tagline: *Judega Bharat, Jeetega India.*

For the INDIA alliance, the crucial missing piece of the jigsaw puzzle still remains seat sharing among mutually suspicious partners, especially in the states of West Bengal, Punjab, Delhi, Kerala, etc. But there was no denying that the monumental hurdle of intent had been crossed. The wager was on the future of the country itself. One data that portended the dismay within was the number of passport-holding Indians who were deserting the illusion of Achhe Din and moving to greener pastures abroad.[27]

The breakfast was over, and I was about to step out for a meeting in Gurugram, when a kindly looking gentleman stopped me in my tracks. 'Mr Jha?' he said. We exchanged pleasantries. Talking heads in India are frequently recognized in public places, as most are familiar with their bark and bite from watching them practically every evening on their TV screens. I was no exception to that rule.

'I am dismayed,' he said. 'It has become intolerably frustrating, listening to the constant social tensions in India. I live abroad in Canada, and I have decided that enough is enough. All we see on TV is Hindu–Muslim conflict stories. I have come here to sell all our ancestral properties and pack our bags forever.' He looked crestfallen. What could I tell him, but a lukewarm 'I understand'. I had heard such hand-wringing many times before.

The gentleman from Canada continued: 'Things have become so bad, that in our family we have constant fights in our WhatsApp groups. My brother-in-law and I are not on talking terms. We are all living on edge, with strained relationships being the rule rather than the exception. It was not like this before.' I nodded. 'I have heard this from many people. Same experience.' Let me narrate another such anecdote, among many others of a similar ilk.

I am a huge cricket buff, so I do occasionally travel to watch matches. I was watching the India vs England One-Day International match at the storied Lord's, the Home of Cricket, in July 2022, when a young man who appeared to be in his mid-thirties occupied the seat next to mine. Perfunctory confabulations followed and judging by the casual impertinence with which his companion spoke to some spectators nearby, it was quite apparent that they felt at home in Westminster. 'Are you a resident here or a visitor like me?' I asked; it was basically a rhetorical enquiry. He sipped his rose wine, and said: 'No, I moved here permanently two years ago. I am a jeweler by profession. The pollution in Delhi was unbearable, and the health infrastructure collapse during the pandemic gave us the heebie-jeebies. There was no way I was going to expose my young son to the nightmare of dengue and mindless traffic jams.' He looked like a comfortably satiated businessman living the high life in a First World country. Strawberries and cream best defined his new universe. There were many who were renouncing Indian citizenship in droves.

People don't leave countries unless there is a compelling push or pull factor. Or both, as is often practically the case. Besides the enormous financial cost of a global relocation, there is the larger emotional upheaval of being sequestered from close family bonds. Unlike the western world, India is not yet molded in the culture of hyper-individualism or materialism, where people seek greener pastures in pursuit of either big green-bucks or their own passions alone. Family considerations have a disproportionately huge influence on personal career and business decisions. Shifting overseas is a tectonic shift, quite literally.[28] Thus, the startling data that nearly 16 lakh people surrendered their Indian passports since 2011 was an alarming figure, a wake-up call. Was this a secular trend or are we experiencing the beginnings of an unstoppable and exponentially rising migration? The #AchheDin in India mirrored the failed Make America Great Again slogan of Modi's chum, Trump.

There are four factors that could have played a role in people crowding the immigration counters.

Firstly, India still suffers from a Third World syndrome. Despite becoming one of the top three world economies (based on purchasing power parity index) and attracting FDI (foreign direct investment) of USD 83.57 billion in 2021–22, most still struggle for basic amenities—clean drinking water, public health infrastructure, efficient inter and intra-city transport systems, educational architecture, organized traffic management, and assured delivery of government services. The second wave of the Covid pandemic, which was a frightening nightmare, has seriously wounded, if not altogether irretrievably damaged the confidence of many. That is why it is the First World countries, such as USA, Canada, UK, Australia, Italy, Singapore, etc., that most are peregrinating to.

Secondly, Ease of Doing Business is a myth. The fact that the World Bank actually scrapped the Ease of Doing Business ranking was because it was being rigged, its publicly known parameters of ranking subject to easy manipulation. India still suffers from bureaucratic cobwebs, the legacy of the pre-1991 days, still lingering in bits and parts. And even where red tape may have become somewhat more elastic, the fact is that the government can still be arbitrary and ad hoc. The MSME sector in India has taken a huge business hit, and for every hyped Unicorn there are hundreds of start-ups that struggle to get elementary business-friendly support. Any surprise that 23,000 dollar-denominated millionaires have left India between 2014–18 alone? The average age of Indians settling abroad is thirty-eight years; they are at the zenith of their entrepreneurial enterprise. That is an enormous loss of human capital.

Third, there is diminishing faith in the country's institutional governance and criminal justice system. Legal roadblocks, institutional harassment, cumbersome delays in closure of disputed cases, bribery and corruption, etc., have corroded business confidence, besides frightening individuals who believe they are up against a tyrannical state power. Although many of these grievous fault-lines have existed since time immemorial, they have got exacerbated in recent times. The airport is the shortest route to salvation.

Lastly, the rise of millennials and zillennials is redefining conversations on the politics they inherit. Globally, the new aware young people are upending the old social order. They are challenging the antediluvian status quo. The fact that India has only 43 per cent in the working-age population who are employed is a reflection of the unemployment catastrophe.[29] Those who go to study abroad, therefore choose to remain there. But the young are also distressed about climate change, gender discrimination, sectarian warfare, authoritarian bullying, rising crime graph and political radicalism. It is therefore hardly a surprise that the highest immigration exits are happening from China, Russia and India, along with Iran, Qatar and Hong Kong.

For sure, attractive destinations in the First World nations is a magnetic draw. But the real reason people are leaving is because they are losing hope in the land they grew up in. For all the Vishwa Guru positioning he sought, Modi had triggered the Great Brain Drain 2.0, not being able to hold his best together. He was not being able to hold India together either. In India, few questioned the government. But when Modi travelled abroad, the truth could not be camouflaged.

'Mr Prime Minister, India has long prided itself as the world's largest democracy, but there are many human rights groups who say that your government has discriminated against religious minorities and sought to silence its critics. As you stand here in the East Room of the White House, where so many world leaders have made commitments to protecting democracy, what steps are you and your government willing to take to improve the rights of Muslims and other minorities in your country and to uphold free speech?' This is what Sabrina Siddiqui, a *Wall Street Journal* correspondent asked PM Modi when the latter had made the magnanimous concession of allowing one question that he would respond to in a press conference in the White House in June 2022, alongside President Joe Biden. Modi, of course, outright denied that India had any minority intimidation issues at all. But bedlam followed. Siddiqui was viciously abused on Twitter and social media as a 'toolkit lobbyist' out to slur India. The fact that she was a Muslim of Pakistani origin accentuated her miseries, eventually forcing the

White House officials to issue a statement in her defence by terming the trolling as 'unacceptable'. The BJP IT cell went on overdrive. Their thin-skinned behaviour, which resulted in a vitriolic outburst, only confirmed Siddiqui's question, exposing Modi's attempt at circumlocution and denial of home truths. A burnt down school library was further proof of the raging campaign of divisiveness in India.

It was not just India's Mughal history that was being deodorized from school textbooks, but even one of their ancient libraries that housed 5,000 rare books, historical documents, old manuscripts, copies of the Quran, artefacts, furniture, etc., which was being burnt down, vandalized, snuffed out of memory. On 31 March 2023, a 113-year-old Madrasa Azizia school in Biharsharif, in Nalanda district of Bihar, was attacked by a 1,000-person mob, New India's rabid militia force.[30] They hurled petrol bombs to reduce the grand library into black soot. They openly made inflammatory statements and carried weapons, which they were only too keen to use. The occasion was ironically, a religious procession for Ram Navami, which is meant to be a unifier. In the name of religion, India was being handed over to charlatans and arsonists. Political patronage for them was assured.

As elections drew near, the BJP raised the noise levels to a crescendo on the Uniform Civil Code (UCC). UCC is part of Article 44, which defines the Directive Principles of State Policy in the Indian Constitution. While deemed desirable by most, it had not been mandated within a time-bound framework, as the founding fathers had left it to India's social metamorphosis over the decades to discover its own common personal code, through a mutually acceptable consensus. Religious diversity meant differing norms for divorce, alimony, remarriage, property inheritance, adoption, etc. But for the BJP, it was one of its Holy Grail agendas, a monochromatic provision in law, suited its majoritarian construct.

Nuh in Haryana was evidence of the spreading specter of polarization under political sponsorship. Historical research has established that communal frenzy is not generated spontaneously, despite the boiling temperature under the serene surface that political parties consistently maintain. It is a just-in-time ready-to-riot model; but planning is an essential prerequisite to make the hysteria escalate. The main purpose is to get a huge headline, and then exploit the spillovers in the following months at the ground level. Nuh was one such trial balloon on 31 July 2023 which performed to expected results. The occasion was perfectly selected; a religious procession called the Brijmandal Jalabhishek Yatra sponsored by RSS's militant offspring, the VHP, through a primarily Muslim-dominated area.

A nefarious cow vigilante by the name of Monu Panesar, a member of the Sangh Parivar's Bajrang Dal, who had pleased Right-wingers with his devilish butchering of two Muslim men (Nasir and Junaid) suspected of cattle trading, announced through a video that he would make a special appearance during the religious walkathon. Panic spread, and quite understandably, fear reigned. After all, Panesar roamed free, with the cocky demeanour of an accused who knew the ruling BJP government was providing him fulsome fostering? A young twenty-two-year-old Imam was murdered, and a mosque burnt to the ground. A ruckus naturally followed, with an outnumbered police force being attacked with stones, water bottles and even guns. Everything that happened was predictable to the perspicacious eye. It is estimated that seven people died, sacrificed at the gate of political fortune-telling. Mahapanchayats, which are powerful congregations of elected village superiors, then upped the ante; they called for a complete economic boycott of Muslims in Haryana, essentially demanding their physical expulsion from the state and economic marginalization in case they still dared to overstay their presence. They were the new 'termites' in the social order who had to be promptly sundered from the state's future. It did not stop there. Adityanath's bulldozer model, adopted by various BJP state governments with undisguised relish, then went into operation. Several homes of the poorest residents in shanty towns were remorselessly pulled down, leaving families, women, children and breadwinners, penniless, broken and shattered. In Modi's New India, the criminal justice system was being inhumanly trampled upon, with spectacular apathy. The wayfarer anarchists were the rulers of the killing fields. They were BJP's vote bank. But India probably, and thankfully, still has traces of a moral conscience left in a few. There were two Indians who chose to call out the campaign of calumny and intolerance. They were G.S. Sandhawalia and Harpreet Kaur Jeevan.

The two judges of the Punjab and Haryana High Court minced no words: 'Apparently, without any demolition orders and notices, the law and order problem is being used as a ruse to bring down buildings without following the procedure established by law. The issue also arises whether the buildings belonging to a particular community are being brought down under the guise of law and order problem and an exercise of ethnic cleansing is being conducted by the State.'[31] Shops burnt, houses razed, lives destroyed, fear in their sunken eyes and sadness in their hearts, most non-resident migrant labourer's left for their homes in Uttar Pradesh, Bihar, etc. It was a tale of segregationist politics disrupting even the most susceptible lives on the outskirts of India's billboard-shining USD 5 trillion economy illusion. It was brutal. The irony was unmissable; the distance between Nuh and Gurgaon is just 45 kilometres. The latter is home to phosphorescent malls, tall, turquoise-coloured glass sheeted skyscrapers which house multinational companies, global management consultancies, big Unicorns, and tech start-ups. The area abounds with wellness centres, souped up gymnasiums, fine dining restaurants and watering holes. DLF is one of the hottest residential addresses in India; biometric tests alone can ensure entry into those hallowed quarters. But Nuh was a reminder to Indians that their New India was founded on prejudice, pilferage of the poor and ransacking of its moral ethos. Minorities, particularly Muslims, were being made to feel unsafe and uncertain about their future in the country they chose to live in after Partition in 1947. But nobody expected the antipathy and bitterness to enter school classrooms.

New India was being inexorably altered by the minute. No one was being spared its venomous indoctrination. Not even a seven-year-old schoolboy in a small village called Kubbapur, near Muzaffarnagar in Uttar Pradesh. The video that surfaced on social media in late August 2023 established the unchallengeable reality of partisanship, particularly Islamophobia, which had percolated down India's veins, permeating its whole body politic. The merchants of abomination were succeeding in converting incited resentment into a retail franchise. A young boy was being repeatedly slapped by his fellow classmates in Neha Public School, one by one, at the strict instructions of the class teacher. Tripti Tyagi goaded the impressionable kids on—kids who were being encouraged to embrace violence and humiliate their contemporary. The boy was a Muslim. The driving imperative was religious identity. Tyagi came up with a cunning pretext; she was physically challenged and could not get up to punish the boy for not completing his homework. Thus, her excuse ran, she had empowered the children to beat him up. This was a modern-day delegation of authority which was at striking odds with the concentration of power in the political hallways of New Delhi. The boy could be seen all swollen up, sad, scared and shriveled. In a way, he was a microcosm of the minority communities in India: frightened and tentative, not aware of what lay ahead for them. Would Tyagi have dared to violate an upper-caste Brahmin boy for, let's say, forgetting his colouring book at home?

The answer is a loud No! This was a flagrant case of communal profiling. In the video, Tyagi could be heard uttering derisory language against Muslims; the normalization of belittlement of their community had been accomplished once again.

The boy's parents promptly removed the innocent victim from the school. They had little choice. The traumatized kid was allegedly so terrified, he could not sleep. How could he? One can imagine the invidious nightmares that he was getting, the dread of what his future would be in his country of birth? The boys who had obediently thrashed him were those with whom he had probably played cricket before, sung songs in a chorus with them, among them the national anthem on Independence Day. But here he was, India's national banner headline. An object of permanent political rhubarb. The BJP's polarization strategy was delivering dividends clearly; they were 'catching them young'. The unwilling conspirators, the reluctant pupils who were ordered to carry out the boy's degradation were all potential Frankenstein's monsters in the making. Presumably, for them, the teacher was only doing her job. In fact, they had all been disciplined soldiers of the school and deserved to earn brownie points for slapping their fellow classmate, perhaps. Tyagi had demanded that the boys should slap their classmate harder, in case, she saw their animal spirits flagging.

Exactly ten years earlier, in the same city of Muzaffarnagar, India had seen the most destructive communal riots after the 2002 Gujarat pogrom. Over sixty people were killed, and thousands were rendered homeless. In the general elections that followed in 2014, the BJP won 71 of the 80 seats, propelling Modi into 7, Race Course Road. As the woeful incident showed, hate once sown mushrooms into a banyan tree. It takes deep roots and expands outwards rapidly towards the sky. It even provides shelter to the perpetrators of hate. And for sure, it blocks the sunlight of compassion and tolerance. Compassion, tolerance and love is something that I learnt a lot about from a soft-spoken caring man when I was a child. He wore a skull cap.

He invariably called me on every auspicious occasion, whether it was the New Year, Diwali, Ramzan, Christmas or Holi. His voice had an unmistakable identity, deeply gruff and somewhat fissured, his long sentences punctuated by an intermittent hiatus, as he spoke with the laboured precision of a man who had seen many moons and experienced the vicissitudes of life. When he asked me about my family's whereabouts, it had a unique solicitude about it, a caring disposition that touched me. When I told him that Insha Allah all was well, he responded with a deep sigh of satisfaction in his inimitable baritone: Bahut Achcha! The conversations were usually one-sided as he enquired separately about everyone's health, studies, career, future plans etc. and I replied with monosyllable's, a calculated mix of restrained exasperation and smothered impatience. But he carried on notwithstanding, his relentless curiosity for the mundane and the meaningless quite unbeatable. Often, I would just interrupt his soliloquy and ask him a diversionary question to prevent long-winded explanations with an orchestrated artifice: what's happening otherwise? Was it really cold in Bhagalpur? When was he likely to go on a holy pilgrimage? He answered them all with delightful exuberance, overjoyed at my seeming interest in his life. He was overjoyed that I asked him about his life; that was the trigger he needed. The conversations thereafter became like one unending monologue of a travel enthusiast returning from an adventurous spree, but it gave me enough room to navigate my e-mails on my mobile phone. Of course, I did the ritualistic interruptions to convey my active engagement with his storytelling, with a recurring 'Really? That's so nice!' When we would finally terminate the imbalanced exchange, he would wait for me to hang up, perhaps secretly hoping that I would linger on, encourage his mindless intrusions into my sanitized corporate life. I didn't give him that opportunity. This old gentleman, who called me with uncanny predictability and indulged in one-sided marathon conversations with me, where I am a mere eavesdropper, was called Nurul Hasan.

In the mid-1960s, Nurul Hasan had met my father when he was a professor of economics at Bhagalpur University, Bihar. He desperately needed a job, and my father had assiduously engineered a temporary role for him in the administrative department of the academic institution. Subsequently, he became a permanent orderly. Hasan was overwhelmed, obligated beyond description. But in those days, instead of attending to clerical or office work, he spent more time taking us siblings out for rickshaw rides, cinema watching, toy shopping and generally entertaining us with his fantasy tales. He was like a quasi-family security guard-cum-odd-jobs-man, passionately overseeing the domestic constitution with painstaking involvement. The joint family system had an extended appendage; Nurul Hasan was its inelastic glue. He was a Muslim, in a household where we were traditional, archetypal Brahmins. We grew up under his watchful eyes, my parents fully reassured that we were in safe hands. Bhagalpur was then considered to be a communal hot button as Hindu-Muslim riots had scarred the local population. But Nurul Hasan was our guardian angel. When my father died in 2002, Hasan called to assuage me; he said that the heavens will be in distinguished company of the late professor, his benevolent guru. It helped. He continued to call me as if he thought it was his moral duty, an unfinished task as it were, after my father's death. I would suffer his intrusions into my chaotic corporate life with monotonous regularity.

Around 2016, Hasan seemed a worried man. His anxiety had a lot to do with getting his son a job as a computer operator. For fear of nepotism and favoritism, I told him that we could not recruit him in our own organization in Mumbai. I don't think he was entirely convinced, given his wonderful experience with my father. Times have changed, I told him. I will check with others, amongst fellow colleagues, who could be more willing, I reassured him. I could visualize him nodding reluctantly in agreement, perhaps telling himself that I was offering impeccable lip service or genuinely did face certain challenges. But the fact is that I did nothing for him. Or his son. Asking a friend in Mumbai to help a young unemployed Muslim boy from Bihar did not seem to be a workable proposition, post-2014. Honestly, I did not even try. I was still trying to understand Modi's New India myself. I needed help too.

In a country which has the third largest Muslim population in the world (200 million), Nurul Hasan is not a solitary example of goodness. If you go to Mohammed Ali Road during Ramzan, you will be submerged more by the prodigious warmth and simple hospitality of the people than those mouth-watering delicacies at Sulaiman Mithaiwala. Some of the most endearing, simple folk with a gentle refined sophistication in their articulation, reminiscent of the Lucknowi tehzeeb, still come from bearded taxi drivers in Mumbai. Muslims in India have added a majestic colourful hue to our social and cultural character. Besides three former presidents, including Dr A.P.J. Abdul Kalam, top-notch civil servants such as Wajahat Habibullah and S.Y. Quraishi, music lyricists and composers such as Sahir Ludhianvi and Khayyam, tabla maestro Zakir Hussain, the inimitable Mohammad Rafi, the spirited animation of cricketers Zaheer Khan, Yusuf Pathan, Mohammad Shami and Mohammad Siraj when representing their country in blue jerseys, the cinematic charm of the Khans, the mesmerizing poetry of Javed Akhtar, it is one exciting, electric, eclectic mix that makes India. Azim Premji has made Wipro into a global software behemoth as much as the Khorakiwalas have done with medical research in Wockhardt. Thus, India's political narrative being redefined using the religious Hindu Rashtra call had me befuddled.

As I thought of my childhood caretaker Hasan, I was sure that India's collective consciousness needed to embrace its multifarious mishmash and resist the dangerous campaign of divineness that had crept up, unchallenged mostly. Economic growth and religious fundamentalism are inversely related. There is a trade-off. That's why Achhe Din had remained just that—a fantasy. Truth is, it was always a pipe dream as the Hindutva chariot traversed across India after May 2014. Maintaining social harmony is always a work in progress in an interconnected world, with communities interspersed all over the country, and the world. In every community, there are good people and bad people. But the bad lot are usually in a minority. But when the good emulate the bad, the lines of distinction get obfuscated. India's plurality remains its most reliable safety net. I was reminded of the famous Urdu poet Rahat Indori Quereshi's famous words: *Sabhi ka khoon hai shaamil yahan ki mitti mein, Kisi ke baap ka hindustaan thodi hai.*

About a few years ago I got a missed call late at night. It was from Nurul Hasan. For the first time in a long while, I returned his call. He was overtly overjoyed. A simple gesture, but it meant the world to him. I promised that I would bring him to Pune, where my father spent the last few years of his life. 'Seriously?' he said, unable to hide his excitement and happiness. It's a promise that I intended to keep. But did not. Nurul Hasan died in 2023, a lone number in one of India's death registers. I wondered how he felt about the broken country that he was leaving behind.

One of the biggest threats to the future of world democracy, already being attacked by populism and demagoguery, is fake news. But with the sudden arrival of Artificial Intelligence (AI), that risk proliferates exponentially. Tech analysts are already calling it the 'Oppenheimer moment'—one that has the sinister strength of world-changing capabilities, like the bombs that befell Hiroshima and Nagasaki in Japan in 1945. Geoffrey Hinton, ex-Google, and considered unanimously to be the Godfather of AI has stated:'Aliens have landed, and people haven't realized because they speak very good English.'[32] Sam Altman, CEO of OpenAI, is deeply worried. 'I am scared. AI needs regulation.' With roughly half the world's population engaged in electoral voting next year in the countries of USA, Britain, India, Indonesia, etc., the challenge to minimize manipulated news and disinformation campaigns will be a tough one. In India, more so, where the AI tools are already being utilized to create deep fakes. It happened with the protesting women wrestlers on 28 May 2023.

Vinesh Phogat and Sangeeta Phogat were detained by Delhi policemen and prevented from walking to the new Parliament building inaugurated by PM Modi. Then a strange twist occurred. The photos on social media showed the protesting wrestlers sporting a happy smile, looking thrilled and delighted that they were arrested as they were being whisked away to a police station.[33] It was a morphed picture, a deep fake; an image-altering algorithm had been at work. The WhatsApp University campaign wished to portray them as duplicitous crusaders for women's rights, who were merely posturing for cheap publicity. Right-wing tech hackers had distorted the real expressions of the wrestlers, which bore their fury and frustrations.[34] The Fourth Industrial Revolution indeed has nuclear capabilities if generative AI could add to man-made fake news. In 2024, all democracies would be vulnerable to filter bubbles, micro-targeting of echo chambers, and the uncontrollable scalability of ai bots to spread false messages. The biggest risk in countries like India will be the ability of AI to augment discrimination, and deepen biases based on group identity, particularly religion and ethnicity.

Says historian and philosopher Yuval Noah Harari in *The Economist*:

In a political battle for minds and hearts, intimacy is the most efficient weapon, and ai has just gained the ability to mass-produce intimate relationships with millions of people. We all know that over the past decade social media has become a battleground for controlling human attention. With the new generation of ai, the battlefront is shifting from attention to intimacy. What will happen to human society and human psychology as ai fights ai in a battle to fake intimate relationships with us, which can then be used to convince us to vote for particular politicians or buy particular products?[35]

The uncertain world of VUCA[36] has a towering mountain to climb with the advent of generative AI. The future is unknown, as it always was, but the black clouds were unmissable.

Out of the blue, it was announced that Arundhati Roy, the Man Booker prize winning author, who was a trenchant critic of the Modi government's fascist ways, would be prosecuted for provocative speech and promoting enmity between groups, for certain comments made about Jammu and Kashmir in the year 2010. After thirteen long years, a moth-eaten old case, was being revived to torment a voice of resistance.

Former Chief Justice of India Ranjan Gogoi, who had controversially accepted a Rajya Sabha nomination from the BJP-led government, along with Jagdeep Dhankar, vice president of India, astoundingly questioned the 'basic structure' of the Constitution itself. Kiren Rijiju, the former law minister, publicly harangued retired SC judges, who berated the government's intimidatory tendencies, issuing ultimatums which bordered on perversity. He even called them part of 'an anti-India gang'. A former SC judge who headed the NHRC praised Modi in eloquent terms, calling him a 'versatile genius'. It reminded one of a former FM's quip:

'Post-retirement job influences pre-retirement judgements.' The judiciary's reputation was in jeopardy. One of the surviving columns of democracy was shuddering. In an extraordinary development, the Modi government tabled a bill in August 2023 to drop the chief justice of India from the three-member panel to select election commissioners, an independent constitutional office, to be substituted by a senior cabinet minister. The subversion of Indian democracy stood assured if such amendments were to become law.

Actor Shah Rukh Khan epitomized my generation—the one that saw the landmark 1991 liberalization, satellite TV, Tommy Hilfiger sweatshirts, Motorola mobile phones, Indian software companies listed on Nasdaq and the multiplex boom, among other things. The among other things also included a darker, more real India that was battling historical demons, the rise of an aggressive, assertive majoritarianism and an economic boom that had created widening income inequalities. Khan's golden period of Bollywood ascension (he was actually lionized unofficially as King Khan) coincided with the Babri Masjid riots, the 2002 Gujarat riots and the rise of populist nationalism in the form of the BJP. Khan may have been the most recognizable Indian abroad, but back home, he was being regularly scrutinized, his every comment or film subjected to Sangh Parivar bloodwork. Khan had to regularly prove his commitment to his Indian passport. His superstardom-driven career nosedived around the same time that he was being reminded by Modi's party that he was a Muslim first. Khan's father had been a freedom fighter for India. Shah Rukh had even worked in a film called *My Name Is Khan*, fully aware of his religious identity, and the suspicious eyes that greeted them in the post-9/11 world.

It was a wet evening in September 2023 in Mumbai, when adhering to family traditions from the days of *Dilwale Dulhaniya Le Jayenge*, we went to see the heavily promoted film *Jawan*, on the first day itself. Khan towered above everyone else, his famous fluffy hair, now tonsured for the role of Rathore, revealing a well-maintained bald moon. He looked like a dangerous man to mess around with. But as the film unfolded, Khan drove the normally sober and restrained South Mumbai multiplex audience into a wild frenzy. Catcalls, whistling, shouting, clapping, it was all there. The only thing missing was the clanging of coins. Khan played a social messiah, a selfless defender of the common Indian. A Robin Hood avatar. But when he spoke to the millions of moviegoers looking them in the eye, asking them to abstain from hate, and avoid religion/caste/money/corruption in choosing their candidates, reminding them of the power of the pinky, the audience went delirious. It was unbelievable. A brilliant but of late beleaguered Bollywood actor, rediscovering himself, was inspiring people who had paid money to watch him entertain them. He had also given them a from-the-heart lesson about their own dormant strength. He had suffered his worst personal agony after his parent's early death and his son had been unfairly incarcerated in a drug abuse charge. Things had not been easy for him; the actor is clearly a master at masquerading his hurt sensibilities. People trusted that he best knew what he was talking about.

As we left the theatre that night, there was that animated buzz in the air that one can sense when suddenly people express their inner thoughts, gleefully acknowledging their own repressed nobility, often weaponized by anger in the past. Their own capacity for introspection and change. Was it a bellwether for a conscience shift in a country that had remained largely detached by everything going wrong around them? *Jawan* would turn out to be Bollywood's biggest blockbuster hit, overtaking Khan's earlier record-setting *Pathaan*. A Khan mania gripped the country, and it seemed surreal that a hardcore masala potboiler with an inane plot would be a palliative for a dismembered social polity. Even if ephemeral—till the next Friday blockbuster would be the new tinsel-town story—in general, everyone felt happy. And one.

The Comptroller and Auditor General of India (CAG) report on 2G Spectrum auctions and misallocations of coal blocks, had brought down the UPA government. The ridiculous, Amazonian figures of notional loss, which had no mathematical logic, became a media circus. The Congress was destroyed. But when the CAG exposed massive scams in the Modi government's highways project called Bharatmala, mostly through inflated costs multiple times higher than what was initially budgeted, the mainstream media looked the other way. The estimated scam could be over Rs 7.5 lakh crore. The Bharatmala project envisaged building 75,000 kms of national highways at a cost of Rs 15 crore per km; but this was subsequently hiked to a whopping Rs 25 crore per km, providing a 66 per cent escalation in commercial value. In the case of the Dwarka Expressway, the escalation was staggering; it went up from Rs 18 crore to Rs 250 crore per kilometer, an unimaginable fourteen times. But none of these were ever allowed to be seriously debated. It was not a level playing field.

The real challenges for India, sadly, never get discussed in Parliament, on television channels or on multiple public platforms with the earnestness they deserve. Barring some liberal think tanks, online news magazines and portals, NGOs, literature festivals, authors from the 'Khan Market gang', YouTubers, etc., India remains in the dark. With acute income inequalities, transparent campaign finance, corruption-free delivery of public goods, public health infrastructure and high-quality affordable education, climate change and environmental protection, animal welfare, egalitarian taxation policies, women's empowerment, police reforms, greater budgetary allocation for sports, neighbourhood relationships beyond Pakistan and China, etc., they do not find airtime. In the last ten years India has wasted itself over programmed antipathy between

Hindus and Muslims, a distasteful diversion from what should have been India's decade of economic prosperity, societal dynamism and a seat at the global high table for responsible statesmanship. Modi's biggest mistake has been his delusion that economic growth and social disharmony can coexist. They can't. They are mutually interdependent; they are inversely related. Life always has trade-offs. Modi blew away two huge public mandates because of his primal preoccupation of humiliating Muslims, making them feel excluded from the mainline India story. Modi may still be remembered as the man in whose tenure the Ram temple was built, but for Ram Rajya, India will have to wait for another prime minister.

India is an inchoate democracy, battling a peculiar inertia to big-ticket changes that can uplift the quality of human life. Politicians have failed India. And I dare say, Indians have failed themselves by being married to mediocrity. That after 2014, the darkest decade since 1947, Modi was still, according to some opinion polls, a strong contender (if not favourite) for winning the 2024 general elections, is what a film critic would call as a 'tragicomedy'.

A country usually become a mirror image of its leader. Nehru was an inclusive, progressive, freedom-loving, far-sighted and erudite intellectual, who dreamt of an India that would be a hallmark of syncretism. He was a rare global statesman. If India today is seeing the tentacles of identity politics subsume it, if it has become a vortex of seething asperity, people mutually suspicious of each other, with civil liberties being ferally crushed, it must seek answers within. Countries are made by the choices their individuals make. Nations are not an abstract, abstruse concept; it's the denizens of the state who determine what it means, what it stands for.

I was ending 2023 by probably entering the Guiness Book of World Records for being the longest suspended member of the Indian National Congress party. On social media, I was regularly trolled for supporting Congress, who according to #ModiToadies had shut the door on me forever for my publicly expressed transgressions. I was shamelessly genuflecting, they said, begging for a homecoming, crawling on both my knees. But the grand old party was not inclined to be accommodating, was the general refrain. I found that weird. I was happy to be the lone outlier in Indian politics—someone who had refused to join another political party, although doing so has become the norm and practice in India. Self-aggrandizement precedes ideological fidelity. Politics has become like a monetary transaction in a vegetable market; everything is negotiable, tradable. There is a reason why I was not up for sale. Or would never be.

I grew up under the gentle guidance of a benign professor of a father who surrounded himself with books. When he was not taking orders from my belligerent mother, or not sleeping or going for his walks, he was reading. Among the books he gifted me, while I was still in school, was *The Story of My Experiments with Truth* by Mahatma Gandhi and *The Discovery of India* by Pandit Jawaharlal Nehru. While I would end up finishing reading them over quite a few years (they competed with Enid Blyton and Archie comics), they moulded my ideological moorings. They defined me as not just the person I was, but the humanity within me that I hoped I would never compromise upon. Or forget. The Congress would go through many trials and tribulations and several kamikaze missions in its political journey. It has itself to blame. But it still possesses the foundational stream of the India that I had grown up in. My own political status was irrelevant in the larger context of a national renaissance that India deserved. I was just happy to be even a cog in the wheel. I don't think anybody understood that. And frankly, I did not care. I felt like Don Quixote. I have always believed that it is better to lose but to fight for the right side of history. Although in May of 2024, I do hope that the right side is winning. India needs to breathe. Again.

I have been a huge movie connoisseur, as you may have already discovered if you have reached the last page of this book. Among my favourite films of all time is the Stephen King-written, cinematic masterpiece, *The Shawshank Redemption*. As two broken men, both tragic victims of circumstances, reunite in the last shot, after years of serving jail time, near the blue waters of the Pacific Ocean, a voiceover says: 'Hope is a good thing; maybe the best of things. And a good thing never dies.'

Hope.

EPILOGUE

'I simply can't build my hopes on a foundation of confusion, misery and death ... I think ... peace and tranquility will return again.'
—*Anne Frank*

I RAN TO answer the doorbell, before anyone else could, because my father would applaud whoever demonstrated a sense of urgent responsibility. My siblings often did not bother, because they were both lazy and were aware of my need for constant parental validation. In front of me stood a man in his early thirties, his jet-black oily hair combed backwards, revealing a large forehead on a bespectacled face with clean-cut sharp features. He had a fountain-pen moustache which was immaculately trimmed; it would have made Hercule Poirot raise an eyebrow in appreciation. In his hand, he carried a large rectangular box, wrapped in a thin bright red film, with the image of Lord Ganesha in bright yellow. He asked for my father.

'He is not in,' I told him. 'These are some pedas for your family. I wanted to say thanks to him personally. But it's okay. I will come again. You see, I just passed my PhD examination. Your father was my academic guide.'

I smiled, and said congratulations and thank you, as I looked forward to devouring the round shaped balls made of flour and sugar. Then out of the blue, the gentleman bent down and touched my feet with both his hands. I was too aghast to respond instantly. For a boy in the ninth grade at school, this was an unexpected, freaky experience. But I collected myself quickly to say, 'Please Sir, why did you do that?' His reply was something I will never forget. 'You are a Brahmin. In touching your feet, we get blessed.' 'But you are much older than me?' I protested. 'That does not matter. You belong to such an upper caste. You are a Maithili Brahmin after all.' As the Sanatan Dharma comment of Stalin Jr reverberated across the country, I was reminded of this unusual, unforgettable episode of my school days.

In television debates, one of those most quoted, least understood and frequently cherry-picked to suit own's own convenient interpretation is Dr Bhimrao Ramji Ambedkar. The Sanatan controversy, thanks to Stalin Jr's reckless allegories which was roguishly electrified by the Sangh Parivar, was a perfect case of flagrant manipulation of truth.[1] For sure, young Stalin used harsh language, which politicians with grey hair and balding plates would usually avoid, but was he actually exhorting for the genocide of the majority community believers, or was he taking about annihilation of caste, as the famous title of Ambedkar's classic treatise highlighted? Truth is, it was Modi's alleged encouragement to his robotic lieutenants to pushback which had a sinister halo around it and exposed BJP's ulterior power play. It was evident that the saffron party was being unconscionable; anyone who has read and known Ambedkar's ideology would know that the Dalit messiah saw India's caste structure as primarily an overarching Brahminical hegemony, an upper-caste monopoly where the Shudras were to be delegitimized, dehumanized for the perpetuation of the former's domination of Hindu society. It would compel Ambedkar to abandon Hinduism altogether and convert to Buddhism in 1956, just before his death. In fact, Ambedkar's call for making Hinduism classless was explicitly strident, 'Because we have the misfortune of calling ourselves Hindus, we are treated thus. If we were members of another faith none would treat us so. Choose any religion which gives you equality of status and treatment. We shall repair our mistake now. I had the misfortune of being born with the stigma of an Untouchable. However, it is not my fault; but I will not die a Hindu, for this is my power.'[2] Ambedkar frequently altercated with several on the subject, but his philosophical warfare with the man of the moment, Mahatma Gandhi, whose own views on the Hindu caste system was perhaps less radical, surprisingly traditional and more opportunistic, made for fascinating contrasts. On caste-segregation decades later, Ambedkar has been proven right, and Gandhi, wrong. Ambedkar would indeed carry out his fateful promise, converting to Buddhism in the October of 1956 along with 3,65,000 of his disciplined followers. He unfortunately died just a few months later.

For BJP, the Sanatan issue was a godsend—a fresh chance to fuel social dedolomitization in the communally susceptible Hindi heartland, by positioning Stalin Jr, whose DMK is part of the INDIA alliance, as being anti-Hindu. In a normal universe such a fabrication of reality would have been dismissed contemptuously as the insidiousness of a malevolent mind. But with powerful TV channels commanding millions of remote controls under his magical spell, Modi and the BJP were always assured of a successful outreach programme. It did not help that the counterattack from a tentative Opposition was lukewarm; the understanding of Ambedkar, an intellectual behemoth who remained a fearless advocate of the socially marginalized, was low. Few understood how one man could be anti-Hinduism, anti-RSS/Hindu Mahasabha, anti-Congress, anti-Gandhi and at the same time be

India's first law minister who drafted the Indian Constitution. That learned individuals, social reformers and political personalities can have myriad beliefs, sometimes conflicting, occasionally influenced by circumstantial developments, or undergirded by personal experiences, or maybe driven by a visionary ideal, had foxed India's politicians of the current age. Everything was only perceived through a binary lens in the post-2014 Modi era; most forgot that both life and politics is actually fought in the large grey zone. Unfortunately for the myopic, avaricious BJP, the strategy, at least in the short-term, boomeranged. The AIADMK, the Tamil Nadu alliance partner of the BJP, fully aware that it would face complete decimation at the polls if it were to remain a mute bystander to the Sanatan debate, pulled the rug from under the BJP's feet. Modi stood checkmated in Chennai. But the BJP could be expected to still manufacture a communal tornado on the subject to reassure Hindus that Modi was its sole custodian. Better late than never, but Rahul Gandhi had other ideas.

In a much-needed, although belated, effort to set the record straight on Hinduism, he wrote in a one-off column in the *Indian Express*: 'A Hindu looks at herself and everyone in this ocean of life with love, compassion and respect because she understands we are all swimming and drowning in exactly the same waters. The action and duty to defend others, especially the weak, is what a Hindu calls her Dharma.'[3] Rahul had intelligently distilled core Hinduism as it is—ecumenical, eclectic and enlightening. It contrasted with the BJP's immoral gameplan of usurping the majority religion and converting it into a majoritarian vote-catching exercise, which had only wrecked India's social tapestry with dark consequences. Rahul and the Opposition were fighting back to save one of India's fast depleting resources, tolerance. It was an uphill task for sure, but it had to be done. They were not alone. One man, a veteran of decades of political experience, decided to take the bull by the horns. He resurrected an issue which is anathema to the saffron platoon—the caste census.

In politics, old is gold. Although most political parties are guilty of not recruiting fresh talent because of internal sloth and power structures, fearing a youthful rebellion down the line, the flip side is that like wine, politicians get better with time. There is no substitute to experience—the experience of dealing with unpredictable voters, reading the tea leaves, being backstabbed by one's most trusted ally, preempting the competitor's wily moves, navigating the shark-infested waters of shady carpetbaggers and political entrepreneurs. One man who has weathered several storms and survived tumultuous hurricanes is Bihar's Chief Minister Nitish Kumar. He would end up giving the struggling Opposition a potent political weapon.

One of the most outstanding success stories emerging from the former PM V.P. Singh's electoral magic wand, the Mandal Commission report on backward classes reservation, was Nitish Kumar. The others being Samajwadi Party strongman Mulayam Singh Yadav and Lalu Prasad Yadav of the Rashtriya Janata Dal. Kumar, who was now head of a splintered Janata Dal (United), had sensed that BJP was going completely unchallenged on its Hindutva turf. BJP's salami tactics of divide and rule were based on its traditional ploy of anti-minorityism, which camouflaged caste discrimination. It was working politically, but the economic trauma of the poorer sections of Hindu society living at the bottom of the pyramid had been exacerbated in the absence of jobs, equal opportunities, food inflation and frequent disruptions, like the pandemic, besides violent consequences for breaching archaic social taboos. It was time to revisit the reality of unfair caste discrimination and the need for appropriate representation in government jobs and educational institutions buffered by state finances. A worried BJP resisted it as it would hurt the vanilla Hindutva vote consolidation strategy that it banked upon. Bihar went ahead and did a caste survey (a caste census, at least nomenclatural-wise was legally prohibited), whose results were announced in October 2023; its findings were earth-shattering. The last official census which was publicly shared was pre-Independence; in 1931.

Bihar's population of 13 crore people was overwhelmingly backward, but the magnitude was beyond astronomical, even if it was on expected lines. Extremely Backward Classes (36.01 per cent), Backward Classes (27.12 per cent), SC (19.65 per cent), ST (1.68 per cent) and General (Unreserved) was at 15.52 per cent.[4] Yadavs at 14.27 per cent formed the largest component of the state's denizens. The numbers indicated the disproportionately poor representation of OBC/EBC's in the larger ecosystem of public institutions of governance. In short, about 84 per cent of Bihar's population was socially backward and mostly economically deprived of a decent life, one that Ambedkar had envisaged decades ago. Nitish Kumar's government had reopened Pandora 's Box, one that the BJP had been clandestinely avoiding for a long time. With that one decision, the INDIA alliance, could have found the magic formula to defeat the progenitors of religious dogmatism and partisan politics. There was no denying that the caste census would be a major factor in the 2024 elections. Other states such as Karnataka and Tamil Nadu also announced their plans to do a state-specific caste headcount. An anxious BJP appeared mummified by the caste calculus trump card of INDIA. It only prompted the party to double-down on its peremptory ways.

Paranjoy Guha Thakurta is among the most intensely voluble and physically frisky people I have met. There is never a pregnant pause or a dull moment with him around. His body language mirrors his verbal messaging; he could as well be a retired Bollywood character actor doing a screen test for a second run in a probably volatile career. He is like a factory's boiler machine, running non-stop, firing away on all cylinders and re-fueling himself without any external support. I think when I first met him, he was perceptibly chagrined that I kept calling him Prannoy. When I joked that his entire name sounded like three different surnames, he forced a reluctant smile, before quickly moving on to what he thought were more pressing matters. Behind that unkempt beard and piercing sharp eyes lurked a feverishly passionate crusader. He was then the editor of *The Economic and Political Weekly*, a fountainhead of Marxist economics. We had been on TV shows a few times, the evidently Left-leaning ideologue scarcely hiding his contempt for my corporate background and my sweet spot for market-friendly reforms. I think Guha secretly despised my pro-capitalism (as opposed to his belief in communism), although he liked my secularism and liberalism and tempered call for responsible capitalism and inclusive growth. We hit it off. Thus, when I heard about Paranjoy being interrogated for several hours by the notorious Delhi Police, my heart sank. This was, in one word, disgusting. The harassment of a thorough gentleman, a spirited thinker and an investigative hack, even radical and polemical maybe, but a terror conspirator? The Modi government was clearly going cuckoo. And Gestapo like. What apparently got their goat was a vocal critic of theirs, Newsclick, an online news portal that saw the BJP as an avatar of Right-wing crackpots determined to annihilate Indian democracy.[5] Naturally, the thin-skinned party had to retaliate. They did. On TV, they call most critics as 'Left-wing loonies'. Modi calls them Urban Naxals. What they really meant is anyone who thinks BJP is a bunch of depressing dunderheads. Liking Karl Marx is a crime in India these days. NewsClick was in serious trouble.

The drumbeats of armed stormtroopers on the march appears like a regurgitation of Nazi Germany; in modern times, they are more stealthy, secretive and arrive unannounced at the crack of dawn. Paranjoy was picked up early in the morning of 3 October

2023, on the day following the anniversary of Gandhi's birth;[6] the irony was not to be missed. By the end of the day, Newsclick's founder and Editor-in-Chief Prabir Purkayastha had been arrested, along with his Human Resource Development head, Amit Chakravarti.[7] Forty-six individuals (employees, contributors, etc.) were made suspects in some allegedly nasty plot to destabilize India. The accusation was that there was Chinese funding of the portal which was being looked into, as if receiving overseas money from Shanghai was an anti-national activity. It appeared, prima facie, as another random hit job to curb press freedom. What gave the game away were the three questions that all those who were being investigated were asked: Did they write about CAA, Delhi riots and farmer protests? What were they supposed to write about? Akshay Kumar's towering performance in Selfie, Virender Sehwag's hair transplant or Vivek Agnihotri's scientific understanding of the Covid vaccine industry? India looked like a farce on a giant Ferris wheel in a circus, revolving like there was no tomorrow. Under the dubious and ill-defined 'threat to national security', even one's dog seemed unsafe. While Newsclick was accused of propagating Chinese propaganda, India's trade with its Asian rival had snowballed into a mammoth high of USD 135 billion, while a certain Chinese/Taiwanese investor who had featured in the Hindenburg-Adani reports as a shady money launderer, seemed to be doing just fine. Nothing added up. McCarthyism was let loose; anyone who was critical of the government was branded as a toolkit carrying conspirator, an Urban Naxal, a traitor to the cause of Bharat. Identifying them and subjecting them to harassment was the new norm.

The last time I met Paranjoy was at a coffee shop in a bookstore around the middle of 2023. In his customary style, he invited me for cappuccino at short notice between his several appointments, maybe because one of them got cancelled. As always, he spoke, while

I listened. He was full of ideas, projects, strategies and programmes. A man who cared for Indian democracy and its Constitution, even if my ripped jeans did not quite agree with his socialist predilections. But he was a worried man. He was convinced that the Modi government had Pegasus spyware on his phone. He made me switch my phone off and gave both our mobile phones at the café's counter, about a few tables away. I think I would be right in believing that when the Delhi Police knocked on his door when the birds had just begun to chatter and the early morning sun had begun to force some to squint, Paranjoy Guha Thakurta was waiting for them. He was in august company.

AAP's Rajya Sabha MP, Sanjay Singh, was taken in for custodial interrogation by the infamous ED in early October 2023 in the Delhi liquor policy controversy, joining his senior colleagues Manish Sisodia and Satyendar Jain in jail. Few seemed genuinely surprised at his incarceration, and that was the real worry. The Modi government's obsessive urge to intimidate political opponents was common folklore; like lynching, hate speeches, cronyism, fake news, communal stress, etc., it had been successfully 'normalized'. Authoritarian leaders follow a familiar pattern; they make the headline-grabbing event into a no-show over a period. They gradually, by brazenly executing their nefarious gameplans periodically, tire the news cycle. An exhausted and bored public either begins to believe their concocted fantasy, or partially adapts to the new environment as a fait accompli, or awaits the intervention of the Supreme Court, that final adjudicator of justice. It helps that given the cynicism of the Indian public with political leaders, the usual response is 'there is no fire without a smoke'. Corruption charges and police cases, pictures of booked leaders being jostled around by frightening men in khaki, do exactly what it is meant to do—damage reputations and sow a seed of doubt. In practically every TV debate where the ruling party was defenceless, their spokespersons would keep repeating, 'But Sonia Gandhi and Rahul Gandhi are out on bail'. The whataboutery became a red herring. It usually works as most people tend to take things at face value. It is a neutral position. The SC though did not seem too convinced.

In a damning observation on Sisodia's bail application, the highest court of India almost rebuked the ED, stating that except a statement by a person who was himself an accused who suddenly turned approver, there was no money trail to establish a kickback against the jailed deputy chief minister of Delhi. 'Where is the evidence against Sisodia? This will fall flat.'[8] Sisodia has been in jail for over eight months. The criminal justice system in India is in tatters. With the investigating agencies under state control weaponized to prosecute adversaries, India's political battleground was not a level playing field. In the case of AAP, a small party that had gained national status, it almost meant temporary extinction with its main brains-trust booked, leaving Arvind Kejriwal as the next one in the line of fire. On a show, the BJP spokesperson, with a combination of sadism and schadenfreude, sniggered: The noose will be soon round Kejriwal's neck. Whatever the ultimate outcome of the corruption allegations, political witch hunt was now a spectator sport. The fangs of fascism were closing in. A worried BJP, seeing a rapidly diminishing support in many states, was playing a dangerous card: Destroy the Opposition itself. Such heavy-handed tactics mostly backfire. The INDIA alliance stood firmly behind AAP leaders, even as several well-meaning Indians were now certain that the 2024 elections were a marker for India's democratic sustainability.

The vulnerability of India's polity was there for all to see. It's hypocrisy and double facedness stared at one and all. BJP leaders remained untouched by the dark long arms of the fearsome law; the Opposition was remorselessly hounded, chased by innumerable men in uniform as well as cleverly disguised avengers. There were many who did suspicious U-turns; abruptly becoming court-appointed whistleblowers from being the primary accused earlier. It was a deadly game of cat and mouse, where the cat wore iron paws and the mouse had their feet chopped. The end result was foregone. And yet, despite the horrid squalls blowing at them, the Opposition had to stand strong. And united. This was not a war for the faint-hearted. Or the weak-kneed. Rahul Gandhi had demonstrated over the Bharat Jodo Yatra that he definitely did not have either. The Opposition, taking cue, hung in together.

The decision of the INDIA alliance to boycott fourteen prominent TV anchors caused the anticipated hoo-hah. Since I know some of them personally, I shall in all fairness, not comment on specific individuals, barring one exception, Arnab Goswami. But more on that in a bit. Honestly, it was a controversial call, as most political decisions are. There is no denying that some TV channels, not just newscasters themselves, had a specific goal: unfairly ambuscade the Opposition while humming encomiums of the ruling party, the BJP. Whataboutery was the name of the game. The government could not be criticized, even if lakhs died during the pandemic, or the youth were twiddling their thumbs, sitting jobless in front of TV screens. It is true that even during the UPA days there was browbeating, and there were those who curried favour. But under the Modi government, the magnitude, intensity, frequency and brazenness of the hostility towards the Gandhi family, Congress, Opposition leaders, etc. had reached levels of jaw-dropping absurdity. The Right-wingers were an odd assortment, but they produced several loudmouthed analysts who hogged airtime with effortless comfort, with the anchors sheepishly indulging in their taradiddle. Most TV shows were lopsided, with the anchors themselves leading the charge, lowering audio feeds of the Opposition, interrupting rudely without any qualms whatsoever whenever they felt on the defensive and giving Opposition spokespeople limited bandwidth to make a compelling case. INDIA alliance was thus wholly justified in feeling shortchanged. And yet, I personally felt that they were making a mistake.

The households who watch news TV are not political junkies; they are fleeting consumers of news information. The majority of TV audiences watch soap operas, reality TV, entertainment and sports shows and now, streaming services. There is a short attention time for most, and at least some of them are reasonably aware of the manipulation or the disinformation which is done on prime-time daily news shows. I have always respected the viewers sitting at home and putting themselves through the ordeal of watching a manic circus in the search of truth. We should never underestimate the intelligence and the instincts of people, though; they are discerning, even if they can be bamboozled by a sustained propaganda for a while. Thus, avoiding TV shows only ends up opening further cleavages for the BJP to wade into, with the anchor playing the victimhood card. Most viewers would not care after a brief flirtation with the moral anguish of INDIA alliance's decision, and would continue to watch the same shows, and buy into the religious scissions being cleverly curated there. In short, the impact of the boycott is a diminishing returns exercise. Life goes on. While it is true that many anchors do not even try to camouflage their burlesque propensities, I believe that the answer lies in fighting them back and not allowing a vacant chair to be further sledgehammered, particularly during election time, when visibility matters, and every available inch of space is crucial. If nothing else, the INDIA alliance spokespersons could repeatedly call out the bias on the shows. But boycotting, although it does draw attention to the alleged discriminatory treatment of Opposition parties, is never a salutary long term magic bullet. It plays into the likes of the Fox News version of Indian television, Republic TV, and its popular celebrity anchor, Goswami, who capitalize on the vacuum.

A flustered Goswami, visibly enraged, castigated the INDIA alliance for possessing an 'Emergency mindset' because of being personally blackballed by them. But what followed was outrageous traducing which bordered on hate speech, with Goswami reading an inflammatory soliloquy from his teleprompter; he talked of the 'declared intent of many of its leaders to eliminate Hinduism, eliminate and annihilate Sanatan Dharma, and uproot Hindu traditions from the soil of our great nation'.[9] If one did a transcript test, this quote of Goswami could have been easily confused with that of an infuriated extremist of the Right wing pouring invectives amid a religious congregation. But this was a much-watched national TV channel which was religiously lionized by extreme Right-wing zealots, in particular. I mention Goswami for just one reason: to publicly confess to one of my worst errors of judgement. For several years when I did shows on his extremely popular show, Newshour, on Times Now, where he worked earlier, I continued to believe, often against a rebelling voice within, that he was a genuine anti-establishment anchor who daily thumped into the Congress/UPA because he cared for public interest issues. But I was embarrassingly off-kilter. Goswami had fooled me with his occasional anti-BJP shows (mostly vitriolic comments made by junior BJP leaders and members of the Sangh Parivar), and sometimes a phone call prior to a programme to brief me on how he was proposing to roast the BJP spokesperson, and why I should be prepared to apply the finishing touches. Hearing Goswami rave and rant against the Opposition was, to say the least, disturbing, no matter his personal ire at being singled out for being a prolific polarizer. Maybe that's why INDIA alliance had decided to say that enough was enough. They had a point for sure. But I would have still preferred to beard the wounded lion in his own den.

Out of the blue, in typical BJP fashion of pulling off staggering surprises, the Modi government announced a special session of

Parliament during 18–22 September 2023. The Opposition was naturally buffaloed; what was the agenda? The BJP went about peacocking that they would know what the agenda was at an 'appropriate time'. The mother of democracy, a self-congratulatory delusion, was in reality the big grandaddy of illiberalism, intolerance and, by a logical corollary, autocratic. Through the usual prism of mainstream media, wild speculation was encouraged; was it about One Nation One Election (Modi's secret fetish), would the government share details of the G20 Summit talks and tom-tom Modi's accomplishing of his cherished Vishwa Guru status, or maybe even a dramatic call for a snap poll, like Atal Bihari Vajpayee did in the mid-term elections of 2004, ahead of schedule? Eventually, it happened to be the one that many had assiduously second-guessed, the Women's Reservation Bill.

Politicians generally always link legislation to self-preservation, or political windfalls (one of the rare exceptions is the RTI Act, a landmark step in government transparency, which became an instrument which was used by the Opposition to grind the originator, the UPA itself, to smithereens). The Women's Reservation Bill (WRB), which envisages 33 per cent of parliamentary and state assembly seats being reserved for women, was not a novel, eureka-kind of breakthrough. In fact, it had been lying frozen in cold storage for years. The WRB had been passed by the Rajya Sabha in 2009 itself when the Congress was in government, but the UPA, a coalition which had significant others in the form of powerful regional satraps such as SP and RJD, was not able to build a national consensus. With elections looming in 2024, the BJP saw the women voters as a crucial vote-catchment bloc. The WRB was not driven by any genuine intent for women's empowerment and gender equality; it was for the BJP, beyond the usual rhetoric, pure electoral arithmetic. Let me explain that. There are innumerable reasons to expose the dichotomy between platitudes and performance, but two fresh episodes established BJP's hypocrisy. Which political party would callously ignore the public shaming of a gangraped woman being paraded naked (the repugnant Manipur tragedy) if they truly cared for women? Could one really be so foolishly naïve as to believe that a government that had become tone-deaf to the plaintive pleas of India's champion women wrestlers for justice against an allegedly serial sexual harasser, who was a powerful political personality of the BJP, really cared about their emancipation? Of course, there were the horrendous instances of Hathras, Kathua and Unnao rapes, where there had been shameful transgressions to protect both party and sympathetic offenders. It was unfortunate, and sickening. So why did Modi & Co. suddenly feel the need to address an issue that should have been sorted out in the first term of the NDA itself, if it was so important? After all, the WRB was one of the rare instances where both the BJP and the Congress seemed to be on the same page. The answer lay in the increasing turnout of women voters in both the state and parliamentary elections. In the 2019 general election, the female voter turnout exceeded their male counterparts for the first time in history. The trend was a critical input to all political parties. The BJP was merely calculating; it had seen which way the wind was blowing. But one politician had pre-empted everyone, demonstrating commendable clairvoyance; it was Congress's Priyanka Gandhi Vadra.

Priyanka's Congress manifesto for the Uttar Pradesh elections of 2022 had an extraordinary promise, hitherto unheard of; she promised 40 per cent of the assembly tickets to women candidates.[10] The slogan was eye-catching: *Ladki hoon, lad sakti hoon*. She was fully aware that the Congress barely stood little chance in the state, but her initiative was bold, pathbreaking, and showed a genuine appreciation of the need for women representatives in a state which has been historically patriarchal. It reminded one of her father Rajiv Gandhi's most groundbreaking reform: the bottom-up creation of Panchayati Raj, wherein village councils were mandated to assure 33 per cent of seats (many would end up seeing more than 50 per cent representation) for women.

With less than 15 per cent of women in the outgoing Parliament, the need for WRB was imperative. India is also ranked among the lowest categories at 148/190 globally on women's participation in a central parliament; Pakistan ranks higher. This anomaly seemed off-the-wall given that currently India has several political parties which are helmed by women; Sonia Gandhi, Mamata Banerjee, Mayawati, Mehbooba Mufti, Supriya Sule, all of them being venerated heavyweights. Once upon a time, Jayalalitha's vote on behalf of her party, the AIADMK, forced the Vajpayee government to resign. And of course, Indira Gandhi as prime minister, when India was battling misogyny (it still does) and inter-caste marriages were considered an unusual social event, even had the poetic Vajpayee hail her as goddess Durga after the defeat of Pakistan in the 1971 war which led to the independence of Bangladesh.[11] Doubtlessly, the time for the WRB had more than arrived. But the Modi government then threw in a spanner in the works; it could not conceal its sleight of hand on the WRB after all.

By stating that the WRB would only be implemented after the decadal census (due in 2021 but delayed on account of Covid) and the delimitation commission's report (due in 2026), at the earliest the Women's Reservation Bill can really be operational is at the 2029 general elections. That is, if one is providential. This wishy-washy, half-baked approach on an issue that deserved top priority revealed the BJP's suspicious commitment on the WRB. The Opposition called it sardonically as 'a post-dated cheque'. But Modi still hoped to garner the women's votes by trumpeting hype on his cylinder, toilets and free foodgrains trifecta. The self-respect of women, their own individual identity and their independence could wait.

An item that many had believed would be introduced during the special session of Parliament but was not, was changing the name of the country from India to Bharat. Modi believes in shock and awe politics, a headline-usurping, TV news anchor furiously screaming, social media wildly fulminating and everyone in near-panicking mode politics. It is a megalomaniacal trait—the visceral need to be frequently, if not permanently, in the voter's headspace. Anxiety usually peaks with two emotional reactions: fear and uncertainty. It is a high-octane combination. With the mainstream media ingratiating his capriciousness with unconcealed glee and a social media engine that was perennially lubricated to fire up melodrama and disinformation, setting an agenda was a cakewalk for the insecure prime minister. He reveled in it. The proposed name change to Bharat would touch the emotional chords of 140 crore people, including young children. No Indian was an exception whatsoever to this manipulated tugging of the heart, whichever name you batted for. Binaries, simple, uncomplicated, divisive, they are Modi's USP; there are many examples. Hindu-Muslim, nationalist-traitors, dynasty-self-made, Harvard vs hard work, Kabrisistan-Shamshan, patriots-urban Naxals, etc. The India-Bharat controversy was a willful experiment in gaslighting India, getting them all antsy for nothing, diverting attention from the issues which plagued the poor aam aadmi and trying to exploit the vulnerabilities of a country that was mostly unaware of its own history. Or even its Constitution.

To ensure that the name-changing drama got maximum mileage, Modi could not have chosen a more baronial platform; invitations to the G20 leaders attending the Delhi summit sent by Droupadi Murmu's office went from the president of Bharat, and not president of India, as has been the official convention since 1947.[12] Indeed, it was a sudden and fustian announcement. I am sure some foreign dignitaries were rechecking their itineraries to reconfirm that they were travelling to the correct destination. For all its pseudo-nationalist hauteur, the BJP was making a significant departure from established government protocol without even discussing the same with the Opposition or sounding out the Indian media and the public. The political vaingloriousness of the BJP and the authoritarian exhibition of Modi were lambent and for all to see. Since Modi does practically everything with the sole intention of converting it into a popular event meant for EVM impact, several skeptics saw through the calculated charade. Did he seriously intend to push through a constitutional amendment for India's name alteration, or was it his usual populist gimmickry to bolster north-Indian Hindutva votes? What had triggered this unwarranted blarney, because on the face of it, it appeared jejune? After all, India's Constitution allows for the usage of both India and Bharat, and until Modi created an unnecessary mawkishness around it, I don't think anybody was even thinking about it.

Article 1 of the Indian Constitution commences with 'India, that is Bharat, shall be a Union of States'; the name was adopted by the founding fathers of a newly liberated nation way back on 18 September 1949 in the Constituent Assembly. Evidently, the BJP leaders had not read it or else they would not have indulged in manufacturing bogus contretemps. The Preamble of India starts with 'We, the People of India.' India is liberally interspersed all over the Constitution. But one man seemed somewhat peeved that the country was being called India. It happened to be the RSS chief, Mohan Bhagwat. In a speech delivered just two days earlier to the big bombshell in the president's invite, Bhagwat had called for India being named Bharat henceforth.[13] Modi is an obedient disciple and owes his job to his ideological bosses in Nagpur. He was only studiously following orders from his strict superiors, clearly. The cultural patina, the Sanskrit origins of Bharat, the historical journey of the word from Vedic times, was meant to instill nationalistic pride in the Hindutva-prone voters, as opposed to the supposedly British hand-me-down, India. It was a pitch pregnant with speciousness, but in India, history is not a super-hit subject anymore. Further, it is being mischievously distorted. The fact that the Indus River could have something to do with the name was not considered. The decibel levels rose higher than the Chandrayaan rocket. Amrit Kaal, Niti Ayog, Sankalp ki Siddhi, Amrit Udyan (the new name of Mughal gardens in Rashtrapati Bhavan), Vande Bharat, etc., there was a planned injection of the Hindi language in the national vocabulary, as it is the one most favoured by northern India, BJP's mainstay. Given the political sensitivity, few addressed it head on. But it was Godzilla-sized; BJP was even passing legislation with names few could be expected to understand in down-south Chennai: Bharatiya Nagrik Suraksha Sanhita (Code of Criminal Procedure), Nari Shakti Vandan Adhiniyam (Women's Reservation Bill). Gradually, the normal usage of English in official use was being substituted by a more traditional Hindi speak. Lost in translation? Ironically, in 2004, when SP veteran Mulayam Singh Yadav, as CM of UP, following his own political compulsions, moved a resolution for changing the name of India to Bharat, he was opposed by the BJP.[14] But a lot of water had since traversed below the bridge. BJP leaders were now calling India 'a symbol of colonial slavery'.[15] The remarkable celerity with which the country's name had become a hot political potato, foxed many. The Opposition had a compelling rationale for BJP's apparent disorientation on a subject so sacrosanct like the country's name itself; the INDIA alliance name itself.

Even the most acerbic critics of the UPA would agree that the newly formed UPA+ alliance had come up with a masterstroke in calling itself, INDIA. How could Modi or the BJP attack the country's name itself? In any case, it was synchronous with the Idea of India. BJP, which relies heavily on ultra-nationalism, swaggering patriotism and national security and Pakistan-bashing as its electoral alpha, seemed bewildered. Their advertising agency was clearly struggling to come up with rejoinder sound bites and their home-grown copywriters seemed to go into a brain freeze. Catchy sloganeering templates are part of BJP's marketing encyclopedia: India Shining, Achhe Din, Sab ka Saath Sab ka Bishwas, Amrit Kaal; pithy catchwords that can be sold to gullible audiences as lofty aspirations. But unfortunately for them, the INDIA vs NDA dust-up, from the point of view of public perception, was a one-horse race. The response from the BJP was vapid and listless. It was also in poor taste.

Modi started equating INDIA alliance with the Popular Front of India, the Students Islamic Movement of India, etc., hinting at political outfits that had a militant character.[16] It was a pathetic effort to paint them as apostates. When that puerile effort went kaput, the BJP spokespersons were ordered to refer to INDIA as Ghamandia, a yawn-inducing pun at wordplay. They were further commanded to call it I.N.D.I.A. in a hilarious gamesmanship to not call the alliance, INDIA.[17] This was kindergarten level maturity being displayed by a political party whose braggadocio on being the largest political party in the world seemed to be inversely related to its cerebral content. That is why the panicky party, which looked spooked, did a dramatic announcement about calling India BHARAT. It was driven by political expediency. A friend casually told me something which I found was a brilliant exposition of Indian democracy; 'I can understand BJP playing communal games. But to polarize the country even with its name, that takes some gall, desperation, immorality and insolence.'

The momentum to rename India as Bharat began to accelerate quickly. In October 2023, it was announced that a special committee set up by the National Council of Educational Research and Training (NCERT), the highest academic body for setting the school curriculum, had recommended that 'India' ought to be replaced with 'Bharat' in all social science textbooks up to Class 12. The Modi government seemed to be in a desperate hurry to push ahead with the country's name-change mission. But even polarization must have its limits.

When I first boarded a flight to New Delhi to start my professional career, a benign-looking retired bureaucrat offered me some unsolicited advice. 'Find a place to live in South Delhi; you might find it more cosmopolitan, diverse and certainly more non-Delhi Delhi,' he quipped with a wicked laugh. I laughed along with him, particularly because I had always been an inveterate Mumbaikar (then called Bombay-ite) by heart. Beyond the butter chicken and paneer rolls, Delhi bored me, particularly with its intellectual pretentiousness, overdose of large single-storeyed government bungalows which reflected its colonial-era hangover of feudal inequality, the dangerous driving on the roads by drunk teenagers and the deathly stillness of wintry nights, when the usually quiet streets became forebodingly creepy. As it happened, I would end up following the superannuated gentleman's counsel and live close to Lutyens' Delhi. In the 2019 general elections, the people from this supposedly educated, enlightened, mixed precinct of South Delhi chose a BJP candidate as their parliamentary representative. His name was Ramesh Bidhuri. He won by a huge margin of 3,67,043 votes.[18]

The new Parliament inaugurated, the milestone Women's Reservation Bill passed, one looked forward, thankfully, to the end of an anti-climactic special session of Parliament. Bidhuri had some other ideas. And they were not good. They were not good at all. The Parliament was discussing a bipartisan matter, the successful landing of the Chandrayaan Mission-3 on the moon, an anodyne, celebratory moment which had received near-unanimous applause. BSP MP Kunwar Danish Ali probably did not agree with the BJP leader's loquaciousness on linking the achievement of the major scientific expedition to the party's unchallenged leader, Modi. That got Bidhuri riled up. He hollered at Ali using profanities normally uttered in cheap YouTube videos made by novices paid for hate magnification.

Bidhuri called the Muslim MP Danish Ali a *bhadwa* (pimp), *katwa* (circumcized genitals), Mullah *ugdawadi* (a militant Muslim) and *atankvadi* (terrorist) in his uncontrollable rage, saturated with religious animosity.[19] This dumbfounding choleric was happening in broad daylight in India's Parliament, where apparently the New India of Modi would assemble to discharge their promised oath to the Indian Constitution. It was sad; a mockery of everything India stood for. But then anti-Muslim commentary was now being chronicled daily, as India was being slowly acclimatized to the vicious '*Hindu khatre me in hain*' testament. When the South Delhi MP became a social media trend no. 1 within hours, he was in a distinguished company of other illustrious leaders of his party. Sitting behind him was the former health minister Dr Harshvardhan, who was seen to be reveling in the revolting outburst of hate. It was a depressing sight. A sad day for India as a whole. Since 2014, the industrialization of hate had been a malicious machination to divide society; now hate speech had made its grand entry into the consecrated halls of India's Parliament itself. It was a singular accomplishment that the BJP could probably take wholesome credit for.

What followed only added insult to injury, inflicted with gratuitous savagery; senior BJP leader Rajnath Singh offered token regret, and the BJP ordered a show-cause notice (at the time of writing this months later, nothing had happened of that inquiry).[20] As many as 200 million Muslims live peacefully in India; a senior leader from their community was literally abused in the foulest of vulgarity while speaking live on camera, but the BJP still needed to do 'an investigation' to unravel the truth. It was a nauseous attestation of BJP's divisive politics. A new nadir had been grazed. This was, to put it in a nutshell, a glorification of religious apartheid. A pained Ali wrote a letter to the Lok Sabha speaker, Om Birla, where his anguish was for all to see. He feared lynching and even considered quitting as a member of Parliament. India's moral degeneration, triggered nearly a decade ago, was perhaps on its homestretch. The constant colloquy on Hindu-Muslim divisions, the manufactured resentments, the triggered hostility was all playing out to a tragic end. One of its victims, within a week of Bidhuri's malice in the Lok Sabha, was twenty-two-year-old Mohammed Ishaq.

Ishaq was murdered by a fiendish mob which was offended that he had stolen prasad during the Ganesh Puja festival.[21] That a Muslim man was lynched to death during a popular Hindu festival for eating sweets given to the gods was emblematic of the malignancy within. This was not normal; it was not just uncivilized, it was barbaric. India has become a vortex of hate. Ishaq was a mentally challenged person; maybe he had no idea of what he was doing. People can usually gauge an individual who may be suffering from serious trauma leading to mental derangement. But the mob that killed Ishaq did not care. They wanted revenge for Ishaq's veering into their sacred space. Religion trumpeted humanity. This ghastly murder took place in Sunderi Nagar, New Delhi, right under the watch of India's nationalistic government. A young Indian citizen lay dead, killed in the prime of his life, his aged, shattered parents devastated to the bone, all because he allegedly chose to sneak in and eat a banana. New India confounded me, it made me sad too, and I was left wondering as to where we were headed.

The sentient could see how the interpolation of divisiveness was challenging India's social climate, deeply disturbed within. But it was a miniscule lot. Over 1,000 million Indians, shoehorned in pigeonholes, in cities and villages, struggle to survive daily. The metronomic erosion of India's democracy, while important, did not figure in their busy day jobs. Further, they were vulnerable to psychological warfare, fake news and digital manipulation. Social media was wreaking havoc with India's headspace. With over 700 million smartphones and 500 million WhatsApp users, news could be made bespoke.[22] Hate was now a retail project, not just a community target.

Within days, Bidhuri, who had made become a global Right-wing celebrity for haranguing Danish Ali, was rewarded with a big political responsibility; he was made the BJP in-charge of the district of Tonk, in Rajasthan.[23] Rajasthan state goes to the polls in November 2023. Tonk district saw the Congress win 3 of the 4 assembly seats in 2018.[24] But why Tonk? The answer was not a surprise. Tonk has a sizable Muslim population of 47 per cent. What better than a man who had mocked them, using the most deplorable language, to polarize voters? After all, 53 is a higher number than 47. In the ocean of hate, some politicians stood unchallenged.

I was studying at XLRI, the business school in Jamshedpur, now in Jharkhand state, when Indira Gandhi was assassinated by her Sikh bodyguards on 31 October 1984. My roommate happened to be a devout Sikh. Tata Nagar, as the city had been christened on account of the massive manufacturing plants of the business group in the industrial township, was infamous for truculent communal tensions. As darkness blanketed the small city, and it was officially confirmed over All India Radio that the prime minister was dead, a shocked nation turned its inconsolable grief into inhuman terrorization. Panic ensued. Jaswinder Singh (name changed) sat on a chair in the middle of the room, his red turban atop a disorganized hill of fat books, while some of us took turns cutting his long hair with borrowed scissors. It was a traumatic night for him. Nearly forty years later, the word assassination still had currency in the tumultuous world of Sikh politics.

When Hardeep Singh Nijjar, a Sikh activist (India had categorized him as a terrorist), was gunned down by two masked men in the parking lot of the Guru Nanak Sikh Gurudwara near Vancouver in British Columbia on 18 June 2023, few had paid much significance to his killing. Inter-gang warfare, personal enmity, bitter rival, etc., were touted as possible reasons for the homicide. But when Prime Minister Justin Trudeau, speaking in the Canadian Parliament on 19 September 2023, said there were 'credible allegations of a potential link' of Indian state-sponsored agents killing Nijjar,[25] a stupefied world took notice. In a sense, within a few days of the conclusion of the orchidaceous flamboyance of the G20 Summit in Delhi, the sheen was off. India was being accused by a leader of the western world of violating a rules-based international order, which in short meant, diligent adherence to democratic norms of political behaviour. Trudeau did not hold back. 'Any involvement of a foreign government in the killing of an Indian citizen on Canadian soil is an unacceptable violation of our sovereignty.'[26]

What followed was the usual diplomatic warfare: angry denials, hard-nosed rhetoric, mutual blame game, social media trolling (no guesses for who had the bigger numbers). Both Canada and India asked a number of their consular staff to leave. It was a belligerent face-off, temporarily, at least. Trudeau, who had frosty exchanges with Modi in New Delhi, publicly stated that he had raised the alarming case of internal surveillance and the bumping off of Nijjar with his Indian counterpart. The mother of democracy was being accused of indulging in cross-border adventurism with a villainous intent. Modi, of course, chose to respond through his more verbose External Affairs Minister Jaishankar, who outright trashed the allegation as rubbish. Khalistan was back in the news. But why?

In the assembly elections of April 2022, it was apparent that the state had moved beyond the miasma of gory bloodshed that had marked Sant Jarnail Singh Bhindranwale's violent leadership of his militant outfit which had terrorized the state. It had claimed more than 20,000 lives and paralyzed Punjab.[27] Every political party, while fearful of Pakistan-engineered separatism, wooed the people by focusing on job creation, eradicating drug addiction among the youth, tighter border patrolling, better farmer subsidies, attracting investments for modern industry, and a host of social programmes and economic incentives. Khalistan, the call for an independent Sikh state, seemed like an abandoned idea, mostly muted, surfacing intermittently overseas on days such as the anniversary of Operation Blue Star, Indira Gandhi's death anniversary, etc. Like the Gujaratis, Sikhs have an innate entrepreneurial zing and are capable of burning the midnight oil to fulfil their dreams. It is hardly surprising therefore that the largest population of Sikhs outside of their home state of Punjab have settled in immigrant-friendly Canada, besides UK and Australia. Nijjar had moved to the cold North American country in 1997. But there had been a series of disquieting murders of Khalistan sympathizers (the Indian government called them as terrorists) which was symptomatic of a pattern. It had not helped that Modi's government had lambasted protesting farmers who had made him eat humble pie on the farm bills as Khalistanis, terrorists, insurrectionists, etc. Something was seriously amiss, and it seemed portentous.

The BJP, of course, saw political manna from god's kingdom in what was essentially an international ignominy. The attractive fable of stealthily knocking off dangerous insurgents on foreign soil suited its macho proclivities, a surgical strike redux. The TV anchors would do the verbal muscle-flexing as per government script. Nothing like a Rambo-like foreign policy in which the government would showcase its 56 inch chest size; these atmospherics mattered as the election season loomed. Of course, there was no denying that several Sikh extremist organizations celebrating the assassins of Indira Gandhi was an ugly spectacle, but then Canada had indeed been a paragon of free speech. The Quebec and Alberta protests were not being proscribed despite their secessionist diatribes. The fact also remained that the deadly bombing of Air India 182 Kanishka over the Atlantic Ocean in 1985 killing 329 passengers, mostly of Canadian origin, was perpetrated by a Khalistani, Jagjit Singh Parmar, could not be ignored. And yet, Khalistan had become a non-issue over the years, as India made rapid strides economically and began to play peacemaker in international disputes. Thus, Nijjar's killing appeared odd. But for the Modi government, rules-based global systems and diplomatic niceties was only meant for editorial columns read by elite English-speaking readership. Electorally, did they even matter?

It helped that the former superpower, USA, a member of the Five Eyes Alliance whose surveillance had apparently provided Canada with the inputs on India's overseas bellicosity, was ambivalent on India's role. But Washington was still forced to ask Modi to cooperate with Canada on the criminal investigations to find the truth behind the material accusations. Time will tell if Trudeau was playing to the domestic populace, where he faced a fierce Conservative Opposition and declining approval ratings, or if he was indeed biting the bullet, fully aware that he had clinching evidence to expose the Modi government's foolhardy bloody experimentations abroad? The million-dollar question hung like the Damocles sword over a country once revered as a temple of Nehruvian democracy. After silencing critics at home with an iron fist, was the cavalier government at such a self-assertive level that they had the confidence to carry out hit jobs abroad? Foreign policy though had become an apparatus for playing to the domestic audiences. The Israel-Hamas war was another such example.

On 7 October 2023, a Jewish holiday, one woke up to the horrific images of thousands of rockets, estimated to be around 5,000 in number, raining over Israel from the nearby Gaza strip.[28] The perpetually on edge, standing on a creaking stage, ready to collapse courtesy even a soft flutter of breeze, the frail Middle Eastern peace, a tenuous arrangement at best between Israel and the Palestinians, had crumbled. What followed was humanity at its despicable worst. Innocent civilians were cold-bloodedly slaughtered; civilians including women, old people and children were taken as hostages by the rampaging Hamas. Israeli leaders called it their 9/11 or Pearl Harbor moment, a lethal attack on their national sovereignty. Promptly, Prime Minister Benjamin Netanyahu declared, 'We are at war', and promised to make Gaza, measuring just 365 square kms, an illegally occupied territory by Israel under a blockade for sixteen years, into 'a desert island'.[29] Hamas, the violent avatar of Palestinian nationalism, which controlled Gaza, promised to double down on its ragtag military mission for what they believed was divine retribution for decades of suppression and humiliation. The Middle East, at most times on the boil, was now a raging ball of fire. Within weeks, approximately 10,000 people were dead,[30] but the body bags were still accumulating by the hour. What was disturbing to watch, however, was the hypocrisy and shiftiness of the western world. To call it unconscionable would be a meiosis. India too was playing an opportunistic card.

Hamas's massacres were unforgivable; Netanyahu was not entirely wrong in angrily calling them ISIS for their vengeful attack. But what Bibi forgot was that his coalition government comprising of extremist far-Right nationalists had successfully subverted their own Supreme Court by limiting its powers of judicial adjudication, alienated citizens over several months, besides deliberately sabotaging prospects of a progressive conversation for an independent Palestine state. It was death by a thousand cuts strategy; in slow-motion bleed all hopes of the quarantined 2.4 million Palestinians living in the West Bank and over 2.1 million in the open prison in Gaza, bordering a mere 37.5 miles with Israel. This was an asymmetrical warfare; Israel is considered to have sophisticated military intelligence, cutting edge armaments (magnanimously supplied by the US, in particular) and a larger trained army as compared to a ragtag, motley crew that was the Hamas resistance. And yet the United States (which under Donald Trump had exacerbated tensions by shifting the US embassy from Tel Aviv to Jerusalem) and the European Union, while correctly condemning the Hamas assault, failed to mention the seventy-five-year-old colonization of the Palestine's territorial rights. The Palestinians were homeless, stateless and helpless in the face of Israel's belligerent occupation, US's crafty politicking, the Arab World's power struggles between Sunni and Shia-ruled states, and an impotent United Nations. The Israeli Defence Minister Yoav Gallant's call for a complete embargo on food, water, electricity and gas for the ghettoized Gazans (he called them 'human animals') was akin to a brazen call for genocide,[31] but no one seemed to mind. Including India. Now how come a country that once saw PM Indira Gandhi and the assassinated PLO leader Yasser Arafat together in a joint mission for Palestine liberation in palpable bonhomie, have changed so much? The answer lay in the compatibility between two authoritarian demagogues, who were masters in majoritarian populism, and followed the same Right-wing playbook. While it is true that India and Israel did break through their diplomatic impasse during the Congress government in 1992, PM Modi's support of Israel, without even mentioning the rebuffed Palestinian cause, which was at the root of the Hamas provocation, was a serious departure from India's foreign policy in the troubled region between the Mediterranean Sea and the Jordan river. The decoupling of the Palestinian homeland cause and the Hamas terror strike is factually incorrect; the Right-wingers though de-hyphenated the siege of Gaza and the West Bank, at the core of the conflict. But the perceptive analyst of Indian politics could see the BJP's ploy; the Hamas intrusion could only add to the burgeoning flames of Islamophobia in India. Anything that could show Muslims in a negative light suited the domestic political narrative. On Twitter, Right-wing trolls flooded the social media feed with hateful messages, fake news, distorted history and a one-sided version of the disputed territories since the two-state solution was proposed by the United Nations in 1948. India was branded as the disinformation capital of the world.[32] Hate was in the air. Foreign policy was now fodder for local politics. The devilish bombing of the Al-Ahli Arab hospital by the Israeli military which killed 500 people led to a furious exchange all over,[33] and conspiracy theories raged, with both sides blaming the other. But the brutal massacre led to an even more polarized exchange in India. It prompted the Indian government, till then conspicuously silent, to expressly articulate its condemnation of the heinous act, while finally, speaking about Palestinian anxieties. Islamophobia in India was singular, and it was being gingerly stoked. While Modi had been vocal on Israel, he had still not tweeted once on Manipur, which continued to simmer and seethe. He had not visited it either. It was six months since the ethnic massacre had happened.

After a long time, nearly five years to be exact, the Congress's fortunes seemed to be on the ascendancy. In the critical state elections for which the results would be announced in December 2023, almost all opinion polls predicted a comfortable win for the party in Madhya Pradesh and Chhattisgarh, with Rajasthan in a close fight against the BJP. In Telangana, it appeared that the BJP had collapsed completely, converting the main battle to a BRS versus the Congress. For the Congress, Telangana had a tremendous strategic value; the state had once been the party's most reliable stronghold even in the most adverse times, augmenting its national tally and giving it a crucial toehold in government formations in New Delhi. A victory in Telangana could also revive its political base in Andhra Pradesh, where it stood completely devastated. In Mizoram too, especially after the Manipur riots, the Congress appeared to be in a position to provide the soothing balm to an electorate which appeared both despondent and in disquietude. Post-December 2023, it was expected that the INDIA alliance would benefit from the momentum of Congress's winning performance, and BJP's diminishing regional footprint. Of course, 2024 was a different proposition, but the winds of change could be seen, and felt.

In the end, the battle for India's future will be written by millions of unknown faces from Kashmir to Kanyakumari, from Kutch to Kibithu, the most formidable banister for its democracy being its salient diversity. Many will queue up to vote as the first rays of morning sunlight start filtering into their eyes in the summer of 2024. The festival of Indian elections will be celebrated with international headlines, with western journalists sipping cutting chai at highway dhabas to capture the dusty fragrance of a bitterly contested election on their video feeds. In homes all across the country, there will be endless chatter, and many tension-soaked relationships will experience painful conflict. Financial analysts will predict likely repercussions on stock markets, the barometer of business confidence. Social media will witness an uncivil war, hashtag trends will wrestle in the ugly filth, and everyone will predict a win for themselves. Until the results are out, every contestant feels like a winner. Edgy as them, nervous to the bone, and both feverish with excitement and trembling with anxiety, bruised yet hopeful, will be India.

Gandhi was assassinated by Nathuram Godse at Birla House, New Delhi on 30 January 1948. His broken Ingersoll watch showed that at exactly 5.17 p.m. on that dreadful evening, the Mahatma breathed his last. But I sometimes wonder if it is possible to kill someone who is already dead. The Mahatma may have inspired decolonization, as Nelson Mandela, Martin Luther King Jr, Barack Obama and several heads of state regularly visited Raj Ghat, but in his own home, he was being murdered again, at close range. India of 2024 seemed to have forgotten the Father of the Nation. It had become a cranky, choleric, confounded cauldron. Those who think that everything is hunky dory, and that India is the next big thing because of hi-tech, digital connectivity, start-up boom and more flight options, live in a hallucinatory world. India's crisis is one of moral existentialism, a metastasizing growth of hate cells gradually corroding its inner being. Those who can see it and are talking about it are finding themselves in jail, facing lawsuits, death threats and living a never-ending fear of retribution. India has, to put it bluntly, abandoned Gandhism. It was heartbreaking, as with the ruthless bombing of Gaza by Israel, killing thousands of young children, the world needed an empathetic, inclusive and compassionate voice telling the opposing camps on a bloodshed spree: An eye for an eye makes the world go blind.

On most days, I drive past an arcadian house, which is mostly hidden off the main road leading to Nana Chowk, surrounded by small, well-maintained, pristine bungalows of the colonial age. Barring the local residents of the area, I am not sure how many people who drive past it are even aware of the enthralling history of the man who lived there from 1917 to 1934 and scripted the great Indian freedom struggle. A few days ago, as I hurried home, I looked towards it out of a customary habit. There were shadowy reflections from the yellow streetlights falling on it; otherwise, it would have been shrouded in darkness. Mumbai moved on at its breakneck speed, millions of sweaty armpits and hurried legs in a complex, byzantine maze of transport and travel, hustling in trains and buses, impatiently queuing up for boarding airplanes, local trains and multiplex tickets, each breathing the air of a country whose future they were to soon determine.

Sometimes, to go forward, we need to go back. We usually have the answers to our problems, but we must find them. Often, we miss what is in front of our eyes. Maybe India's answers lie in the forgotten address called 19, Laburnum Road, Gamdevi, Mumbai.

ACKNOWLEDGEMENTS

I WOULD LIKE to acknowledge Kanishka Gupta, my literary agent, for instantly liking the synopsis of the manuscript that I sent to him. I am grateful to Swati Chopra, associate publisher of HarperCollins, for agreeing to my vision for the book and constantly reminding me of my deadlines. The rest was easy, barring the usual kickups between a publisher and an author. Anju Christine was generous enough to do a thorough job of deodorizing the script of any grammatical blemish. Saurav Das needs to be congratulated for the book design and creative dry runs.

Veronica Vaz, my research associate, and Ganesh Sapaliga, my Man Friday, were exceptionally meticulous with the finer details of sourcing, citations and references. They were also fun to work with, the occasional exasperation notwithstanding.

My family too had a minor role to play. Mohini patiently heard my rumblings and offered insightful guidance, which helped me understand a Gen Z reader's kaleidoscopic mindset. Maithili had a complex creative model that helped choose the book's cover. If you like it, full credit goes to her recommendation. If you don't, well, that is also her responsibility. Pallavi was as most wives are; inscrutable. When she disagreed, she did so rather unambiguously.

When she was silent, it meant it was tolerably efficient. On a rare occasion, I sighted a nod of approval.

Lastly, I need to thank myself for writing the book despite Mumbai's chaotic madness, the distracting TV shows that I was part of where I endured some insufferable rogues, routines that I was unwilling to compromise on such as a tennis court visit, being still emotionally gutted with the loss of my illegitimate son, and yet never losing my faith in the goodness of humanity.

NOTES

Scan this QR code to access the notes.

ABOUT THE AUTHOR

Sanjay Jha is a former national spokesperson of the Indian National Congress party. A former banker and an internet entrepreneur, he began his political innings in 2004. He is the bestselling author of *My Illegitimate Son: A True Story* (2023), *The Great Unravelling: India After 2014* (2020) and *The Superstar Syndrome: The Making of a Champion* (2013), where he was a co-author. A new edition of *The Great Unravelling*, titled *2014: The Great Unravelling*, comes out in 2024.

As a former managing editor and co-founder of CricketNext.com, Jha was at the forefront of those who warned about the looming Indian Premier League scam. He has been a frequent contributor to mainstream media publications such as *The Times of India*, *Deccan Herald* and *The Indian Express*. He appears regularly on television panels as a political analyst.

Jha lives in Mumbai with his wife, two daughters and a few dogs.

2014

THE GREAT UNRAVELLING

Since May 2014, under a resurgent Bharatiya Janata Party, the Nehruvian—read liberal, secular, scientific—Idea of India appears to have come utterly undone. Institutions of governance that weathered great turbulence in the past are now disintegrating. The economy, once the celebrated 'India story', is in a shambles. Large sections of the media genuflect to the ruling dispensation. Meanwhile, the grand old party of India remains trapped in its glorious yesterday and unsure about its future.

In *2014*, named after the year the BJP-led National Democratic Alliance first came to power, Sanjay Jha takes a long, hard look at what all of this means for India. What are the reasons for the Congress's acute lack of oppositional ability? Can the party look beyond the easy fallback of the Gandhi-family charisma and embrace transformational change? Can it sell its vision—of inclusive growth and social justice—to a nation that seems mesmerized by a polarizing rhetoric and the rise of muscular, populist nationalism?

Though Jha asks tough questions of the government and his former party, he has not lost faith in Mahatma Gandhi's India. He writes of renewal, of hope. And the Congress, he firmly believes, is central to that revival of India.

HarperCollins *Publishers* India

At HarperCollins India, we believe in telling the best stories and finding the widest readership for our books in every format possible. We started publishing in 1992; a great deal has changed since then, but what has remained constant is the passion with which our authors write their books, the love with which readers receive them, and the sheer joy and excitement that we as publishers feel in being a part of the publishing process.

Over the years, we've had the pleasure of publishing some of the finest writing from the subcontinent and around the world, including several award-winning titles and some of the biggest bestsellers in India's publishing history. But nothing has meant more to us than the fact that millions of people have read the books we published, and that somewhere, a book of ours might have made a difference.

As we look to the future, we go back to that one word— a word which has been a driving force for us all these years.

Read.

Harper
Collins

HARPER
PERENNIAL

HARPER
BUSINESS

HARPER
BLACK

हार्पर
हिन्दी

HarperCollins
Children'sBooks

HARPER
DESIGN

HARPER
VANTAGE

Harper
Sport